THE
Malt Whisky
FILE

The Essential Guide for
the Malt Whisky Connoisseur

JOHN LAMOND AND
ROBIN TUCEK

CANONGATE

This book is dedicated to

Karen and Kirsty
and
to the memory of
Jack and Marjorie Tucek

First published 1995
Revised and reprinted 1996
Reprinted 1997
Second edition 1997
Reprinted 1998 and 2000

Revised third edition first published simultaneously in
Great Britain, the United States and Canada in 2001
by Canongate Books Limited
14 High Street
Edinburgh EH1 1TE
Scotland

10 9 8 7 6 5 4 3 2

British Library Cataloguing-in-Publication Data
A catalogue record for this book is available from the British Library
ISBN 1 84195 072 6

Cover design by Paddy Cramsie

Printed by Litografia Danona S. Corp., Oiartzun, Spain

Contents

Tasting notes by
John Lamond

Background and history by
Robin Tucek

Introduction

I t's a tough job, but someone's gotta do it. Keeping up to date within the whisky industry used to be easy. It was a relatively moribund giant; happy to sell its bottles which until recently had been on ration and seeing sales climb ever skywards. The tail end of the '80s and early '90s saw an end to that. Take-overs/mergers currently seem to be de rigueur, while new expressions of the old, familiar product abound. It makes life interesting, if complicated, for someone like me.

The Scotch Whisky industry used to be the most conservative of industries. Now there are fashions appearing, and some facets of the industry have become chic! I refer, of course, to wood. Wood has become the new black.

What most aficionados don't seem to realise is that, when in 1915 the industry was forced to age its product for a minimum of three years, all sorts of cask were used initially – as long as they were constructed from oak. All of a sudden the distillers had to obtain sources of used casks. New oak is not suitable for ageing Scotch, or Irish, whisky, as the spirit is too delicate – yes even those powerful malts such as *Ardbeg* or *Laphroaig* would be swamped by the flavours of a new oak cask. So they used casks which had previously held sherry and other wines, rum, brandies, Bourbon and liqueurs (see the entry for *Clydesdale* on page 70). I have even heard rumours of butter casks or herring casks being used and dread to think what the latter tasted like.

Amongst the plethora of new releases, it is easy to miss one or two, for which I apologise, and inevitably there had to be some restriction on the size of the edition. I have gone back to re-taste several whiskies. This in itself is a considerable task, as it is only possible to taste three whiskies objectively at one sitting. After the third, the anaesthetic effect of the spirit dulls the palate and objectivity has been compromised. I will admit to tasting at two sittings, 11.30am–12.30pm and 4.30pm–5.30pm (the palate is more receptive when you are hungry), as the publisher's deadline approached.

The take-overs mentioned above have naturally meant that we have lost a number of characters from the industry. However, the product seems to develop them organically and I have noted that some of the younger – and even some of the female – members of the industry are becoming characters as they too become steeped in the spirit and its heritage.

It may be much-maligned, but the industry, and by that I mean its people, is in good health.

In this, the third edition under the Canongate imprint, I have brought the mainstream malts and bottlings up to date and endeavoured to include some more of the independent bottlers' contributions. Some of the larger distillers have never accepted the existence of these companies. The Scotch Malt Whisky Society brought the whole subject of independent bottlings to a head back in 1983. Their system of numbering the distilleries got round the problem of the distillery owners' branding and introduced many consumers to cask strength, single cask bottlings for the first time. A number of companies now supply the needs of those adventurous consumers. This diversity is one of the factors which makes the industry such a fascinating place.

Although the compilation of this edition was a little fragmented and Canongate's deadline was extended by a couple of weeks, I did enjoy most of it. I hope that, even if you have a previous edition, this wee book gives you pleasure.

Slainté!

JOHN LAMOND
MASTER OF MALT

A Guide to the Regions

No two single malt whiskies are alike. Even malts produced by sister distilleries using the same source of water have their own distinct individuality. But, although single malt whiskies cannot be neatly packaged and parcelled, certain whiskies do have shared characteristics which can, broadly defined, help to identify a malt's original provenance. For example, some, but not all, Islay malts share similarities, as do some Speyside whiskies, particularly those in that elastic glen, Glenlivet.

Traditional Regions
The traditional regions are Highland, Lowland, Islay and Campbeltown, although the latter's once numerous distilleries have now dwindled to just two. The Highland region may also be sub-divided into Speyside, Northern Highland, Eastern Highland, Perthshire and Island (not to be confused with Islay) malts.

Islay Malts
Islay malts are the weightiest, most pungent and most heavily peated and are therefore generally the easiest to identify. These malts take their characteristics both from the peat used to dry the barley and their closeness to the sea. These factors give them what is often described as a seaweedy, medicinal taste and a distinct peaty flavour.

Lowland Malts
Lowland malts are dry, when compared with their Highland counterparts, and, although often quite spirity, are light whiskies with generally fewer individual differences than those of other regions.

Northern Highland Malts
Northern Highland malts are sweeter and have more body and character than their Lowland relations. They can have very distinctive and subtle characters, with a rich mellowness and fullness of flavour, but, equally, they can show a dry peatiness or a delicate fragrance.

Speyside Malts
The Speyside malts are the sweetest whiskies. Although they do not have as much body as some Highland malts, their flavours are richer and more complex with fruity, leafy and honeyed notes and a subtle delicacy of aroma which, once recognised, should be easy to identify.

Eastern Highland Malts
Eastern Highland malts come from the area between the North Sea coast and Speyside. Often full-bodied, they tend to have a dry, fragrant, fruity-sweet flavour, together with a touch of smokiness.

Perthshire Malts

The Perthshire malts, although Highland by definition, come from the area bordering the Lowland region. They tend to be medium-sweet, clean-tasting whiskies which are both light and fruity. Their identity may be best considered as falling somewhere between that of Lowland and Speyside whiskies.

The Island Malts

The Island malts from Skye, Jura, Mull and Orkney are characterised by a peaty, smoky nose and flavour. Some could be said to resemble Islay malts while others are more like Northern Highland whiskies.

Campbeltown

If it is possible to categorise Campbeltown nowadays, then it must fall between the Lowlands and the Highlands in dryness, but shows a distinct smoky character with good body and a salty tang.

Irish Malt Whiskey

Irish malt whiskey (note the "e" in whiskey) is much lighter, smoother and fresher than its Scottish counterpart. This is, in part, due to the fact that it is mostly triple distilled, although there are a couple of Scottish single malts also produced in this way. Irish whiskey has traditionally used unpeated barley, unlike most Scotch whisky. The new Cooley Distillery company produces some peated whisky, however.

Although it is possible to map out generalised characteristics for single malts, each distillery produces a malt which has its own unique personality. It has its own micro-climate, wild yeasts, source of water and specific malting requirements. All of these factors (and even the shape of the still used) will have an effect on the individual character and flavour of a malt.

The Art of Nosing

I t seems somewhat perverse that those who most appreciate the finest spirit in the world should spend a great deal of their time not drinking it. They do not even go so far as serious-minded wine connoisseurs who swill it round their mouths before ejecting it. No, the master blender will use nothing other than his nose – and his experience – to assess and evaluate malt whisky. He noses rather than sips to preserve his ability to "taste" after the first sample. The reasoning behind this is simple: unlike wine or other less alcoholic substances, a distilled spirit will anaesthetise the taste buds, the very taste mechanisms which need to be used time and time again.

Aromatics

Our sense of aromatics (or "volatiles" as they are sometimes called) is derived from an organ known as the olfactory epithelium. This is located at the back of the nasal passage, and is directly linked to the brain. This helps to explain why we cannot taste so well when we have a cold.

Using the nose to detect aromatic ingredients provides a more immediate route to this area than via the back of the throat. The palate can detect only four taste elements: salt, sweet, sour and bitter. All other flavour characters are created when the palate warms the contents of your mouth and causes aromas to rise through your nasal passages to the olfactory epithelium. The palate should merely confirm the aromas detected by the nose, although there will be slight differences and the strength of individual flavours may vary.

Our sense of smell is one of the most under-used of the human senses, being relegated in most cases by sight and taste to a subordinate role and only called into use for rather crude analysis of whether something smells "good" or "bad". In fact, it is one of the most subtle of the senses, capable of detecting even faint changes in style or balance, and has a large "vocabulary" of its own. The tasting vocabulary used throughout this book has evolved over the years and, we hope, is easily comprehended by the reader.

The Master Blender

A master blender has an "educated" nose and can detect more than 150 separate flavours or characters in a whisky. Some of these will tell him that the product has been adversely affected in some way during maturation; others will indicate the type or style of wood in which it has matured. But although your senses are not as highly tuned as the blender's, each whisky has a sufficient number of different characteristics to enable you to distinguish one from another.

The Nosing

In general, the nosing of malt whiskies is carried out in a small, tulip-shaped or similar glass which, being bulbous at the base and reducing to a relatively narrow rim, releases the aromatics and concentrates them at the rim, where the nose can pick up aromas. The sample is always diluted, or cut, with water; this releases the esters and aldehydes and thus makes the aroma more pronounced. The amount of water to be added depends on the alcoholic strength of the spirit which is being nosed. As a rough guide, malt whisky in the strength band 40% to 43% alcohol by volume (abv) should be cut with one third water, preferably a soft water – Scottish spring water – or clean tap water. Avoid waters with high mineral contents.

Higher Strength Whiskies

Other, higher strength whiskies should be cut with a greater quantity of water to reduce the sample to approximately the same strength. A high strength whisky of, for example, 60% abv, should be diluted with an equal volume of water for sampling. There is a very good reason for this. The olfactory senses are adversely affected by the high alcohol level, even to the extent of feeling pain. Dilution removes the likelihood of this pain being inflicted. The quantity used for sampling should be fairly small, to allow plenty of room for the aromatics to collect in the glass. There is enough spirit for an adequate assessment in a 25ml measure of whisky diluted with water.

You will find that different elements in the sample become dominant at different periods of the nosing. You may become confused by concentrating too hard and, very often, your first opinion will be the correct one. As you become more expert, you will discover a greater range of aromas in the glass. For example, one person may detect a hint of rubber in a whisky, while that same characteristic may come over to another as something else – liquorice, for example. The difficulty with either tasting or nosing is in the descriptions used by individuals to describe sensation or flavour. Attempts have been made to categorise these flavours and John Lamond produced a *Malt Whisky Wheel* for *Aberlour*. This helped identify the principal flavour characteristics, and their taste relationships, using taste bands rather like spokes on a bicycle wheel.

While it is possible to create a common language to describe the aromas, the sense of smell is very subjective. Malt whisky is a gregarious spirit, so that the next time you are with friends discussing flavour, let your nose lead your opinions. You can still have as much fun trying to describe the aromas in your own words as you will get from finally drinking the whiskies. This is the fascination of single malts.

File Notes

There are three types of Scotch whisky: *malt* whisky, *grain* whisky and *blended* whisky. *Malt* whisky is produced only from 100% malted barley. *Grain* whisky is produced from a variety of cereals which may, or may not, include a proportion of malted barley. *Blended* whisky is a combination of *Malt* whisky and *Grain* whisky, mixed together in the same bottle.

Single Malts

Most of the whiskies covered in this book are *single malt* whiskies. These are the products of individual malt whisky distilleries. For example, *Aberlour, Edradour, Laphroaig* or *Macallan*. However, the actual distillery name does not have to be identified on the label for a whisky to be called a single malt. Single malt may come from different casks of various ages, but they must all be from the same distillery. Not all distillery owners bottle their single malts under the name of the distillery. For example, the single malt from Macduff distillery is bottled as *Glen Deveron* by its owners.

Vatted Malts

Vatted malts are whiskies from more than one malt distillery which have been blended together, according to the specifications of the blender, to produce a fine, consistent product with a personality of its own. This whisky may well be given an individual name, such as *Sheep Dip* or *Poit Dhubh*. A *vatted malt* may not contain any *grain whisky*, otherwise it is *blended whisky*. Some *vatted malts* have been included in a section at the end of this book, as have some *single malts* bottled under "brand names" of independent bottlers.

Pure Malt

All Scotch malt whiskies, whether single or vatted, are *pure malt*. They are produced only from malted barley. If a whisky contains even one millilitre of *grain* whisky, then it is a *blended* whisky.

Grain Whisky

Grain whisky is produced from a mash of various cereal grains usually, but not exclusively, made from wheat, maize and barley. Both *malted barley* (barley which has started to germinate and then been dried to arrest its germination) and *unmalted barley* (barley which remains dormant) are used in the production of *grain whisky*.

Scotch Whisky

All *Scotch* (and *Irish*) whisk(e)y is produced by first grinding the particular cereal grain(s) to a coarse flour and then steeping this in hot water in a *mash tun*. The resultant liquid, called *wort*, is then cooled to between 22°

and 24°C and run into a **wash back**. Yeast is then added. Once the yeast has been fermented out, a strong ale called **wash** remains, which is about 9% abv. This pot ale is then distilled by heating it in **copper stills**, either in a continuous still, called a **Coffey** still, for **grain** whisky, or twice in the case of **malt** whisky using a pair of **pot** stills. Three stills are used for **Irish** whiskey and the Scottish malts *Auchentoshan*, *Benrinnes* and *Rosebank*, these all being **triple distilled.** Pot stills are usually onion-shaped, with tall, tapering swan necks designed to help the alcohols condense, after which they are collected, cooled and put into casks.

A whisky, however produced, may only be legally described as **Scotch** whisky if it has matured in oak cask in Scotland for a minimum of three years. It must also have been bottled at a minimum strength of 40% alcohol by volume. There is no legal requirement for Scotch whisky to be bottled in Scotland. The same legal restrictions also apply to **Irish** whiskey in Ireland.

Whisky casks are made of oak, from the genus *Quercus*. The species *Q. cerris* (French oak), *Q. falcata* (Spanish oak), or *Q. alba* (American white oak) are used. Oak is a natural substance and therefore variations in density, quality and porosity are inherent. To complicate and confuse the issue further, the wood is split by hand and the casks are constructed by hand. Thus each cask is unique in that it is larger or smaller than its neighbours, its staves vary in thickness and no two pores are the same size. Its influence on the maturing spirit which it holds is therefore going to be different from that of any of its neighbours.

That is why the recipe for each blended whisky is different. A blender cannot state categorically that the blend for his "Hamish's Choice" Blended Whisky is, for example:

     23 casks of Glenardle, 10-year-old
     2 casks of Harport, 18-year-old
     15 casks of Royal Lochmaben, 7-year-old
     13 casks of Leith grain, 5-year-old etc.

because the proportions of each constituent whisky will vary with each blend. When you enjoy a bottle from a single cask bottling, you are drinking a very finite resource; you are consuming heritage.

A **hogshead** will yield roughly 300 bottles (bottled at cask strength) after 10 to 12 years, a **butt** 500, a **barrel** 200. The variations in the oak cask mean that the distiller cannot deliberately repeat   exactly this magic of creation.

Generally the whisky drunk pre-1900 was young, only the landed gentry being able to afford to mature their spirit. The ageing cask could be new or previously have held wine, or rum, or butter, or herring, or anything

Continued on page 12

Scotland's Malt Distilleries

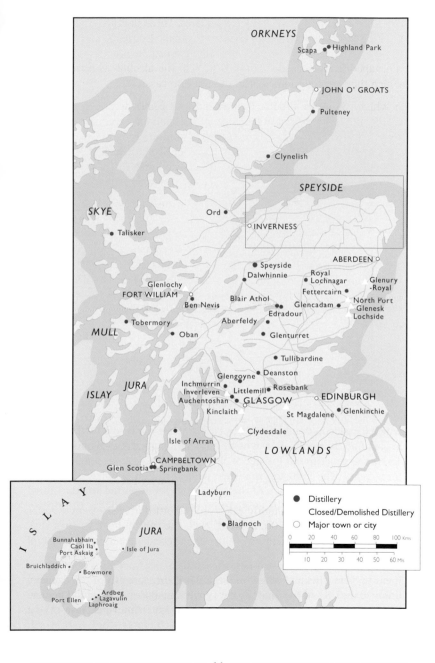

ORKNEYS

Scapa • Highland Park

○ JOHN O' GROATS

• Pulteney

• Clynelish

SPEYSIDE

SKYE

Ord •

○ INVERNESS

• Talisker

ABERDEEN ○

• Speyside
Dalwhinnie

Royal
Lochnagar   Glenury
-Royal
Fettercairn

Glenlochy
FORT WILLIAM ○   Blair Athol •   North Port
• Ben Nevis   Glencadam •   Glenesk
Edradour   Lochside

• Tobermory   Aberfeldy •

MULL   • Oban   • Glenturret

• Tullibardine

JURA   Glengoyne • Deanston

Inchmurrin
ISLAY   Inverleven   Littlemill • Rosebank
Auchentoshan •   GLASGOW   ○ EDINBURGH
Kinclaith   St Magdalene • Glenkinchie

• Isle of Arran   • Clydesdale

LOWLANDS

CAMPBELTOWN
Glen Scotia •• Springbank

Ladyburn

• Bladnoch

● Distillery
Closed/Demolished Distillery
○ Major town or city

0   20   40   60   80   100 Kms

10   20   30   40   50   60 Mls

ISLAY

JURA

Bunnahabhain
Caol Ila •
Port Askaig   • Isle of Jura

Bruichladdich •

• Bowmore

Ardbeg
Port Ellen • • Lagavulin
Laphroaig

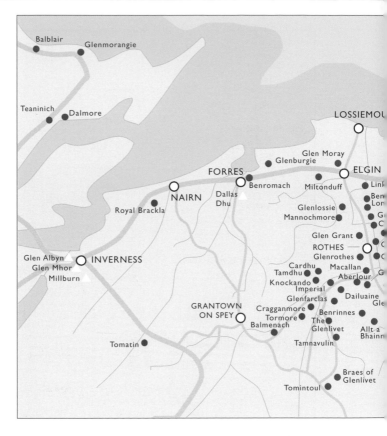

which a cask could hold. Until the 1850s, whisky was sold by the distiller in cask and the publican or whisky merchant bottled it as required. From 1916, the government insisted whisky be aged in cask for a minimum of three years. The industry was then obliged to find supplies of casks in which to age their product. At this time, all sherry imported into the United Kingdom was shipped in cask, to be bottled in the UK by the British merchants. Once emptied, the casks were surplus to the importers' requirements.

Ever keen to save a few pennies, the canny Scots were thus able to pick them up very cheaply. Likewise, because of the strength of the coopers' union in the USA at the time the laws governing Bourbon production were being created by Congress, it was written into American law that a Bourbon barrel could be used only once. When empty, they were worth only their value as firewood. Once again the thrifty Scots stepped in and

hisky Distilleries

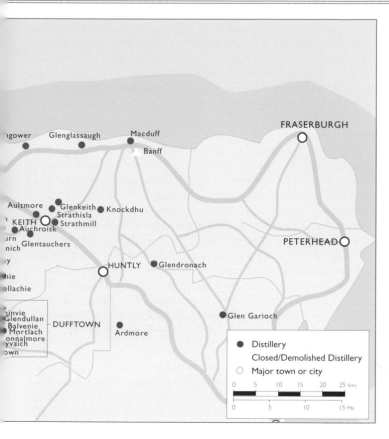

established another economic source of cask. The situation has now changed in that, since 1983, the Spanish government has decreed that all sherry must be bottled in Jerez and sherry butts are now reusable by the Jerezanos. New sherry casks are now a considerable cost element to the whisky distiller.

With casks being used as many as four or five times over, the most usual type of cask used for filling Scotch whisky and Irish whiskey is known as a *refill* cask. The casks are carefully checked by coopers between each fill to ensure that there will be no leakage of precious spirit. *First fill* sherry casks are nowadays very rarely used to fill new grain whisky, second, third and fourth refill casks being the usual choice for such whiskies.

One element which has developed in importance in the past 20-25 years is the distiller's awareness of the origins of the cask. So much so that some now have them made to order by Spanish or French coopers and loan them to a sherry bodega. *Glenmorangie*, preferring Bourbon casks, has even gone to the length of buying an oak forest in the Ozark mountains in Missouri to ensure continuity of supply of a particular quality of oak. The cask has moved a very long way from being a vehicle for transporting whisky or a container of a handy size for sale, and companies are now experimenting with whiskies aged in oak casks that have previously held port, brandy and rum. Sometimes whiskies are filled in one type of cask, e.g. Bourbon, and then "finished" for their last few months or so of maturation in another, e.g. sherry.

The respect of age

Much is made of the age of a whisky, and great respect and often considerable prices are given to whiskies of more senior years. The age of a whisky, if given on a bottle, must be that of the youngest whisky contained in that particular bottling. If all of the whisky used except for one centilitre is 21 years old and that centilitre is 11 years old then the whisky may only carry an age statement that it is not more than 11 years, although it could be described as being of a younger age, e.g. 10 years. The date of distillation of a particular cask, as well as the date of bottling, may be given on a label, but the age of the whisky itself, unless given in days, may be given only as not more than the number of complete years that the whisky has remained in cask. For example, if a whisky was distilled in May 1960 and bottled in April 1973, then the whisky is 12 years old, although it could be sold as an 11- or 10-year-old or less, or even not be given an age statement.

Whisky is usually about 70% abv when distilled, slightly higher in the case of triple distilled whisky. The remainder of volume is water from steam condensed with the distillation. It is a clear, colourless spirit, with few subtleties of flavour, and the actual volume of alcohol will vary slightly from batch to batch. With the exception of a few selected casks, it is now industry practice to reduce all casks by the addition of water to a standard 11 degrees over proof, 63.4% abv. While in cask, a whisky loses about 2% a year in evaporation. This is known as the *Angel's Share*. A whisky matures and changes in cask, the spirit leaching out tannins and other flavours from the oak cask, and absorbing notes from the air passing through the porous wood while it lies slumbering in the warehouse. Just as the type of cask can make quite a difference to the whisky, so can the location at which it lies. A cask of Islay malt, maturing in a warehouse next to the Atlantic Ocean, for example, will give a very different whisky to a similar cask maturing in a warehouse at Broxburn or Leith. Most whisky is reduced further in volume in the bottling hall, being reduced to 40% by volume for the standard European strength and 43% by volume for the general export strength. A few selected casks may be bottled at a higher strength. *Cask strength* whisky is whisky that is bottled straight from cask without the further addition of any water.

The longer a whisky remains in cask, the more flavour it will acquire and the less spirit will remain. A 21-year-old whisky, for example, will usually have more complex flavours than a 12-year-old whisky, although the degree of change is greatly dependent on the quality and type of cask used for filling. It will certainly be more expensive. Some whiskies are known to mature more quickly than others, Lowland whiskies generally being the quickest maturing, while others age particularly well, as is the case with many of the Speyside malts. However, although greater age means a more expensive whisky, it does not necessarily mean a better one. It is all a matter of personal taste. Some will not care much for a very woody, tannic 25-year-old malt, preferring a soft, honeyed 18-year-old and yet others may choose a sherried 12-year-old. As with most things in life, it is a matter of personal preference.

The following are some of the independent bottlers, starting with the two most important and influencial, Gordon & MacPhail and William Cadenhead:

Gordon & MacPhail
Established as licensed grocers in Elgin, Moray, in 1895, Gordon & MacPhail has not long celebrated its centenary. Scotland's leading independent bottler, and largely responsible for the availability of so many bottled single malts, Gordon & MacPhail were shipping single malt whiskies round the world when many of today's best-selling single malt whiskies were unheard of outwith the distillery. The company is now also a distiller, being the owner of Benromach distillery. They are a very independently minded and spirited company and justly proud of what they have achieved in bringing single malt whisky to the world's attention.

William Cadenhead
Established in Aberdeen in 1842 and now based in Campbeltown, William Cadenhead are Scotland's oldest established firm of independent bottlers. The business is owned by J. & A. Mitchell of Springbank. Cadenhead believes in bottling whiskies that are uncoloured and without chill-filtration. The company has for several years run a malt whisky shop at 172 Canongate, Edinburgh. In 1995, a second, franchised, Cadenhead shop opened in Covent Garden, London.

The Adelphi Distillery Ltd
Established in 1993 by the great-grandson of the former owner of the Adelphi distillery, Glasgow, which closed in 1902, the company specialises in cask strength, non chill-filtered, non coloured single malts.

Blackadder International
Blackadder International bottles non chill-filtered, non coloured single malt whiskies under the *Blackadder* and other labels.

Douglas Laing & Co Ltd
A Glasgow-based family business run by brothers Fred and Stewart Laing. Established over 50 years.

Hart Brothers
This Glasgow-based company offers a selection of single malt whiskies, bottled from casks selected by Donald and Alistair Hart.

James MacArthur
Established in Edinburgh in 1982 and specialising in rarely available malts from closed distilleries.

Murray McDavid
Director Gordon Wright was formerly at Springbank.

The Scotch Malt Whisky Society
This Edinburgh-based society bottles cask strength whiskies for members. Each cask is bottled under a numerical code, so as not to identify the source distillery on the label.

Signatory
The Signatory Vintage Malt Whisky Company, to give it its full name, was established in Leith in 1988. Signatory bottles an extensive selection of single malt whiskies.

The Vintage Malt Whisky Company
Another young company, based in Bearsden, Glasgow, they specialise in vatted and single malts under their own brand names.

Judging and understanding the differences
Each of our tasting notes contains its own numerical rating system. This system, developed by John Lamond and Robin Tucek, is designed to give you an approximate idea of *Sweetness*, *Peatiness* and *Availability* for each whisky. It is intended as a helpful guide only and is not meant to be used as a qualitative or quantitative rating system for malt whiskies. In our opinion, malt whisky is too much of a personal preference to justify any attempt to give rating scores to individual whiskies. After all, one man's *Macallan* is another woman's *Laphroaig*. Some will choose *Bowmore* and others *The Balvenie*. We would not wish to position any malt before any other – all are to be respected and enjoyed for their relative qualities, all are made to similar quality levels and *all* are aged in oak casks. Only *you* can decide the whiskies which are your favourites.

The Malt Whisky File Tasting Codes

The scale runs from 0 to 10, with 0 being the driest and least peated end of the scale, 10 the sweetest and most pungent. The ratings are a statement of fact; a guide to help you find those malt whiskies which are most akin to your own taste. If, for example, you like a malt with a *Sweetness* factor of 7 and a *Peatiness* factor of 4, then those other malts which have a similar rating should be of interest to your palate.

Most bottlings from the independents are of limited availability. We have given such bottlings a maximum *Availability* rating of 4. If the vintage listed is finished, then they normally follow up with the next vintage which, making allowances for individual cask influences, will usually be very similar to its predecessor. The *Availability* factor 0 means that this whisky is no longer available, 1 to 3 mean that these whiskies are difficult to obtain; 4 to 6 are available from the more specialist shop, 7 to 10 are increasingly more widely available. The *Availability* rating is based on the UK market, including Duty Free. We have not shown availability for Japanese whiskies.

Following the success of the independent companies in marketing single cask and cask strength whiskies, several of the major brand owners have now followed suit, making some very interesting whiskies available. These whiskies are often bottled with little or minimum filtration and it is increasingly frowned on to add caramel colouring to them. Such limited edition bottlings are an important and growing market but, because of the extra production costs involved, these whiskies are very much a specialist interest. Because each single cask of whisky can be such an individual product, they cannot possibly have the same consistency of style and taste as the more widely available malt whisky brands, each of which is bottled after blending together several carefully selected casks from the owner's warehouses of maturing whiskies.

The popularity of single malt whisky today owes much to the efforts of the specialist bottler in making such whiskies available when, with one or two notable exceptions, the brand owners showed little interest in producing malt whisky for anything other than blending. With the growth in interest and availability of single malt whisky, certain brand owners have let it be known that they do not like the independents bottling casks filled at their distilleries as single malts. This is a pity, as distilleries' own bottlings are always clearly identified for what they are, while the independents recognisably make their own name a clear endorsement of quality as part of their own label design. Some independent bottlings can be quite superb, with each cask bottled having its own differing and interesting personality. However, the better and rarer of these bottlings usually carry a price premium. With today's consumer increasingly wanting to know exactly what it is he is drinking, it is clearly neither realistic nor fair to the consumer to expect such whiskies to be bottled without their origin being disclosed. Some distillery owners keep all of their cask fillings for their own use and this would seem to be the sensible approach for those distillers not happy about other companies bottling their own distillery's product.

Vocabulary

We feel that, as any tasting note is necessarily a very personal and subjective thing, some of our descriptions may need explanation, in particular for readers outwith Scotland. *Tablet* is a Scottish confection, similar to a firm fudge, very sweet and sugary. We have "created" some words which pedants might object to – for this we apologise. Some of these are: *toffeeyed*, meaning having the character of toffee; *cerealy*, having the aromas of the grain from which the malt is produced; *mashy*, retaining the aromas of malt and sugars from the mash tun.

Labels

In some cases, the labels depicted above the tasting notes are not the vintage tasted. This is usually because of the bottler "following" on with the next vintage – which has not yet been tasted. The current vintage should be very similar to the previous vintage when the whisky is bottled at a similar age. It is only where there are much greater older, or younger, age differences that these nuances become more noticeable.

Water

Although water from a kitchen tap is safe to drink in many parts of the world, it can often be far from ideal as an accompaniment to malt whisky. In some areas, the water is naturally quite chalky or has a high mineral content. In others, for reasons of public health, various additives are put into water supplies. In Britain, for example, varying amounts of chlorine are added to drinking water and this can affect the nose of a whisky.

In a perfect world, the water added to whisky would come from the distillery's own water supply. As an alternative, clear, pure soft spring water with a low mineral content, such as one of the bottled Scottish waters, is eminently suitable (use still rather than sparkling).

Finally, don't be put off adding water. The belief that nothing but more malt whisky should be added to malt whisky is a misconception. Taste the difference for yourself: one glass with one third water and one without.

Mail Order Whiskies

Whiskies by post

The following offer a mail order whisky service, as do many of the specialists listed on page 255–6:

Blackadder International/Adlands, e-mail: blackadder@blackadder.com

Gordon & MacPhail, 58–60 South St, Elgin, Moray, IV30 1JY

The Scotch Malt Whisky Society, The Vaults, 87 Giles St, Leith, EH6 6BZ

The Whisky Connoisseur, Thistle Mill, Biggar, ML12 6LP

William Cadenhead, 172 Canongate, Edinburgh, EH8 8DF

Abbreviations used in tasting notes

DCL	The Distillers Company Limited, now United Distillers & Vintners (UDV), a part of Diageo plc
D.o.b.	Distillery's own bottling
IDG	The Irish Distillers Group
IDV	International Distillers and Vintners, part of Diageo plc
SMD	Scottish Malt Distillers. The malt distilling operational arm of DCL. Merged with SGD, Scottish Grain Distillers, to form SMGD, Scottish Malt and Grain Distillers. Now UMGD, United Malt and Grain Distillers. Part of Diageo plc.

How to use this book

The pages are arranged in alphabetical order by distillery name. In cases where two distinct styles of whisky are still produced at the same distillery, e.g. Longrow and Springbank, each whisky has its own alphabetical entry. Where the whisky is from an independent bottling source, this has been noted in the tasting notes.

Visitors – [V] indicates that the distillery welcomes visitors.

Key to geographical area of production

Arran – [A]	Ireland – [IR]
Campbeltown – [C]	Speyside – [S]
Highland – [H]	Lowland – [L]
Islay – [I]	

Hints on Pronunciation

Unless you are an expert Gaelic speaker, you may have difficulty in pronouncing some of the names of the malts in this book or of the areas in which they are produced. The following list contains those names that may cause a problem, with their phonetic alternatives.

Aberlour	Aber-lower
Allt-a'Bhainne	Olt-a vane
Auchentoshan	Ochentoshen
Auchroisk	Othrusk
Balmenach	Bal-MAY-nach
Bruichladdich	Brew-ich-laddie
Bunnahabhain	Boon-a-havun
Caol Ila	Kaal-eela
Cardhu	Kar-doo
Clynelish	Klyn-leesh
Craigellachie	Krai-GELLachy
Dailuaine	Dall-YEWan
Dallas Dhu	Dallas Doo
Drumguish	Drum-oo-ish
Edradour	Edra-dower
Glen Garioch	Glen Gee-ree
Glenglassaugh	Glen Glass-och
Glen Mhor	Glen Voar
Glenmorangie	Glen-MORanjee
Glentauchers	Glen-tochers
Glenury-Royal	Glen-you-ree
Islay	Eye-la
Knockdhu	Nock-doo
Laphroaig	La-froyg
Ledaig	Led-chig
Old Pulteney	Pult-nay
Pittyvaich	Pit-ee-vay-ich
St Magdalene	Magdaleen
Strathisla	Strath-eye-la
Tamdhu	Tam-DOO
Tamnavulin	Tamna-VOO-lin
Teaninich	Tee-an-inich
Tomintoul	Tomin-towel
Tullibardine	Tully-bard-eye-n

and finally...

Slainté (Cheers!)	Schlan-jer

Aberfeldy

Built between 1896 and 1898 by Perth-based blenders, John Dewar & Sons Ltd. Run by SMD since 1930, Dewar's having joined DCL in 1925. The distillery building is most impressive. The still house and tun-room were rebuilt in 1972–3 using the original stonework. Four stills. Sold to Bacardi during 1998, Aberfeldy is the jewel in their portfolio. Award-winning visitor centre.

Location – Immediately to the east of the village of the same name; next to the former railway line and the main A827 road and overlooking the River Tay.

Notes – Previously about a dozen distilleries had been opened in the Aberfeldy neighbourhood by men who had been smugglers in earlier times. The distillery lies in a beautiful setting, with close by woodland housing a rare colony of red squirrels. Tommy Dewar set off on a two year world tour in 1892. He returned with 32 new agents in 26 different countries.

Water – The Pitilie Burn.

12 yrs, 40% abv

Sweetness – 5   *Peatiness* – 6   *Availability* – 6

Colour – Amber with old gold highlights.   *Nose* – Medium-bodied, medium-dry, gentle & creamy with a slight cherry fruitiness & a floral edge.   *Palate* – Medium-dry, round, quite full-bodied & toffeeyed with a good, tangy cocoa peat character.   *Finish* – Long, smooth & creamy with a touch of milk chocolate on the tail.   *Notes* – D.o.b.

15 yrs, 43% abv

Sweetness – 7	Peatiness – 7	Availability – 6

Colour – Straw/amber with gold highlights. *Nose* – Quite full and ripe with rich oaky vanilla, a creamy lanolin oiliness with a slight nuttiness. *Flavour* – Full, smooth, round and medium-sweet with layers of oak at the back. *Finish* – Full, round and rich, smooth and almost luscious. *Notes* – United Distillers bottling.

25 yrs, 40% abv

Sweetness – 5	Peatiness – 6	Availability – 4

Colour – Mid-amber with old gold highlights. *Nose* – Round, mature, quite soft with rich, medium-sweet vanilla, notes of coffee, toffee, a definite touch of honey & an almost grapey character. *Palate* – Medium-dry, soft, quite full-bodied & elegant with sweet vanilla/toffee, a hint of banana & cocoa-flavoured peat. *Finish* – Very long, soft, complex & ethereal with notes of dark chocolate & espresso coffee. *Notes* – D.o.b.

1982, 43% abv

Sweetness – 6	Peatiness – 6	Availability – 1

Colour – Straw with pale yellow highlights. *Nose* – Medium-sweet, fresh, malty and quite delicately peated with a rich lemon peel character. *Flavour* – Smooth, round, medium-sweet and fruity with a good, soft peat character. *Finish* – Long, clean and fresh with a soft shortbread sweetness on the tail. *Notes* – *Cooper's Choice* bottling from the Vintage Malt Whisky Company.

Aberlour

ABERLOUR, BANFFSHIRE [S] [V] EST. 1826

Founded in 1826 by James Gordon & Peter Weir. Rebuilt in 1879 after a fire. This is the date which appears on the label. Re-equipped with four stills in 1973. The Aberlour Glenlivet Distillery Company is a subsidiary of Campbell Distillers, itself a part of Pernod-Ricard.

Location – Aberlour is situated about a quarter of a mile below the Linn of Ruthrie, a 30 foot cascade on Ben Rinnes which falls into the pool which gives rise to the Lour Burn. The distillery is about 300 yards from the Lour's confluence with the River Spey.

Notes – Aberlour is a delightful village by the Lour at the foot of Ben Rinnes, from the summit of which, ten counties (from Caithness in the north, to Perthshire in the south) are visible. The early Christian missionary, St Dunstan (or St Drostan as he was known in Scotland), used the waters of the Lour for baptisms.

Water – A spring on Ben Rinnes.

10 yrs, 40% abv

Sweetness – 7	Peatiness – 4	Availability – 10

Colour – Deep amber/golden. **Nose** – Full, rich, sweet and slightly toffee-like. **Flavour** – Quite full-bodied and sweet with a well-balanced richness. **Finish** – Good, full and long. **Notes** – D.o.b.

15 yrs, 43% abv

Sweetness – 7	Peatiness – 3	Availability – 4

Colour – Deep amber with old gold highlights. *Nose* – Medium-sweet, fresh and clean with a slight green fruity note and a delicate peatiness. *Flavour* – Medium-sweet, medium-bodied, round and smooth with a very gentle peatiness. *Finish* – Long, very delicately peated, elegant and complex. *Notes* – D.o.b. as *Cuvee Marie d'Ecosse*.

21yrs, 1970, 43% abv

Sweetness – 7	Peatiness – 6	Availability – 5

Colour – Deep, bright amber with rich old gold highlights. *Nose* – Quite fresh, lanolin, oily character, ripe, almost walnut character with a touch of hedgerow greenness at the back, full-bodied and delicately peated. *Flavour* – Medium-dry, full, fresh, walnuts, creamily smooth with a touch of spice and a hint of citrus. *Finish* – Long, clean and creamy with a gentle smokiness on the tail. *Notes* – D.o.b.

1990, 61.8% abv

Sweetness – 8	Peatiness – 4	Availability – 1

Colour – Very pale, watery straw with silver/lemon highlights. *Nose* – Light-medium bodied, medium-dry, youthful, quite a floral, apple blossom note and a perfumed malty character, quite soft and almost vinuous. *Palate* – Soft, sweet, medium-bodied, a youthful floral note and quite rounded. *Finish* – Long and rich with notes of dark chocolate in the lingering peat. *Notes* – Clydesdale Original bottling.

1976, 43% abv

Sweetness – 8	Peatiness – 3	Availability – 4

Colour – Mid-amber with old gold highlights. *Nose* – Full, round, medium-sweet, honeyed with a note of beeswax and aromas of toffee, coffee, cocoa & chocolate orange. *Palate* – Soft, ripe apple skins, good body, smooth, creamy, medium-sweet & delicately peated with touches of ginger & espresso. *Finish* – Long & elegant with ripe peaches & tangy coffee on the tail. *Notes* – D.o.b.

ABERLOUR SHERRY WOOD FINISH, 15 yrs, 40% abv

Sweetness – 7	Peatiness – 3	Availability – 6

Colour – Mid-amber with bronze highlights. *Nose* – Quite full-bodied, sweet, really rich, quite soft & honeyed with aromas of hazelnuts, ripe lemons & tangerines. *Palate* – Smooth, round, medium-sweet, creamy & delicately peated with notes of citrus, vanilla & chocolate. *Finish* – Very long, quite soft & elegant with a little belt of clean peat on the tail. *Notes* – D.o.b.

ABERLOUR ANTIQUE, No age statement, 43% *abv*

Sweetness – 8	Peatiness – 3	Availability – 3

Colour – Quite deep amber with bronze highlights. *Nose* – Full-bodied, medium-sweet with a slightly green apple perfumed hedgerow character, rich and softly oaky. *Flavour* – Rich, sweet, quite full-bodied and with a touch of spice. *Finish* – Long, sweet and lingering. *Notes* – D.o.b.

ABERLOUR 100, No age statement, 57.1% *abv*

Sweetness – 8	Peatiness – 3	Availability – 3

Colour – Quite deep amber with old gold/bronze highlights. *Nose* – Quite full-bodied, almost stickily sweet, rich and honeyed with a slight green apple character. *Flavour* – Sweet, soft and round, with good body, a slight green edge and a touch of spice. *Finish* – Long, slightly chewy, sweet and lingering. *Notes* – D.o.b.

ABERLOUR A'BUNADH, No age statement, 59.6% abv

Sweetness – 7	Peatiness – 4	Availability – 4

Colour – Mid-amber with old gold highlights. *Nose* – Quite big-bodied, mature, sweet & darkly nutty with a touch of a ripe maltiness & cooking apples. *Palate* – Rich, medium-sweet citrus & apples with a dark nuttiness & good cocoa-flavoured peat integration. *Finish* – Long, quite smoky, warm & spicy with a dollop of dark chocolate. *Notes* – D.o.b.

Allt-a-Bhainne

A modern building of contemporary architecture, built in 1975 by Chivas Brothers Ltd, a subsidiary of the Seagram Company of Canada. As a reminder of the traditional distillery, four small pagoda roofs are set on the main roof. Sold to Pernod Ricard in 2001.

Location – Sited on the southern slopes of Ben Rinnes to the north of the B9009, some eight miles south-west of Dufftown.

Notes – Allt a'Bhainne is the Gaelic for Burn of Milk.

Water – A spring on Ben Rinnes.

13 yrs, 1979, 43% abv

Sweetness – 9	Peatiness – 4	Availability – 1

Colour – Pale straw with lemon highlights. **Nose** – Quite soft and sweet with a rich, ripe fruitiness – dried apricots, lightly smoky with a floral note at the back. **Flavour** – Soft, quite sweet, smooth and round with a fruity character and gently peated. **Finish** – Long, smooth, soft and almost stickily sweet. **Notes** – Cask no. 026329, distilled 10/79 and bottled 2/93 for The Whisky Castle of Tomintoul.

1980, 60.5% abv

Sweetness – 8	Peatiness – 6	Availability – 1

Colour – Deep amber with old gold highlights. **Nose** – Full, rich, unctuous, almost rancid, over-ripe character, toffee, vanilla, tablet and coffee. **Flavour** – Medium-sweet, ripe, rich, toffee, tablet with a tang of smokiness. **Finish** – Smoky and rich. **Notes** – Wm Cadenhead bottling – cask no. 100027.

Ardbeg

The original distillery was run by a notorious band of smugglers, before excisemen overran the place, destroying the buildings. John McDougall established the present distillery in 1815. Owned from 1979 by Hiram Walker and operated by Allied Domecq, Ardbeg had been closed before being purchased in early 1997 by the Glenmorangie Distillery Co Ltd.

Location –A very romantic, lonely site at the water's edge on the south coast of Islay.

Water – Supply from Lochs Arinambeast and Uigidale.

10 yrs, 46% abv

Sweetness – 2	Peatiness – 10	Availability – 8

Colour – Amber with pale gold highlights. *Nose* – Big-bodied, dark & pungent, good, solid peat character and an underlay of rich lemon zest citrus, dry, but with a hint of sweetness, round with a delicate note of iodine. *Flavour* – Full-bodied, earthily, smokily peaty and rich with touches of coffee/chocolate & tarry ropes/creosote. *Finish* – Long, tangy and quite pungent, the citrus notes reprise, together with dark chocolate and a little seaweed. *Notes* – D.o.b.

15 yrs, 43% abv

Sweetness – 2	Peatiness – 10	Availability – 8

Colour –Amber with old gold highlights and a hint of lemon. *Nose* – Big, dark & powerful, a chunky peatiness with iodine, crabmeat and crashing breakers, dry, but rich, soft, sweet vanilla & a round, nutty character. *Palate* – Big-bodied, dark & very heavily peated, good richness with notes of chocolate, tarry ropes & quite chewy tannins. *Finish* – Long, very tangy and initially very rich with notes of honey, orange, espresso coffee and dark chocolate. *Notes* – D.o.b.

17 yrs, 40% abv

Sweetness – 2	Peatiness – 10	Availability – 8

Colour – Quite full amber with old gold highlights & a touch of lemon. **Nose** – Quite gentle & delicate peat, fruity! – orange/citrus. good body, slightly off-dry. **Palate** – Big-bodied and powerful, good peat & richness – a touch of sweetness. **Finish** – Long, elegant, very rich & complex with a touch of spice. **Notes** – D.o.b.

30 yrs, 40% abv

Sweetness – 1	Peatiness – 9	Availability – 1

Colour – Amber with gold highlights. **Nose** – Big, dry, pungent, dark and tarry; quite elegant, full-bodied, a relatively slight sea character with hints of creosote and cocoa. **Flavour** – Big, dry, pungent and tarry, not overwhelmingly peaty and gently chewy. **Finish** – Long with just a hint of richness, quite elegant and almost delicate. **Notes** – Allied Domecq bottling.

32 yrs, 49% abv

Sweetness – 1	Peatiness – 10	Availability – 2

Colour – Deep amber with bronze highlights. **Nose** – Big, pungent, powerful & sea-tainted, really quite medicinal with aromas of tarry ropes, creosote, citrus, chocolate. **Palate** – Dry with a slight touch of richness, a big sea/smoky peat character & gently chewy. **Finish** – Long, softly chewy, medicinal, elegant & powerful. **Notes** – Douglas Laing bottling.

1991, 46% abv

Sweetness – 1	Peatiness – 10	Availability – 2

Colour – Pale straw with pale lemon highlights. **Nose** – Big, sea-tainted, characters of seaweed, hospital wards & bandages & a slightly earthy, cocoa note to the peat. **Palate** – Powerful, earthily peaty, pungent & dry with an edge of citrus sweetness. **Finish** – Long, clean, quite ethereal & powerful. **Notes** – Murray McDavid bottling.

1978, 43% abv

Sweetness – 1	Peatiness – 10	Availability – 4

Colour – Full amber with bronze highlights and a hint of ruby. **Nose** – Quite full peat, but not overpoweringly, a touch of sweetness – like granulated sugar, a dark, earth peatiness. **Palate** – Big-bodied, but delicate, the flavour expands on the palate. **Finish** – Very long, amazingly complex with notes of spice, chocolate & green coffee. **Notes** – D.o.b.

FROM ARDBEG, 21 YEARS OLD

ADELPHI

Distillery

LIMITED

EDINBURGH SCOTLAND

1826

PURVEYORS OF RARE MALT WHISKIES AGED IN WOOD AND BOTTLED DIRECT FROM THE CASK

PURVEYORS OF RARE MALT WHISKIES AGED IN WOOD AND BOTTLED DIRECT FROM THE CASK

21 yrs, 1976, 49.2% abv

Sweetness – 1	Peatiness – 10	Availability – 1

Colour – Pale amber with pale gold highlights. *Nose* – Full-bodied, pungent, dark and earthy with a dry, medicinal peatiness and a sweet vanilla touch. *Flavour* – Dry, powerful, dark, smoky and gently chewy with an edge of richness. *Finish* – Long, dry and finishes relatively delicately after the initial explosion. *Notes* – Adelphi bottling from cask no. 453.

1976, 52.8% abv

Sweetness – 0	Peatiness – 10	Availability – 2

Colour – Deep amber with bronze highlights. *Nose* – Big-bodied, rich & fruity – apples & an orange tang, toasted vanilla & quite a big peat character, more gentle than cask no. 2392. *Palate* – Big-bodied, quite a bit softer & less rich than cask no. 2392, also drier & less earthy. *Finish* – Dry, gently chewy, big & medicinally smoky. *Notes* – D.o.b. ex-cask no. 2394. Only available at the distillery and to members of the Ardbeg committee, the distillery's organisation for fans of the whisky.

1976, 55.3% abv

Sweetness – 1	Peatiness – 10	Availability – 2

Colour – Deep amber with old gold highlights. *Nose* – Big-bodied & medicinal with a rich sherried edge, showing citrus & sultanas, a big, slightly earthy peat character & notes of toasted oak, treacle, creosote & tarry ropes. *Palate* – Powerful & rich with quite a sweet edge, notes of chocolate & coffee & enormously peaty. *Finish* – Long, pungent & earthy with a perfumed edge & a whiff of cocoa. *Notes* – D.o.b. ex-cask no. 2392. Only available at the distillery and to members of the Ardbeg committee, the distillery's organisation for fans of the whisky.

1974, 40% *abv*

Sweetness – 1	Peatiness – 10	Availability – 2

Colour – Amber with gold highlights. *Nose* – Big-bodied, dark and pungent with a burnt peaty character and hints of ozone. *Flavour* – Big, powerful and slightly salty with a burnt mahogany peatiness and quite firm tannins. *Finish* – Big, long, chewy and pungent with a salty touch on the tail. *Notes* – Gordon & MacPhail bottling.

1967, 52% *abv*

Sweetness – 1	Peatiness – 10	Availability – 1

Colour – Quite deep amber with bronze highlights. *Nose* – Big-bodied and pungent with a dark nuttiness, rich and full with a medicinal note – iodine/creosote/tarry rope. *Flavour* – Big, powerful and gently chewy with a burnt smokiness. *Finish* – Long, medicinal and smoky with a note of burnt Christmas cake richness on the tail. *Notes* – Signatory bottling.

ARDBEG 'LIMITED EDITION', 1975, 43% *abv*

Sweetness – 2	Peatiness – 10	Availability – 3

Colour – Amber with old gold highlights. *Nose* – Full-bodied, powerful sea character to the peat, a deep fruitiness. Almost apricot and really rich toffee/tablet vanilla. *Palate* – Dry, but really very rich, round, quite pungent, toffeeyed and gently chewy tannins. *Finish* – Long, elegant and complex, tangy and darkly peaty with good richness on the tail. *Note* – D.o.b. Distilled 1975, bottled 1999.

Ardmore

B uilt by Wm. Teacher with two stills and doubled in size twice – four stills in 1955 and eight stills in 1974. The distillery was built as part of a major expansion programme for the company's popular blended whiskies. Now operated by Allied Distillers Ltd, a part of Allied Domecq.

Location –Situated alongside the Aberdeen to Inverness railway line, below the 1,425 ft Knockandy Hill. Close by is Leith Hall.

Notes – Wm. Teacher use the make in blending *Teacher's Highland Cream*. The stills remain coal fired and the steam engine, boiler front and other relics of the original distillery are preserved. One of the largest malt whisky distilleries in Scotland, Ardmore also houses extensive research laboratories.

Water – A spring on Knockandy Hill.

1977, 40% *abv*

Sweetness – 6	Peatiness – 6	Availability – 4

Colour – Pale amber with pale gold highlights. *Nose* – Quite full and smoky with a slight green touch, medium-dry with a touch of richness. *Flavour* – Medium-bodied, quite smoky and medium-dry with good richness. *Finish* – Sweet with a good underpinning of smokiness, a touch of spice and quite chewy. *Notes* – Gordon & MacPhail bottling.

18 *yrs*, 46% *abv*

Sweetness – 8	Peatiness – 6	Availability – 4

Colour – Full amber with golden highlights. *Nose* – Light, slightly sweet and oaky. *Flavour* – Malty, richly sweet and full. *Finish* – Creamy and oaky. *Notes* – Wm Cadenhead bottling.

Auchentoshan

DALMUIR, DUMBARTONSHIRE   [L]   EST.   CIRCA 1800

T he name Auchentoshan is believed to derive from the Gaelic words "achad oisnin" possibly meaning "corner of the field". Not much is known of the distillery's early years, but a Mr Thorne has been recorded as owning it in 1825. It is now one of three distilleries owned by Morrison Bowmore Distillers, itself owned by Suntory of Japan. Although not the only distillery to experience war damage (see Banff) it had the misfortune to suffer heavily when Clydebank's shipyards were the target of enemy bombing, an event which caused extensive damage and great loss of spirit!

Location – The distillery is situated close to the Erskine Bridge on the A82, between Duntocher and the River Clyde.

Notes – Although geographically situated south of the Highland Line, the source of Auchentoshan's water supply is north of the line. Thus the distillery is a Lowland one, but its water supply is Highland. The make is triple distilled and very lightly peated. The first distillation takes an hour, the second five, the third nine hours.

Water – Near Cochna Loch in the Kilpatrick Hills.

No age statement, 40% *abv*

Sweetness – 2	*Peatiness* – 7	*Availability* – 7

Colour – Straw with lemon/gold highlights. *Nose* – Fresh and dry with a touch of green cereals and quite good body. *Flavour* – Dry and smooth with a slight richness and a touch of perfume. *Finish* – Quite perfumed with a touch of richness. *Notes* – Bottled as *Auchentoshan Select*. Carries no age statement. D.o.b.

Sweetness – 4	*Peatiness* – 4	*Availability* – 5

Colour – Very pale straw with a slight green edge. *Nose* – Fresh, clean and floral. *Flavour* – Light, soft, quite sweet and slightly fruity. *Finish* – Finishes quite well, although light. *Notes* – D.o.b.

21 *yrs*, 43% *abv*

Sweetness – 2	*Peatiness* – 4	*Availability* – 3

Colour – Mid-amber with old gold highlights. *Nose* – Soft, round, nutty and quite full-bodied with an almost buttery character. *Flavour* – Dry, soft and smooth with a hint of richness, gentle tannins and medium bodied. *Finish* – A hint of sweetness at first, nutty, long, quite delicate and complex. *Notes* – D.o.b.

AUCHENTOSHAN THREE WOOD, no age statement, 43% *abv*

Sweetness – 2	*Peatiness* – 4	*Availability* – 4

Colour – Deep amber with ruby/bronze highlights. *Nose* – Quite full, round, warmly nutty, with an almost over-ripe cheesy note and a cooked-fruit (Madeira-like) character, lightly peated. *Flavour* – Rich, but quite dry & intense, with a gentle touch of nutty, oaky tannin, softly peated with a touch of vanilla toffee. *Finish* – Long, with notes of dried fruit, toffee & nuts & a touch of spice. *Notes* – D.o.b. One of the very few malts which does *not* benefit from the addition of water before tasting.

Auchroisk

MULBEN, BANFFSHIRE [S] EST. 1974

*T*he Singleton of Auchroisk, to give the whisky its full name, is produced at the Auchroisk distillery. That name being rather a mouthful, the company's own bottlings are marketed as "The Singleton". Independent bottlings are under the name Auchroisk. The distillery is managed by Justerini & Brooks (Scotland) Ltd, a subsidiary of IDV, which is itself part of Diageo plc. Eight stills.

Location – On the north side of the A95 between Keith and Aberlour.

Notes – A new distillery producing its first make in 1975. Despite being a modern complex, the buildings are in the Scots vernacular style and the distillery received a Saltire Award (for outstanding architectural achievement in a traditional Scottish style). Sherry casks are used predominantly. Auchroisk is a showpiece distillery and has an old steam engine from Strathmill preserved in its entrance hall.

Water – Dorie's Well.

THE SINGLETON OF AUCHROISK, 10 *yrs*, 40% *abv*

Sweetness – 7	*Peatiness* – 5	*Availability* – 8

Colour – Mid-amber with old gold highlights. *Nose* – Quite full-bodied and medium-sweet with a dark peaty note, good nutty richness and a dark fruity character. *Flavour* – Medium-bodied and quite sweet, round with a touch of greenness to the peatiness and a definite toffee character to the richness. *Finish* – Long and smooth with a vanilla tablet sweetness. *Notes* – D.o.b.

THE SINGLETON OF AUCHROISK, 1981, 43% *abv*

Sweetness – 7	Peatiness – 5	Availability – 4

Colour – Amber with gold highlights. *Nose* – Full-bodied, clean, medium-sweet and fresh with a slightly green unripe peachy fruitiness and a delicately perfumed smokiness at the back. *Flavour* – Medium-sweet, quite smoky, creamily smooth with an almost chocolatey flavour. *Finish* – Long and round with a hint of coffee. *Notes* – D.o.b.

THE SINGLETON OF AUCHROISK, 1983, 40% *abv*

Sweetness – 4	Peatiness – 3	Availability – 2

Colour – Full amber with old gold highlights. *Nose* – Quite rich and medium-sweet with a dark nuttiness and reasonable weight. *Flavour* – Medium-bodied, round, dark, nutty and medium-dry. *Finish* – Almost dry, slightly bitter and with a toffee-like tail. *Notes* – D.o.b.

THE SINGLETON OF AUCHROISK, 1976, 40% *abv*

Sweetness – 7	Peatiness – 4	Availability – 1

Colour – Amber with gold highlights. *Nose* – Rich, quite full-bodied and minty with a peachy sweetness and good weight. *Flavour* – Quite full-bodied and smooth with a sherried nuttiness, a vanilla oaky-oiliness and quite delicately peated. *Finish* – Quite long, nutty and dark with a smokiness on the tail. *Notes* – D.o.b.

12 *yrs*, 1978, 59.3% *abv*

Sweetness – 8	Peatiness – 3	Availability – 1

Colour – Pale straw with lemon/yellow highlights. *Nose* – Fresh, fruity-citrus and cherries, quite full-bodied with a touch of raisins at the back. *Flavour* – Sweet, fruity, smooth and round with good oaky tannins and quite spirity. *Finish* – Smooth and spirity with a hint of cloves and quite long. *Notes* – Wm Cadenhead bottling as *Auchroisk*.

1989, Natural strength, 59.8% *abv*

Sweetness – 6	Peatiness – 3	Availability – 1

Colour – Water-white with silver/white highlights. *Nose* – Very young, mashy and medium-sweet, floral with a slight fruity note and very light peat. *Flavour* – Young, mashy, vegetal and medium-sweet. *Finish* – Long and spirity. *Notes* – Clydesdale Original bottling as *Auchroisk*.

Aultmore

KEITH, BANFFSHIRE [S] EST. 1895

Built by Alexander Edward of Sanquhar, Forres, with two stills. The first of the make was produced in early 1897. It became a part of DCL in 1925 and was transferred to SMD's management in 1930. Rebuilt in 1970–1 and doubled to four stills. Now operated by UMGD, a part of Diageo plc.

Location – An isolated building standing on the A96 Keith to Elgin road close to the turning to Buckie.

Notes – Until 1969 a steam engine had been providing power, operating 24 hours a day, seven days a week since 1898. The old engine is still kept for show.

Water – The burn of Auchinderran.

SPEYSIDE
SINGLE MALT *SCOTCH WHISKY*

AULTMORE

distillery located between *KEITH* and *BUCKIE* began production in 1897. The name, derived from the *Gaelic*, means "*big burn*". Ideal supplies of *water* and *peat* from the *Foggie Moss* made this area a haunt of *illicit distillers* in the past. *Water* from the *Burn* of *AUCHINDERRAN* is now used to produce this *smooth, well balanced single MALT* ⅟₂ *SCOTCH WHISKY* with a *mellow* finish.

AGED **12** YEARS

43% vol Distilled & Bottled in *SCOTLAND.* AULTMORE DISTILLERY Keith, Banffshire, *Scotland.* 70 cl

12 yrs, 43% abv

Sweetness – 5	Peatiness – 4	Availability – 6

Colour – Pale straw with lemon highlights. *Nose* – Rich, round, medium-bodied, a cooked mash character, appley and spirity. *Flavour* – Medium-bodied, lightly peated and medium-dry. *Finish* – Smooth, malty and quite long. *Notes* – D.o.b.

14 yrs, 1985, 60.1% abv

Sweetness – 7	Peatiness – 5	Availability – 2

Colour – Mid-amber with pale old gold highlights. *Nose* – Full, rich, medium-sweet with a toasted cereal character & toffee/caramel/vanilla notes & delicate peat at the back. *Palate* – Rich, quite sweet & toffeeyed, quite full-bodied with a slight hint of greenness to the peat. *Finish* – Long, quite ethereal & clean with a cereal note. *Notes* – Adelphi bottling from cask 2900.

Balblair

EDDERTON, ROSS-SHIRE [H] EST. 1790

The present distillery was built in 1872 when the then owner, Andrew Ross, decided to extend the business, the new buildings being higher up the slope of the hill. The older buildings were converted into a bonded warehouse. Extended from two to three stills in the 1970s by owners Hiram Walker and operated by Allied Domecq. Sold to Inver House Distillers in 1996. The fermenting of ale on the site is said to have taken place as long ago as 1749.

Location –Less than a quarter of a mile from the Dornoch Firth, about six miles from Tain on the A9.

Notes –Distilling in the area predates Balblair by a considerable number of years, there being many suitable sources of water and peat in abundance. Indeed, the Edderton area is known as "the Parish of the Peats" and once abounded in smuggling bothies. One of the malts associated with *Ballantine's* blended Scotch Whisky.

Water – The Allt Dearg, a burn four miles from the distillery.

16 yrs, 43% abv

Sweetness – 6	Peatiness – 4	Availability – 6

Colour – Amber with gold highlights. *Nose* – Quite full-bodied, medium-sweet & fresh with a slight green fruit (peaches & apples) character. *Palate* – Quite soft & round with toffee & vanilla flavours, good body, quite a delicate peatiness & medium-dry. *Finish* – Long, quite dark & tangy with a hint of tarry rope. *Notes* – D.o.b.

BALBLAIR ELEMENTS, No age statement , 40% abv

Sweetness – 8	Peatiness – 3	Availability – 7

Colour – Amber with gold highlights. *Nose* – Quite full-bodied, rich, malty and medium-sweet with a slight fresh green peatiness, a floral hedgerow note and a light floral character. *Palate* – Sweet, rich, full-bodied, quite fresh and quite delicately peated with notes of toffee & vanilla, very smooth. *Finish* – Long, quite tangy, rich and malty. *Notes* – D.o.b.

Balmenach

The distillery was established in 1824 by James McGregor. At the time, it was at the centre of an area which was full of smugglers' bothies and illicit distilling was a way of life. Bought by SMD in 1930 and extended from four stills to six stills in 1962. A Saladin Box malting system was installed in 1964 and used until the mid-1980s. Purchased by Inver House in December 1997.

Location –The distillery lies in a bowl in the hills off the A95 main road heading towards Bridge of Avon from Grantown-on-Spey. The distillery stands about a mile from the former Cromdale station on the Spey Valley railway line.

Notes – A branch line was built to the distillery in the late 1880s and the steam engine which worked the line is preserved on the Strathspey railway at Aviemore. Local lore tells that farmer James McGregor was visited by an excise officer just after the 1823 Excise Act had been passed. He was shown round the farm and experienced typical hospitality with a bottle of fine whisky. The officer then pointed out an outbuilding and asked what it was used for. "That's just the peat shed," came the reply. The officer said nothing, and continued to enjoy his whisky. After a few more drams, the officer made to leave. "If I were you, Mr McGregor," he said, "I'd take out a licence for that peat shed." McGregor took the hint and took out the necessary licence. In 1690 the Jacobites were defeated by William of Orange in a battle on the hills above the village of Cromdale.

Water – The Cromdale Burn.

SPEYSIDE
SINGLE MALT
SCOTCH WHISKY

Sometime in the early (19th, after *walking*
in the *CROMDALE* hills *with*
his 2 *BROTHERS*, *James McGregor* settled
and established

BALMENACH

distillery. Spring water from beneath those
same HILLS is still used to produce
this *RICH flavoured* single *MALT' SCOTCH*
WHISKY of *exemplary* quality.

AGED **12** YEARS

43% vol   Distilled & Bottled in *SCOTLAND.*
BALMENACH DISTILLERY, Cromdale, Moray, *Scotland.*   70 cl

12 yrs, 43% abv

Sweetness – 7	Peatiness – 5	Availability – 6

Colour – Quite deep amber with bronze highlights. *Nose* – Quite full-bodied, heather floral characters, medium-sweet, rich and sherried with a light honeyed nuttiness. *Flavour* – Full-bodied, sherried and nutty with a touch of oily vanilla. *Finish* – Long, nutty and medium-sweet with a touch of tannin. *Notes* – United Distillers bottling.

1981, 62.6% abv

Sweetness – 6	Peatiness – 5	Availability – 4

Colour – Very pale, watery straw with pale lemon highlights. *Nose* – Very mashy, youthful character, lightly spirity with a sweetness at the back. *Flavour* – Medium-sweet, rich and unctuous with gentle tannins, a hint of austerity at the front of the palate and lightly peated. *Finish* – Quite short, but smooth with a light chewiness. *Notes* – Wm Cadenhead bottling.

1972, 40% abv

Sweetness – 6	Peatiness – 7	Availability – 2

Colour – Mid-amber with light bronze highlights. *Nose* – Medium-sweet, quite full-bodied, dark, rich, brazil nutty and smoky, oaky with a good unctuous richness. *Flavour* – Medium-dry, nutty, of good body with a soft richness and smoky oak. *Finish* – Long and slightly chewy with a slight perfumed smokiness. *Notes* – Gordon & MacPhail bottling.

1971, 40% abv

Sweetness – 5	Peatiness – 7	Availability – 2

Colour – Amber/straw with yellow/gold highlights. *Nose* – Quite smoky & peaty, medium-bodied with a slight green nuttiness. *Flavour* – Dryish, smoky, quite full and delicately peaty with an edge of sweetness. *Finish* – Dry with oaky tannin and reasonable length. *Notes* – Gordon & MacPhail bottling.

18 yrs, 1977, 43% abv

Sweetness – 5	Peatiness – 7	Availability – 1

Colour – Very pale straw with pale yellow highlights. *Nose* – Medium-dry and quite full-bodied with a slightly earthy peat character and a slight burnt vegetal note. *Flavour* – Medium-dry, smooth and creamy with good body and an earthy peatiness. *Finish* – Long and quite elegant with a slight edge of richness. *Notes* – Blackadder bottling; distilled 18 November 1977.

Balvenie

DUFFTOWN, BANFFSHIRE [S] EST. 1892

Built next to William Grant's Glenfiddich distillery in 1892. The stills came second-hand from Lagavulin and Glen Albyn. Three further stills were added to make eight in all (two in 1965 and one in 1971). Floor malting is still carried out at Balvenie, this supplying about 15% of the distillery's malt requirements. The peat used is hand-cut locally, and dried and seasoned before being used to fire the malt kiln. The stills at Balvenie are heated using the heat waste from Glenfiddich to produce steam heat to boil them.

Location – Situated just below Glenfiddich on the lower slopes of the Convals, the hills which dominate Dufftown.

Notes – *The Balvenie* is an excellent example of just how different single malts can be. Standing next door to its more famous sister, *Glenfiddich*, it draws its water from the same source and shares the same supply of malt – even the distiller is the same person – and yet the two whiskies are very different in character. In 1992, 100 years after Balvenie was built, the Grants opened another new distillery, Kininvie, next door.

Water – The Robbie Dhu (pronounced "doo") springs.

THE BALVENIE FOUNDER'S RESERVE, 10 *yrs*, 40% *abv*

Sweetness – 8	*Peatiness* – 3	*Availability* – 8

Colour – Straw with good golden highlights. *Nose* – Full and rich with a green edge, medium-sweet with an appley aroma. *Flavour* – Medium-dry, smooth, oaky and malty. *Finish* – Of reasonable length, quite rich. *Notes* – D.o.b.

ESTᴰ 1892

SINGLE MALT

Distilled at

THE BALVENIE

Distillery, Banffshire

SCOTLAND

DOUBLEWOOD

MATURED IN TWO WOODS

AGED **12** YEARS

| FIRST CASK | SECOND CASK |

Traditional Whisky Oak | Original Sherry Oak

maturation *Mellows* the spirit and *Builds Character*. This is the *Customary Practice* of other SINGLE MALT Scotch Whiskies. The result is a *Rich*, MELLOW flavour of great *Depth* & *Unusual* COMPLEXITY

maturation *Increases Complexity*, *Depth* and *Fullness* of Flavour. This *Second Cask Ageing* is at the HEART of The Balvenie Doublewood.

MALT SCOTCH WHISKY

THE BALVENIE DISTILLERY COMPANY, BALVENIE MALTINGS, DUFFTOWN, BANFFSHIRE, SCOTLAND AB55 4BB

70 cl e   PRODUCT OF SCOTLAND   40% vol

THE BALVENIE DOUBLEWOOD, 12 *yrs*, 40% *abv*

Sweetness – 7   *Peatiness* – 3   *Availability* – 7

Colour – Quite full amber with old gold highlights and a hint of lemon. *Nose* – Quite full mashy/spirity and ripe with a slightly walnutty character and a fresh, almost Riesling-like diesel touch. *Flavour* – Medium-sweet, slightly spicy, smooth and round with a dark nuttiness, a chocolatey/malty character and delicately peated. *Finish* – Fresh, warm, rich, quite tangy, long and with the walnut character of the nose. *Notes* – Partly aged in a Bourbon cask, its maturation is finished off in a sherry cask, hence its name *Balvenie DoubleWood.* D.o.b.

THE BALVENIE SINGLE BARREL, 15 yrs, 1978, 50.4% abv

Sweetness – 7	Peatiness – 3	Availability – 4

Colour – Bright, pale mid-amber with yellow-gold highlights. *Nose* – Quite full-bodied, ripe, rich and medium-sweet with an unctuous oily, honeyed vanilla-oak character, delicately peated with hints of green apples. *Flavour* – Medium-sweet, quite full-bodied, smooth and round with a backbone of oaky tannin, an oily-vanilla texture and a slight green edge to the peatiness. *Finish* – Very long and complex with hints of bitter chocolate, hazelnuts, toffee, honey and a nice green coffee tang. *Notes* – D.o.b. Bottle no. 134 from cask no. 199. This cask was filled on 17.1.1978 and bottled on 13.10.1993. Sold as *The Balvenie Single Barrel*.

THE BALVENIE PORT WOOD, 21 yrs, 43% abv

Sweetness – 5	Peatiness – 4	Availability – 2

Colour – Mid-amber with bronze highlights and a slight ruby hue. *Nose* – Soft, round, quite full-bodied and sweet with a rich toffee and vanilla oak character, a touch of beeswax and a note of soft, ripe peach. *Flavour* – Quite dry with chewy tannins, good body and richness and quite delicately peated. *Finish* – Long and gently chewy with a touch of beeswax. *Notes* – D.o.b., finished in a port pipe.

Banff

BANFF, BANFFSHIRE [H] EST. 1863

Built by James Simpson junior to replace an earlier distillery of the same name built in 1824. Rebuilt after a fire in 1877. Owned by SMD since 1932. Two stills. Closed and dismantled in 1983.

Location – Half a mile west of Banff on the B9139.

Notes – One of the first distilleries located to take advantage of the railways. On Saturday, 16 August 1941 a single German plane machine-gunned and bombed no. 12 warehouse. Exploding casks flew through the air and a local newspaper reported, ". . . thousands of gallons of whisky were lost, either burning or running to waste over the land . . . even farm animals became intoxicated". Cows were not milked because they could not be got to their feet. Banff was known locally as "Inverboyndie distillery".

Water – Springs on Fiskaidly Farm.

CONNOISSEURS CHOICE

Connoisseurs Choice, a range of single malts from various districts of Scotland

In the Highlands are situated the greatest number of malt whisky distilleries

SINGLE HIGHLAND MALT SCOTCH WHISKY

DISTILLED AT

BANFF

DISTILLERY

Proprietors: Slater, Rodger Ltd

DISTILLED 1974 DISTILLED

SPECIALLY SELECTED, PRODUCED AND BOTTLED BY

70cl   GORDON & MACPHAIL   40%vol
ELGIN · SCOTLAND
PRODUCT OF SCOTLAND

34 yrs, 43% abv

Sweetness – 4	Peatiness – 5	Availability – 2

Colour – Deep amber with ruby-tinted highlights. *Nose* – Big, burnt, dark. Mature & dry, softly pungent, medium-dry & quite gently peated. *Palate* – Quite big-bodied, medium-dry, softly pungent, with chewy tannins & a delicate peatiness. *Finish* – Long, oaky, almost medicinal & quite chewy. *Notes* – Douglas Laing Bottling.

17 yrs, 1976, 60.5 % abv

Sweetness – 6	Peatiness – 6	Availability – 1

Colour – Mid-amber with yellow/gold highlights. *Nose* – Fresh and clean with a soft green fruitiness, hints of perfume and a cedar note. *Flavour* – Fresh, smooth, medium-dry and quite round with good body and gentle tannins. *Finish* – Of reasonable length, it has a light earthy smokiness with a green edge. *Notes* – Wm Cadenhead bottling.

Ben Nevis

LOCHY BRIDGE, FORT WILLIAM [H] [V] EST. 1825

Founded by "Long John" Macdonald in 1825. Owned by various Macdonalds until taken over by Ben Nevis Distillery (Fort William) Ltd in 1955, which installed a Coffey still. Later sold to Long John International Ltd (a part of Whitbread) in 1981, when the Coffey still was removed. Four pot stills. Sold by the Whitbread group to the Japanese company, Nikka, early in 1989.

Location – Situated two miles north of Fort William on the A82.

Notes – A cask of *Ben Nevis* was presented to Queen Victoria on her visit to Fort William on 21 April 1848. The cask was not to be opened until the Prince of Wales reached his majority 15 years later.

Water – Allt a' Mhuilinn (The Mill Burn), which flows from two small lochans, Coire Leis and Coire na' Ciste, situated at over 3,000 ft up Ben Nevis.

10 yrs, 46% abv

Sweetness – 5	Peatiness – 6	Availability – 6

Colour – Mid-amber with old gold highlights. *Nose* – Fresh with a dark nuttiness, medium-dry with a leafy demerara sugar character, rich and quite full-bodied, quite intense and showing fruit – orange and almost a grapiness. *Palate* – Quite full, soft, fresh & medium-sweet with a dark peat character, a touch of spice and sweet, oaky vanilla. *Finish* – Long, rich & smooth with a touch of toffee & chocolate. *Notes* – D.o.b.

21 yrs, 55.6% abv

Sweetness – 5	Peatiness – 6	Availability – 2

Colour – Quite deep amber with bronze highlights. *Nose* – Full-bodied, rich, oaky and medium-sweet with a firm peatiness. *Flavour* – Full-bodied, dark and nutty with a rich peatiness, medium-sweet with quite gentle oaky tannins. *Finish* – Long, powerful and delicately smoky with a tangy touch of spice and just an edge of sweetness on the tail. *Notes* – D.o.b.

22 yrs, 46% abv

Sweetness – 3	Peatiness – 6	Availability – 2

Colour – Deep, peaty amber with good gold highlights. *Nose* – Spirity, malty, dryish, lightly peated and slightly leafy. *Flavour* – Dry, lightly peaty, spirity and slightly spicy. *Finish* – Smooth, clean and enjoyably long. *Notes* – Wm Cadenhead bottling.

15 yrs, 1984, 63% abv

Sweetness – 5	Peatiness – 6	Availability – 2

Colour – Full amber with bronze highlights. *Nose* – Dry, round, slightly nutty, quite soft, medium-dry and fresh with a rich, dark peatiness. *Palate* – Big, warm, medium-dry, rich & quite intensely honeyed with a fairly solid peat note and nice chewy tannins. *Finish* – Long, tangy, quite complex & very rich. *Notes* – Blackadder bottling from cask no. 255 distilled in November 1984.

15 yrs, 1977, 60.9% abv

Sweetness – 6	Peatiness – 5	Availability – 1

Colour – Straw with yellow/pale gold highlights. *Nose* – Full-bodied with a dark peatiness and a rich, medium-dry tang of orange peel. *Flavour* – Soft, medium-sweet, rich and velvety smooth with a gentle peatiness. *Finish* – Long, fresh, clean and rich with a lightly toffeeyed tail. *Notes* – Wm Cadenhead bottling.

1972, 60.5% abv

Sweetness – 5	Peatiness – 6	Availability – 2

Colour – Pale amber with gold highlights. *Nose* – Quite full, earthy, medium-sweet, quite peaty for the region with hints of hazelnuts. *Flavour* – Medium-sweet, smoky and smooth with a little tannin and a green freshness. *Finish* – Long and gently smoky with a touch of spice. *Notes* – D.o.b. from cask no. 619.

26 yrs, 1967, 58% abv

Sweetness – 4	Peatiness – 5	Availability – 3

Colour – Mid-amber with old gold highlights. *Nose* – Medium-sweet, quite rich and fresh with a touch of oily oaky vanilla, a green character and medium-bodied. *Flavour* – Medium-dry, quite full and rich with a slight oily smoothness. *Finish* – Long and gently smoky with good rich sweetness and a tail of bitter toffee. *Notes* – D.o.b.

Benriach

Founded in 1898 as the whisky market moved suddenly into recession. It was then closed in 1900 and did not open again until 1965, when it was rebuilt by The Glenlivet Distillers Ltd. Owned by The Seagram Company of Canada from 1977. Sold to Pernod Ricard in 2001. Four stills.

Location – Situated three miles south of Elgin to the east of the A941.

Notes – The floor maltings are still in use. Previously only available from independent bottlers, Seagram introduced their own bottling in 1994. The sister distillery to the much prized Longmorn next door, both distilleries were built within four years of each other in the boom years of the 1890s. Like Longmorn, it is an important constituent of the flagship Seagram blend, *Chivas Regal*.

Water – Local springs.

BENRIACH DISTILLERY
EST. 1898
A SINGLE
PURE HIGHLAND MALT
Scotch Whisky

Benriach Distillery, in the heart of the Highlands,
still malts its own barley. The resulting whisky has
a unique and attractive delicacy

PRODUCED AND BOTTLED BY THE

BENRIACH
DISTILLERY Cº
ELGIN, MORAYSHIRE, SCOTLAND, IV30 3SJ
Distilled and Bottled in Scotland

AGED 10 YEARS

70 cl ℮ 43%vol

10 yrs, 43% abv

Sweetness – 6	Peatiness – 3	Availability – 7

Colour – Quite pale straw with lemon highlights. *Nose* – Fresh, green appley bubble-gum character, lightly malty and lightly peated, medium-sweet. *Flavour* – Medium-dry, soft, quite full-bodied with a chocolatey richness and touches of spice and coffee. *Finish* – Rich with a tang of coffee, quite long and lingering. *Notes* – D.o.b.

1969, 40% abv

Sweetness – 6	Peatiness – 3	Availability – 4

Colour – Pale straw with gold highlights. *Nose* – Sweet, distinctive fruitiness, fresh and appley. *Flavour* – Sweet, appley, distinctive, reminiscent of Calvados. *Finish* – Spicy and good with the apple flavour lingering. *Notes* – Gordon & MacPhail bottling.

Benrinnes

The original distillery was located at Whitehouse Farm, three quarters of a mile to the south east and was washed away in the great flood of 1829. The present building was founded in 1835 by William Smith & Co as an extension of the farm steading. Acquired by Dewar's in 1922, and thereby became a part of DCL in 1925. Run by SMD since 1930, the licensees were A. & A. Crawford Ltd. Major reconstruction took place between 1955 and 1956. Doubled from three to six stills in 1966. Now part of United Distillers plc.

Location – Situated one and a half miles south of the A95 on a loop of an unclassified road which runs between the A95 at Daugh of Kinermony and the B9009 at Succoth in Glen Rinnes.

Notes – A form of triple distillation is practised.

Water – The Scurran and Rowantree Burns.

SPEYSIDE
SINGLE MALT
SCOTCH WHISKY

BENRINNES

distillery stands on the
northern shoulder of BEN RINNES
700 feet above *sea level*.
It is ideally located to exploit
the *natural advantages* of the
area-pure *air*, *peat* and
barley and the *finest* of *hill* water,
which rises through *granite*
from *springs* on the *summit*
of the *mountain*. The resulting
single MALT SCOTCH WHISKY,
is *rounded* and *mellow*.

AGED **15** YEARS

Distilled & Bottled in SCOTLAND
BENRINNES DISTILLERY
Aberlour, Banffshire. Scotland.

43% vol 70 cl

---

15 yrs, 43% abv

Sweetness – 8	Peatiness – 4	Availability – 4

Colour – Amber with old gold highlights. *Nose* – Medium-bodied, biscuity-yeasty, fresh, vanilla and medium-sweet with a slight floral note. *Flavour* – Medium-sweet, round, smooth, biscuity and honeyed. *Finish* – Nice, sweet, round, biscuity and honeyed. *Notes* – United Distillers bottling.

14 yrs, 1982, 43% abv

Sweetness – 7	Peatiness – 5	Availability – 1

Colour – Pale amber with bright gold highlights. *Nose* – Quite full-bodied, medium-sweet and rich with a slight hint of green apples and a rubbery peatiness. *Flavour* – Quite big-bodied, medium-dry and slightly smoky. *Finish* – Dry, long and gently chewy. *Notes* – Signatory bottling from cask nos. 95/1171/4, distilled 25 November 1982.

16 yrs, 1980, 43% abv

Sweetness – 6	Peatiness – 6	Availability – 2

Colour – Pale straw with pale yellow highlights. *Nose* – Quite a mashy cereal note, soft and medium-dry with quite gentle peatiness. *Flavour* – Medium-sweet with an almost fragrant peatiness, smooth round and of good body. *Finish* – Long, fragrant & clean. *Notes* – Blackadder International bottling from cask no. 1350, distilled 19 March 1980.

1968, 40% abv

Sweetness – 6	Peatiness – 6	Availability – 2

Colour – Straw/gold with good bright highlights. *Nose* – Sweet, nutty and slightly fatty in an unctuous way. *Flavour* – Medium-sweet, smoky, spicy and oaky. *Finish* – Good, smoky and dry, smooth and creamy. *Notes* – Gordon & MacPhail bottling.

Benromach

Built by the Benromach Distillery Company. Bought by Associated Scottish Distilleries Ltd in 1937, who sold it to DCL in 1953. It was managed by SMD and licensed to J. & W. Hardie. The still house was rebuilt in 1966 and the mash house was rebuilt and the tun-room modernised in 1974. Two stills. Bought by Gordon & MacPhail in 1992, who reopened it in 1996.

Location – North of Forres on the north side of the railway line.

Notes – In 1925 the mash tun was wooden. Benromach was designed by Elgin architect Charles Doig and has high pitched gables and narrow mullioned windows in the Scots vernacular style of the 17th century.

Water – Chapeltown springs near Forres.

12 yrs, 40% abv

Sweetness – 7	Peatiness – 4	Availability – 5

Colour – Amber with yellow highlights. *Nose* – Medium-bodied and medium-sweet with a rich, almost bubble-gum fruitiness and a touch of apple with good background peat. *Flavour* – Medium-sweet, round and smooth with good, quite chunky peat flavours. *Finish* – Long, very gently smoky and quite complex. *Notes* – D.o.b.

15 yrs, 40% abv

Sweetness – 7	Peatiness – 5	Availability – 4

Colour – Amber with pale gold highlights. *Nose* – Full, malty, rich & medium-sweet with a slightly green vegetal note & darkish peat character, showing notes of heather honey & lemon curd. *Palate* – Medium-dry, rich & quite creamy with gently chewy oaky tannins & a good dark peat character. *Finish* – Long & softly chewy with creamy toffee on the tail. *Notes* – UDV bottling.

1974, 40% *abv*

Sweetness – 7	Peatiness – 4	Availability – 2

Colour – Amber with gold highlights. *Nose* – Quite soft, medium-sweet and malty, quite delicately peated, showing characters of toffee, ripe, sweet apples & almost peaches. *Palate* – Quite big, soft, medium-sweet & honeyed with a quite delicate peatiness. *Finish* – Long, clean, rich and quite elegant with a toffee apple character. *Notes* – D.o.b.

1969, 40% *abv*

Sweetness – 7	Peatiness – 4	Availability – 2

Colour – Mid-amber with yellow/gold highlights. *Nose* – Fresh and medium-dry with an oily-oaky aroma, soft and smooth with a touch of green apples. *Flavour* – Medium-dry, quite rich and soft, sweetness develops in the palate, gently peated. *Finish* – Quite long and lightly smoky with a touch of spice in the tail. *Notes* – D.o.b.

BENROMACH CENTENARY, 17 *yrs*, 43% *abv*

Sweetness – 7	Peatiness – 5	Availability – 4

Colour – Amber with pale gold highlights. *Nose* – Medium-sweet, round and slightly malty with notes of vanilla & cereals. *Palate* – Medium-sweet, round and malty with a quite delicate, but also quite solid peatiness. *Finish* – Long and clean, showing creamy vanilla. *Notes* – D.o.b.

BENROMACH LIMITED EDITION, 17 *yrs*, 43% *abv*

Sweetness – 5	Peatiness – 7	Availability – 4

Colour – Amber with old gold highlights. *Nose* – Fresh and medium-dry with a quite solid, earthy peat character & sweetly charred, oaky vanilla, a rich vegetal touch with hints of cocoa & coffee. *Palate* – Medium-sweet, of good body, with a quite dark, yet subtle, peatiness, gently chewy oaky tannins and a rich, fruity character. *Finish* – Long, richly smoky, smooth and quite spicy. *Notes* – D.o.b. as 'Special Centenary Bottling'.

Ben Wyvis

INVERGORDON, ROSS-SHIRE   [I] [V]   EST. 1881

B uilt within the Invergordon grain distilling complex in 1965 by Invergordon Distillers Ltd, Ben Wyvis had two stills. These were closed down in 1977 and subsequently dismantled. Its make has never before been bottled and is therefore extremely rare.

Location – Within the Invergordon grain complex to the west of the town of the same name.

Notes – Invergordon is the deepest port in Britain. A regular port of call for cruise ships, the Cromarty Firth, on the shores of which the harbour is situated, is a storage area for deep sea oil rigs.

Water – Loch Glass.

1968, 51% *abv*

Sweetness – 7	Peatiness – 4	Availability – 1

Colour – Amber with yellow highlights. *Nose* – Quite full-bodied, medium-sweet, slightly honeyed vanilla note with sweet, soft oak, beeswax & lemon oil. *Palate* – Quite soft, round, smooth and of good body, with gently chewy tannins & delicately peated. *Finish* – Long, rich & elegant with lingering shortbread flavours. *Notes* – Signatory bottling.

Bladnoch

Founded in 1817 by John & Thomas McClelland. Sold by Dunvilles, the Irish whiskey distillers, in 1936 for £3,500, this "representing a considerable loss for the premises and plant". Closed in 1938 and reopened in 1956. Run by United Distillers plc and closed in 1993. Now owned by Raymond Armstrong trading as Bladnoch Distillery Ltd. Recommenced distilling in November 2000.

Location – The southernmost distillery in Scotland. Situated on the river of the same name, just a mile outside Wigtown.

Notes – Close to the distillery is Baldoon Farm, where stands the ruined castle to which Janet Dalrymple, the "Bride of Lammermoor", came to die after her marriage to David Dunbar of Baldoon.

Water – The River Bladnoch.

10 yrs, 43% abv

Sweetness – 4	Peatiness – 4	Availability – 6

Colour – Straw/amber with yellow highlights and green tinge. *Nose* – Fresh, quite full, fruity and floral, medium-dry with an attractive grape spirit-like aroma. *Flavour* – Fresh with good weight, a sweet edge and a touch of spice. *Finish* – Fresh with nice sweetness and quite light. *Notes* – United Distillers bottling.

22 yrs, 50% abv

Sweetness – 8	Peatiness – 2	Availability – 2

Colour – Amber with yellow highlights. *Nose* – Medium-bodied, fresh, quite fat & rich, medium-sweet & lightly peated with notes of apple, orange, dried bananas & sweet, oaky vanilla. *Palate* – Sweet, rich, lightly peated, quite full-bodied with flavours of vanilla & banana. *Finish* – Long, rich, quite fresh & appealingly fruity. *Notes* – Douglas Laing & Co Ltd bottling.

Blair Athol

Although originally founded almost 30 years earlier, the present distillery was established in 1826, when revived by John Robertson. It passed into the hands of John Conacher & Company in 1827. It closed in 1932 and, although purchased by Arthur Bell & Sons the following year, it did not come into production again until 1949 after rebuilding. Extended from two to four stills in 1973. Now part of Diageo plc.

Location – Not at Blair Atholl, as its name suggests, the distillery is to be found on the southern approach road to Pitlochry, just off the main A9.

Notes – The Conacher family, who owned the distillery for a time in the 1800s, are said to be descended from the chivalrous young Conacher who so admired Catherine Glover, the Fair Maid of Perth. The distillery has a large modern visitor centre. Blair Athol is well worth a visit, having an excellent audio-visual presentation as part of a tour of the distillery. Blair Athol malt (note the difference in spelling from the town) plays an important part in the Bell's blend.

Water – From a spring on the nearby 2,760 ft. high Ben Vrackie.

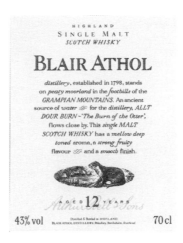

12 yrs, 43% abv

Sweetness – 7	Peatiness – 6	Availability – 6

Colour – Pale, mid-amber with gold highlights. *Nose* – Quite full with touches of nuttiness and greenness, medium-sweet with a fresh smokiness. *Flavour* – Medium-sweet and quite full-bodied, spicy and round with a definite smoky tang. *Finish* – Fresh, quite long and smoky with a sweetness on the tail. *Notes* – D.o.b.

8 yrs, 40% abv

Sweetness – 5	Peatiness – 5	Availability – 0

Colour – Straw/golden. *Nose* – Fresh, clean and lightly peated. *Flavour* – Sweet, almost almondy. *Finish* – Quite good and distinctive. *Notes* – Arthur Bell Distillers bottling.

23 yrs, 1966, 57.1% abv

Sweetness – 6	Peatiness – 5	Availability – 1

Colour – Mid-amber with yellow/gold highlights. *Nose* – Medium-sweet, quite good body and round with nice vanilla-oak and a citrus oil tang. *Flavour* – Soft, smooth, medium-sweet with a dry oakiness, quite gentle tannins and good body. *Finish* – Long with a distinctive perfumed sweetness and a gentle smokiness. *Notes* – Wm Cadenhead bottling distilled October 1966.

18 yrs, 1977, 50.4% abv

Sweetness – 5	Peatiness – 5	Availability – 1

Colour – Straw with yellow highlights. *Nose* – Light-bodied, sweet and malty with a hint of darkness to the peat character and a touch of liquorice and apple. *Flavour* – Medium-sweet, quite lightly peated and gently chewy with an appley flavour. *Finish* – Long and chewy with a touch of spiciness. *Notes* – James MacArthur bottling.

Bowmore

In 1776, an Islay merchant, David Simpson, obtained permission from the local laird to build dwellings and "other buildings". The "other buildings" were soon converted into a distillery. Bought by Stanley P. Morrison in 1963, the distillery is now owned by Morrison Bowmore Distillers, who were themselves purchased outright by Suntory of Japan in 1994. The company had been part owned by Suntory for some years previously, having had a long-term trading relationship with the Japanese company.

Location – Bowmore stands, almost fortress-like, on the shores of Loch Indaal.

Notes – Bowmore uses a revolutionary waste heat recovery system to reduce energy costs. The distillery donated a warehouse to the village of Bowmore which has been converted to a swimming pool. The waste heat from the distillery is used to heat the swimming pool. The distillery was built early in the village's history, at the foot of Hill Street, and has proved important to its economic survival. It is said to be the oldest legal distillery on the island.

Water – Laggan River.

BOWMORE LEGEND, No age statement, 40% *abv*

Sweetness – 1	*Peatiness* – 8	*Availability* – 9

Colour – Light amber with gold highlights and a touch of green. *Nose* – Full, pungent, a touch perfumed and a phenol character with a little greenness. *Flavour* – Dry with an edge of richness, perfumed and quite pungent. *Finish* – Long, gently smoky and perfumed. *Notes* – D.o.b. Sold as *Bowmore Legend.*

10 yrs, 40% abv

Sweetness – 0	Peatiness – 8	Availability – 8

Colour – Mid-amber with gold highlights. **Nose** – Full, dry, pungent with a touch of burnt heather and perfumed. **Flavour** – Dry, heather-perfumed, fresh and smoky, quite full-bodied with whiffs of ozone. **Finish** – Long, characterful and smoky. **Notes** – D.o.b.

12 yrs, 40% abv

Sweetness – 0	Peatiness – 8	Availability – 7

Colour – Full, amber, very bright. **Nose** – Lightish, peaty, burnt heather with a characteristic tang of ozone/iodine and even a whiff of chocolate! **Flavour** – Smooth, refined flavour with a pronounced smoky peatiness. **Finish** – Good, long and dry. **Notes** – D.o.b.

17 yrs, 43% abv

Sweetness – 2	Peatiness – 8	Availability – 6

Colour – Quite full, deep amber with old gold highlights. **Nose** – Rich, medium bodied with a pungency, but delicate, and aromas of violets. **Flavour** – Round, quite full-bodied, smoky and rich with gentle tannins. **Finish** – Soft, gently smoky, quite elegant and slightly salty. **Notes** – D.o.b.

21 yrs, 43% abv

Sweetness – 2	Peatiness – 8	Availability – 5

Colour – Mid-amber with old gold highlights. **Nose** – Quite big-bodied, dark and smoky, rounded and quite dry with just a hint of ozone. **Flavour** – Big, round, burnt heather roots, quite pungent with a delicate floral note at the back. **Finish** – Long with a hint of sweetness/richness and finely smoky with a touch of bitter chocolate on the tail. **Notes** – D.o.b.

25 yrs, 43% abv

Sweetness – 3	Peatiness – 7	Availability – 3

Colour – Quite deep amber with pale bronze highlights. **Nose** – Quite full-bodied, rich with a slightly green hedgerow freshness, a floral smokiness and burnt vanilla notes. **Flavour** – Full-bodied, fresh and round, medium-dry but rich, a slightly perfumed dark peaty smokiness and a touch of oaky tannin. **Finish** – Long, gently chewy, almost floral, quite delicately smoky with a hint of seaweed and bitter chocolate – very complex. **Notes** – D.o.b.

1989, 46% *abv*

Sweetness – 2	Peatiness – 8	Availability – 2

Colour – Straw with pale yellow highlights. *Nose* – Medium-bodied, quite floral – violets, burnt heather roots & with quite a dark peat note. *Palate* – Quite big-bodied, rich, floral, round & darkly peaty. *Finish* – Long, quite rich & sea-tainted. *Notes* – Murray McDavid bottling.

BLACK BOWMORE, 1964, 50% *abv*

Sweetness – 2	Peatiness – 7	Availability – 1

Colour – Very deep, dark mahogany/teak with deep bronze highlights. *Nose* – Big-bodied, full, dark, nutty and rich, quite delicately peated, dry with slight notes of burnt mahogany. *Flavour* – Big, powerful, full-bodied, quite tannic with dark nutty flavours, smooth, although chewy. *Finish* – Long, full-flavoured, quite chewy with a smoky/nutty character, a good perfumed peatiness and a rich salty tang on the tail. *Notes* – D.o.b. Known as *Black Bowmore*, this is from a very rare old sherry cask bottling. There were three issues of *Black Bowmore*, the first and the last being the most rare.

BOWMORE MARINER, 15 *yrs*, 43% *abv*

Sweetness – 2	Peatiness – 8	Availability – 5

Colour – Amber with gold/bronze highlights. *Nose* – Rich, gloriously chocolatey and with good body; a delicate note of burnt heather roots and a peatiness at the back. *Flavour* – Quite full-bodied, smoky, clean and round with a richness at the back. *Finish* – Long, fresh and smoky with an appealing green edge. *Notes* – D.o.b.

Braeval

Originally called Braes of Glenlivet, Braeval was built between 1973 and 1974 by Chivas Bros Ltd, a subsidiary of the Seagram Co Ltd of Canada. Originally three stills, with two more being added in 1975 and a sixth in 1978. Sold to Pernod Ricard in 2001. Although a very modern distillery, it is nevertheless of a most attractive design, with a decorative, albeit non-functional, pagoda-style roof.

Location – High up above the remote hamlet of Chapeltown off the B9008, it is one of the most isolated distilleries in Scotland.

Notes – This whisky is at last becoming available through independent bottlers. The distillery's name was changed to Braeval to avoid confusion with its illustrious sister, The Glenlivet.

Water – The Pitilie Burn.

Vintage 1979
Single Highland Malt Scotch Whisky
Matured in sherry casks for 15 years
Distilled at the Braes of Glenlivet Distillery

15 yrs, 43% abv

Sweetness – 7	Peatiness – 5	Availability – 2

Colour – Quite deep amber with bronze highlights. *Nose* – Quite full-bodied, round and gently peaty; rich and creamy with a slightly perfumed character. *Flavour* – Round, smooth, full-bodied, medium-sweet with a not unpleasant, slightly perfumed, green edge. *Finish* – Long, smooth, medium-dry and slightly nutty. *Notes* – Signatory bottling distilled on 6 June 1979.

8 yrs, 1987, 60% abv

Sweetness – 7	Peatiness – 4	Availability – 2

Colour – Pale straw with pale, watery lemon highlights. *Nose* – Medium-dry, of quite good body, a young mashy character with a slight touch of citrus, a hedgerow greenness and a soft maltiness. *Flavour* – Soft, medium-sweet, quite good body and round with a touch of peat at the back. *Finish* – Clean, of reasonable length, with good sweetness. *Notes* – Wm Cadenhead bottling.

Brora

Brora was known as Clynelish until 1969. Established by the Duke of Sutherland, who had cleared his tenant-farmers off the land to make way for sheep. Having moved some of the inland farmers to the coastal strip, the distillery was established to create a market for the farmers' grain. Owned by SMD, now a part of Diageo plc, since 1930.

Location – Just off the A9 at Brora.

Notes – After the modern distillery had been built in 1967–8, the old Clynelish reopened in April 1969, housed in the former mash house, which had been rebuilt. It subsequently ceased distillation in May 1983. The old buildings are now used as warehouses and the visitor centre for the "new" Clynelish. Brora had two stills.

Water – The Clynemilton Burn.

1981, 43% abv

Sweetness – 3	Peatiness – 8	Availability – 2

Colour – Pale amber with yellow highlights. *Nose* – Big-bodied, fresh & medium-dry with quite a solid peat character, a green, almost leafy, touch, a slight edge of sweetness & a menthol note. *Palate* – Medium-dry, of good body and a big smoky peat character. *Finish* – Long, darkly smoky & slightly peppery. *Notes* – Signatory bottling.

22 yrs, 58.7% abv

Sweetness – 4	Peatiness – 8	Availability – 1

Colour – Amber with gold highlights. *Nose* – Big bodied, quite pungent, a dark, smoky, almost sooty, burnt tang with richness at the back. *Flavour* – Quite big with a soft peatiness, but a burnt character, medium-sweet, quite rich and with big tannins. *Finish* – Long, with an almost burnt character, spicy with chewy tannins. *Notes* – D.o.b.

Bruichladdich

BRUICHLADDICH, ISLAY, ARGYLL [I] EST. 1881

Built by Robert, William & John Gourlay Harvey (of the Dundashill & Yoker Harveys). Became the Bruichladdich Distillery Company (Islay) Ltd in 1886. Doubled from two to four stills in 1975. Owned in recent years by Invergordon Distillers, who were taken over by JBB (Greater Europe) plc in late 1993. A lot of very old machinery and distillation techniques were employed in the distillery, making it an exciting distillery to visit. Mothballed abruptly at the end of January 1995, it was sold in December 2000 to the Bruichladdich Distillery Co Ltd, a consortium of 25 shareholders. Production started again in May 2001.

Location – Sited on the western shore of Loch Indaal on the A847 to Port Charlotte and the picturesque village of Portnahaven.

Notes – The distillery is the most westerly in Scotland and, despite this, it has a lighter, more delicate character than the other Islay malts. It is thought that this is because it is sheltered from the prevailing winds – and weather – by the Rhinns of Islay, a range of hills which lie between Bruichladdich and the open sea.

Water – A reservoir in the local hills.

10 yrs, 40% abv

Sweetness – 2	Peatiness – 7	Availability – 7

Colour – Pale golden with slight green tinges. *Nose* – A delicate peatiness, fairly light and with no great pungency. *Flavour* – Full and flavoursome, smoky and dry without the heavier notes of other Islays. *Finish* – Of good length and with a well-defined finish. *Notes* – D.o.b.

15 yrs, 40% abv

Sweetness – 3	Peatiness – 6	Availability – 4

Colour – Straw with amber/gold highlights. *Nose* – Rich, delicately peated, but with an underlying sweetness. *Flavour* – Slightly sweet with hints of nuttiness and very little of Islay's heavier characteristics. *Finish* – Spicy, warm, long, with sweet oak, but finally dry. *Notes* – D.o.b.

21 yrs, 43% abv

Sweetness – 3	Peatiness – 6	Availability – 4

Colour – Light amber with yellow/gold highlights. *Nose* – Quite light, fresh and rich with a faint touch of ozone. *Flavour* – Medium-bodied, fresh, almost dry, but with an edge of richness – an intriguing mixture of sweetness and dryness. *Finish* – Tangy, fresh, rich and clean and gently smoky. *Notes* – D.o.b.

32 yrs, 1964, 49% abv

Sweetness – 4	Peatiness – 5	Availability – 0

Colour – Very dark, deep amber with bronze highlights and a ruby hue. *Nose* – Dark, slightly sweet, nutty (sweet hazelnuts) and full-bodied with an edge of burnt heather roots, and a soft, vanilla-oaky character. *Flavour* – Wonderfully soft and mature, very delicately peated, gently chewy with a sweetly dark edge. *Finish* – Long, elegant, complex and very gently smoky with a slight hint of fruitcake sweetness. *Notes* – *Piper's Preferred* bottling from an oloroso cask. Sold in Germany.

1991, 57.9% abv

Sweetness – 3	Peatiness – 7	Availability – 2

Colour – Pale, watery straw with pale lemon highlights. *Nose* – Light, fresh, quite soft and lightly malty with a perfumed note to the delicate peat. *Palate* – Medium-bodied, quite rich and delicately peated with a floral note. *Finish* – Long and quite elegantly youthful with a darkly soft peat note on the tail. *Notes* – Clydesdale Original bottling.

1967, 44.7% abv

Sweetness – 4	Peatiness – 5	Availability – 2

Colour – Deep amber with blood red highlights. *Nose* – Quite delicate, but rounded, warm & nutty with a slight hint of burnt mahogany & notes of toast, honey, beeswax & toffee. *Palate* – Soft, round, smooth & rich with very delicate chewy tannins & creamy toffee. *Finish* – Long, ethereal & complex, showing beeswax, honey & citrus on the tail. *Notes* – Signatory bottling.

Bunnahabhain

Became part of Highland Distilleries Ltd in 1887 when amalgamated with William Grant and Co of Glenrothes. Extended from two to four stills in 1963.

Location – Situated towards the north east tip of Islay on the bay from which it takes its name.

Notes – Bunnahabhain means "mouth of the river". Prior to the building of this distillery which is the island's most northerly, the adjacent area was inhospitable and uninhabited. Now a small hamlet has built up around the distillery.

Water – River Margadale.

12 yrs, 40% abv

Sweetness – 3	Peatiness – 6	Availability – 9

Colour – Straw with golden highlights. *Nose* – Distinctive, quite light and flowery. *Flavour* – Smoother, softer and less pungent than other Islays. *Finish* – Smooth, round, lovely and long. *Notes* – D.o.b.

25 yrs, 1964, 46% abv

Sweetness – 5	Peatiness – 6	Availability – 0

Colour – Straw with yellow highlights. *Nose* – Medium-sweet, rich, ripe and fruity with a dark tarriness at the back and a floral note. *Flavour* – Medium-sweet and rich with oaky tannins, quite smooth and creamy. *Finish* – Rich, full-bodied and quite long with an earthy smokiness on the tail. *Notes* – Master of Malt bottling.

17 yrs, 1979, 43% abv

Sweetness – 4	Peatiness – 6	Availability – 2

Colour – Pale amber with yellow highlights. *Nose* – Fresh, medium-dry, rich, fruity with notes of lemon, apple and sweet vanilla and quite gently peated. *Flavour* – Medium-dry with an edge of richness, a soft fruity touch and gentle peat. *Finish* – Long, malty and softly smoky. *Notes* – Blackadder International bottling from cask no. 8770 distilled 5 September 1979.

17 yrs, 1979, 58.4% abv

Sweetness – 3	Peatiness – 5	Availability – 2

Colour – Full amber with old gold highlights. *Nose* – Full, ripe and nutty with a fine, delicate peatiness, medium-dry with a slight hint of liquorice/trout fishing basket. *Flavour* – Smooth, medium-dry and nutty with good body and a very gentle peatiness. *Finish* – Nuttily soft, lingeringly complex and round. *Notes* – Signatory bottling from butt no. 5110, distilled 18 April 1979.

1979, 46% abv

Sweetness – 3	Peatiness – 6	Availability – 2

Colour – Pale straw with pale yellow highlights. *Nose* – Medium-bodied, fresh, slightly vegetal (cabbage), peppery & spicy with quite a soft hint of richness. *Palate* – Quite big-bodied, medium-dry, round & gently peated with soft, chewy tannins. *Finish* – Long with vegetal & menthol notes. *Notes* – Murray McDavid bottling.

Bushmills

Bushmills was granted a licence to distil in 1608, making it by far the earliest legal distillery of all. Operated by Irish Distillers which, in 1988, was the target of a hard-fought takeover battle between British giant Grand Metropolitan and French rival Pernod-Ricard, which the latter won.

Location – Near the Giant's Causeway on the north coast of Ulster.

Notes – Bushmills is triple distilled, although it is not alone in this respect. Auchentoshan, Rosebank and Benrinnes also use forms of triple distillation. Bushmills is also available in duty-free markets at 43% abv. Irish whiskey is unpeated, unlike most Scotch whisky. Irish Distillers own two distilleries: Bushmills and the modern Midleton complex near Cork. Irish blends such as *Jameson, Original Bushmills, Black Bush, Powers, Paddy* and *Tullamore Dew* are produced from whiskeys distilled at these two distilleries. In 1920, there were 23 distilleries in Ireland and 134 in Scotland.

Water – Saint Columb's Rill.

10 yrs, 40% abv

Sweetness – 7	Peatiness – 0	Availability – 9

Colour – Amber with yellow-gold highlights. *Nose* – Fresh, clean and grassy with a bubble-gummy sweetness (medium-sweet) and a slight grassy character. *Flavour* – Medium-sweet with quite good body and round with a nice vanilla wood note. *Finish* – Clean, long and fresh. *Notes* – Irish Distillers bottling.

16 yrs, 40% abv

Sweetness – 5	Peatiness – 0	Availability – 6

Colour – Mid-amber with old gold highlights and an edge of ruby. *Nose* – Full-bodied, fresh and slightly green with a gooseberry character, it has a rich, woody nuttiness and is medium-sweet with a nutty toffee character. *Flavour* – Almost dry with good body, smooth, dark and nutty; round with a slight gooseberry ripeness and a touch of toffee. *Finish* – Long, with a good, nutty richness, a dark complexity and an almost mahogany-flavoured chewiness. *Notes* – Irish Distillers bottling; aged in a mixture of Bourbon barrels and sherry butts, then finished off for six months in port pipes.

BUSHMILLS DISTILLERY RESERVE, 12 yrs, 40% abv

Sweetness – 6	Peatiness – 0	Availability – 1

Colour –Mid-amber with old gold highlights. *Nose* – Clean, rich and creamy, with notes of toffee, almonds, rich vanilla, marzipan and a fresh grapey fruitiness. *Palate* – Medium-sweet, rich, quite full-bodied, tangy, smooth, quite elegant and thoughtful. *Finish* – Long, round & rich with lingering sweet vanilla. *Notes* – D.o.b. only available from the distillery.

Caol Ila

PORT ASKAIG, ISLAY, ARGYLL   [I] [V]   EST. 1846

Built by Hector Henderson on what, when you are standing at the distillery, seems a very isolated spot. The distillery was taken over in 1863 by Bulloch Lade & Co, who extended and rebuilt it in 1879. It came under DCL's control in 1927 and management has been by SMD, now UMGD, since 1930. It was completely rebuilt, apart from warehouses, between April 1972 and January 1974, when it was extended from two stills to six. Now a part of Diageo plc.

Location – Another distillery which is literally at the end of the road, in this case, the northern end of the A846.

Notes – Caol Ila's still house has arguably the finest view in the Scotch whisky industry. It overlooks Caol Ila (the Gaelic name for the Sound of Islay) to the Paps of Jura. Hot water from the condensers is pumped through a sea water condenser, cooled and returned for re-use in the still house condensers. Never one of United Distillers' mainstream malts and thus mainly available as a single from independent bottlers, it is nevertheless an important and extensive building block for blended whisky. It is now one of the key malts in *Bell's* 8-year-old blend.

Water – Loch Nam Ban (Torrabolls Loch).

ISLAY
SINGLE MALT *SCOTCH WHISKY*

CAOL ILA

distillery, built in 1846 is situated near *Port Askaig* on the *Isle of Islay*. Steamers used to call twice a week to collect *whisky* from this remote *site* in a cove facing the *Isle of Jura*. Water supplies for mashing come from *Loch nam Ban* although the sea provides *water* for *condensing*. Unusual for an *Islay* this *single MALT SCOTCH WHISKY* has a *fresh aroma* and a *light* yet *well rounded* flavour.

A G E D **15** Y E A R S

43% vol   Distilled & Bottled in *SCOTLAND*. CAOL ILA DISTILLERY Port Askaig. Isle of Islay, *Scotland*.   70 cl

15 yrs, 43% abv

Sweetness – 2	Peatiness – 9	Availability – 5

Colour – Straw/pale amber with lemon-yellow highlights. *Nose* – Full, quite pungent and peaty, smoky, burnt heather roots with a touch of unripe greenness. *Flavour* – Big, full, smoky and pungent with an edge of sweetness. *Finish* – Long, rich and smoky with a touch of bitter chocolate and spice. *Notes* – D.o.b.

10 yrs, 43% abv

Sweetness – 2	Peatiness – 10	Availability – 2

Colour – Straw with yellow highlights. *Nose* – Big-bodied, dry, malty & rich with a powerful, earthy peat character. *Palate* – Full-bodied, quite soft (relatively), rich & gently chewy with a solid peat character. *Finish* – Long, smooth, earthy & rich. *Notes* – Hart Brothers bottling.

10 yrs, 46% abv

Sweetness – 1	Peatiness – 9	Availability – 1

Colour – Pale straw with pale gold highlights. *Nose* – Rich, creamy, quite full and round, with burnt heather roots. *Palate* – Dry, big-bodied with very smoky burnt heather roots. *Finish* – Long and rich with a good peat character. *Notes* – Cadenhead bottling.

19 yrs, 43% abv

Sweetness – 1	Peatiness – 9	Availability – 2

Colour – Very pale straw with lemon highlights. *Nose* – Full-bodied, pungent and dry with the aroma of burnt heather roots. *Flavour* – Full, pungent, smoky and dry with just a hint of sweetness on the edge. *Finish* – Long, characterful and smoky with oaky tannins. *Notes* – Blackadder International bottling.

1989, 46% abv

Sweetness – 2	Peatiness – 9	Availability – 2

Colour – Straw with yellow/lemon highlights. *Nose* – Full and big-bodied, fresh and heavily earthy-peated with a green edge and a hint of menthol. *Palate* – Big-bodied, pungent, intense and powerful with an earthy peatiness and a slight sea character. *Finish* – Long, intensely smoky, rich with an edge of sweetness & a touch of salt. *Notes* – Murray McDavid bottling.

1980, 43% abv

Sweetness – 2	Peatiness – 9	Availability – 2

Colour – Quite pale amber with pale gold highlights. *Nose* – Big, powerful, quite an earthy peatiness with a layer of ripe coconut, fresh, almost dry, quite rich & slightly perfumed. *Palate* – Almost dry, big-bodied, quite heavily peated and rich with a slightly vinuous note. *Finish* – Long, fresh, quite smoky & powerful with a touch of coconut on the tail. *Notes* – The Vintage Malt Whisky Co Ltd bottling.

1974, 40% abv

Sweetness – 2	Peatiness – 9	Availability – 2

Colour – Bright gold/amber with gold highlights. *Nose* – Peaty, malty, earthy, more than a hint of the sea, but with a rich, almost perfumed fruitiness to it. *Flavour* – Dry, round, quite full-bodied and peaty. *Finish* – Smoky and dry, but rich. *Notes* – Gordon & MacPhail bottling.

Caperdonich

Following the industry slump at the end of the 19th century, Caperdonich was closed in 1902 and did not produce again until 1965 following rebuilding. Extended from two to four stills in 1967 under Seagram's ownership. Sold to Pernod Ricard in 2001.

Location – Situated at one end of the small town of Rothes, across the road from its sister distillery, Glen Grant.

Notes – The distillery was built to supplement the output of Glen Grant and was known as Glen Grant No. 2. The whisky, using the same water, is lighter and fruitier than *Glen Grant*. The two distilleries were originally joined by a pipe which carried spirit from Caperdonich to Glen Grant across the town's main street. Rothes supports five distilleries, with Caperdonich the last to be built. Glen Grant, established in 1840, was the first.

Water – The Caperdonich Well, adjacent to the Glen Grant Burn.

1979, 40% *abv*

Sweetness – 8	Peatiness – 8	Availability – 3

Colour – Pale straw, almost yellow. *Nose* – Sweet, ripe, grapey with a hint of cloves and apples. *Flavour* – Sweet and spirity with a slight flavour of cloves. *Finish* – Quite good for its youth, but shortish. *Notes* – Gordon & MacPhail bottling.

16 yrs, 1972, 40% *abv*

Sweetness – 7	Peatiness – 3	Availability – 0

Colour – Honey-amber with old gold highlights. *Nose* – Full, fruity, almost raisin-like, nutty and delicately peated with hints of demerara sugar. *Flavour* – Quite full and oaky with good peatiness, smooth and medium-sweet. *Finish* – Long, creamy and spicy with oaky tannins. *Notes* – Master of Malt bottling.

Cardhu

KNOCKANDO, MORAY   [S] [V]   EST. 1824

Built on Cardow farm, the distillery was also known by that name until recently. The original licensee was John Cumming, who had previously gained a string of convictions as a whisky smuggler. Acquired by John Walker & Son in 1893, it became part of DCL in 1925. Managed by SMD since 1930. Rebuilt in 1960 and extended from four to six stills. Now part of Diageo plc.

Location – Situated high up above the River Spey on its north bank, on the B9102 between Knockando and Craigellachie.

Notes – A "flagship" of UDV, the malt has long played an important role in the success of Johnnie Walker's famous Red and Black Label brands. Cardhu means "black rock".

Water – Springs on the Mannoch Hill or the Lyne Burn.

12 yrs, 40% abv

Sweetness – 8	Peatiness – 7	Availability – 9

Colour – Pale mid-amber with a definite green tinge. *Nose* – Quite full-bodied, rich, medium-sweet and smoky with a green apple character. *Flavour* – Round and mellow, sweet with a delicate peatiness. *Finish* – Long, peaty and sweet. *Notes* – D.o.b.

1974, 56% abv

Sweetness – 7	Peatiness – 7	Availability – 2

Colour – Deep amber with ruby-tinted bronze highlights. *Nose* – Big-bodied, medium-sweet & rich with a slight charred oak character, a dark liquorice & almost petrol note. *Palate* – Big, quite chewy tannins, round, medium-dry & quite soft with the charred character. *Finish* – Long & campfire smoky. *Notes* – Signatory bottling.

Clydesdale

Clydesdale distillery was said to have been built by Lord Belhaven and his first tenant was Patrick Chalmers. Lord Belhaven pulled out in 1848. Clydesdale Distillery Co Ltd was founded in 1894 and this was one of the founding members of Scottish Malt Distillers Ltd in 1914.

Location – On the south east side of Glasgow Road, Wishaw, where the local Glasgow–Lanark railway crosses the road.

Notes – Production ceased in 1919, although the premises were used by DCL as bonded warehouses until 1988 when the buildings were demolished.

Water – A burn rising in the Cambusnethan peat moss.

Unknown – circa 1900, 45% *abv*

Sweetness – 7	*Peatiness* – 3	*Availability* – 0

Colour – Quite dark amber with bronze highlights. *Nose* – Quite full-bodied, rich and sherried, dark nuttiness (Brazil nuts), quite soft vanilla with a dryness at the back. *Flavour* – Round, quite full, sherried, rich, soft, medium-sweet, nuttiness and a greenness. *Finish* – Long, rich, a touch of oakiness, creamy and nutty with a nice spicy tang. *Notes* – One of two bottles taken from the distillery in 1917 and kept by the Campbell family of Wishaw for use at funerals. This sample was also tasted by one of Scotland's master blenders who was of the opinion that it had been aged in a liqueur cask, a common practice at the turn of the century when casks for ageing were at a premium.

Clynelish

The original Clynelish distillery was the old, now closed, Brora distillery next door. It was founded by the Marquess of Stafford, later the first Duke of Sutherland. It was intended as a ready market for barley produced by crofters who had been evicted from inland farms and moved down to the coastal plain. Established as a brewery in 1817, it was turned into a distillery two years later. Operated by UMGD and now part of Diageo plc. Six stills.

Location – Just off the A9 north of Brora on the north side of the extensive plain which forms the mouth of Strath Brora.

Notes – Brora was known as Clynelish until 1969. After the modern distillery had been built in 1967–8, the old Clynelish reopened in April 1975, housed in the rebuilt mash house. It subsequently ceased distillation in May 1983. There is no little confusion as Brora is often called "Clynelish". The whisky from the old distillery was only bottled as *Clynelish* prior to 1967. Between 1967 and 1983, production from the old distillery was stencilled as "Brora" on casks.

Water – The Clynemilton Burn.

14 yrs, 43% abv

Sweetness – 4	Peatiness – 6	Availability – 6

Colour – Pale amber with good green/gold highlights. *Nose* – Rich, medium-dry, a citrus fruitiness, quite full and round with good smokiness at the back. *Flavour* – Smoky with a soft sweetness, quite full-bodied and almost luscious – very complex. *Finish* – Long and elegant with a touch of bitter chocolate. *Notes* – D.o.b.

9 yrs, 61% abv

Sweetness – 6	Peatiness – 5	Availability – 1

Colour – Straw with yellow highlights. *Nose* – Fresh, medium-dry and vinuous with a green fruity character and a quite solid peatiness. *Palate* – Medium-sweet, fresh and of good body, with a quite solid dark peaty note and a nice, smooth maltiness. *Finish* – Long, round, sweet & rich with an elegant chocolate peat note. *Notes* – Cadenhead bottling.

12 yrs, 40% abv

Sweetness – 6	Peatiness – 5	Availability – 4

Colour – Mid-amber with yellow/gold highlights. *Nose* – Clean with good body and a richness at the back, gently peated and medium-dry with a light apple touch. *Flavour* – Good body, medium-sweet, smooth, creamy and gently peated with an apple character at the back. *Finish* – Quite long with good sweetness and a creamy. peatiness. *Notes* – Gordon & MacPhail bottling.

1983, 43% abv

Sweetness – 4	Peatiness – 7	Availability – 2

Colour – Pale straw with pale lemon highlights. *Nose* – Slightly closed, rich, medium-dry with a hint of mint, good creamy peat integrated and notes of demerara sugar and toffee. *Palate* – Medium-dry, rich, round, smooth & quite creamy with a good dollop of peat & quite solid body. *Finish* – Long, intense, rich, fresh and quite delicately, almost earthily smoky on the tail. *Notes* – The Vintage Malt Whisky Co Ltd bottling.

14 yrs, 1984, 54% abv

Sweetness – 3	Peatiness – 7	Availability – 2

Colour – Straw with yellow highlights. *Nose* – Quite full-bodied, fresh, malty & medium-dry with a slight peanut character, a solid peat note & a slight green floral & citrus note. *Palate* – Dry, but with a soft, rich edge, big-bodied & gently chewy with a quite solid peat note. *Finish* – Long, quite fresh & malty with a hint of cocoa. *Notes* – Adelphi bottling from cask no. 3077.

28 yrs, 1965, 50.7% abv

Sweetness – 3	Peatiness – 6	Availability – 2

Colour – Mid-amber with yellow/gold highlights. *Nose* – Quite full-bodied, fresh, round and medium-sweet with an unctuous sweet-oak character. *Flavour* – Dry, but with a nice edge of sweetness, rich, round, good dry oaky tannins, nutty and softly unctuous. *Finish* – Long, elegant and gently smoky with just a touch of sweetness at the front. *Notes* – Signatory bottling.

Coleburn

Built by John Robertson & Son. Became part of DCL in 1925 and managed by SMD from 1930. Two stills.

Location – Situated to the east of the A491, four miles south of Elgin. It is "faced on one side by a plantation of Scotch firs and birches, and swept by the cool mountain breezes of Brown Muir" according to Robertson's original announcement in 1896.

Notes – The distillery was built from warm-coloured Moray sandstone and roofed with blue Welsh slates. A problem which faced the architect was the provision of a lavatory to the excise office – it took 18 months to resolve! The excise officer's house took even longer to be completed. Closed in 1985 and unlikely to reopen.

Water – A spring in the Glen of Rothes.

1965, 40% *abv*

Sweetness – 8	Peatiness – 5	Availability – 2

Colour – Warm peaty/gold with amber highlights. *Nose* – Sweet, nutty-almondy oily rich. *Flavour* – Medium-sweet, delicate, slightly spirity, rich. *Finish* – Smooth and creamy with good length. *Notes* – Gordon & MacPhail bottling.

1972, 40% *abv*

Sweetness – 7	Peatiness – 6	Availability – 3

Colour – Straw/amber with yellow/gold highlights. *Nose* – Medium-bodied, quite heavily peated, fresh and nutty with a touch of greenness. *Flavour* – Medium-dry, smoky, quite heavy with a richness and an unripe green character. *Finish* – Smoky with richness at the back and light touches of oaky tannins. *Notes* – Gordon & MacPhail bottling.

Convalmore

Founded 2 June 1893 by the Convalmore-Glenlivet Distillery Co Ltd. Purchased from the liquidator in March 1905 for £6,000 plus stock at 2s 6d (12.5p) per gallon by W. P. Lowrie & Co Ltd, who were controlled by James Buchanan & Co Ltd from 1906. Fire broke out on 29 October 1909 and the malt barn, kiln, malt mill, mash house and tun-room were destroyed. After the distillery had been rebuilt, it was used for experiments into the continuous distillation of malt. W.P. Lowrie & Co joined DCL in 1925 and production was carried out by SMD from 1930. Doubled from two to four stills in 1964. Closed in 1985 and the site sold to Wm Grant & Sons in 1990.

Location – Just north of Dufftown on the A941.

Notes – The distillery accommodated a signals detachment of the 51st (Highland) Division from 1940 to 1942 and then gunners of the 52nd (Lowland) Division until 1944.

Water – Springs in the Conval Hills.

1969, 40% *abv*

Sweetness – 8	Peatiness – 5	Availability – 4

Colour – Very pale straw, almost watery. *Nose* – Sweet, with the smell of a field of grain after rain in summer. *Flavour* – Medium-sweet, nutty, spicy. *Finish* – Spicy and of reasonable length. *Notes* – Gordon & MacPhail bottling.

31 *yrs*, 1962, 48.9% *abv*

Sweetness – 6	Peatiness – 5	Availability – 2

Colour – Mid-amber with old gold highlights. *Nose* – Gently smoky with a slight burnt oak character. *Flavour* – Quite big-bodied, medium-sweet with an appley malic character. *Finish* – Quite fresh with a touch of liquorice and good length with a delicate smoky edge. *Notes* – Wm Cadenhead bottling.

Cooley

RIVERSTOWN, DUNDALK, CO. LOUTH, EIRE [IR] EST. 1987

The Cooley Distillery plc was established in 1987. The company took over the site of an old industrial distillery at Riverstown, Dundalk and installed Coffey and pot stills. The first whiskey was distilled in 1989.

Location – At Riverstown, Dundalk, not far from the border of the Irish Republic and Northern Ireland.

Notes – The Cooley distillery produces two different styles of Irish malt whiskey, a traditional unpeated malt and the peated malt the company markets under its *Connemara* brand.

Water – A spring on Slieve Na gCloc in the Cooley Mountains.

CONNEMARA, No age statement, 40% *abv*

Sweetness – 5	Peatiness – 6	Availability – 4

Colour – Mid-amber with old gold highlights. *Nose* – Quite full-bodied, fresh ad medium-dry with a round fruitiness and a good measure of slightly green peatiness. *Flavour* – Medium-sweet, with good body, a nice weight of peat and a round dark nuttiness. *Finish* – Long and clean with a good background smokiness. *Notes* – Peated Irish single malt from Cooley.

THE TYRCONNELL, No age statement, 40% *abv*

Sweetness – 7	Peatiness – 0	Availability – 4

Colour – Straw with yellow highlights. *Nose* – Fresh and clean with a touch of liquorice, a good ripe richness, medium-sweet and quite round with a slight unctuous character. *Flavour* – Medium-sweet, fresh, round and smooth with quite good body. *Finish* – Long and clean with an almost barley-sugar sweetness and a slight citrus note. *Notes* – Unpeated Irish single malt from Cooley.

Cragganmore

Built by John Smith, the lessee of Glenfarclas from 1865 to 1869, manager of Macallan in the early 1850s, Glenlivet from 1858 and Clydesdale in the early 1860s. The distillery never closed for even a fortnight in any year up until the summer of 1901, when reconstruction began. Extended from two to four stills in 1964. Now a part of Diageo plc.

Location – Cragganmore occupies a site north of the A95 between Grantown-on-Spey and Ballindalloch, close to the River Spey. It was the first Speyside distillery to be sited to take advantage of railway transport, the former railway line (now the Speyside Way footpath) passing its doors.

Notes – Originally available only at the distillery or through independent bottlers, the make is now widely available as one of UDV's *Classic Malts* portfolio. An interesting feature is that the spirit stills have flat-topped, T-shaped lyne pipes instead of the usual swan necks. The stills have cooling worms rather than condensers.

Water – The Craggan Burn, a spring on the Craggan More Hill.

CRAGGANMORE DISTILLER'S EDITION, 1984, 40% *abv*

Sweetness – 6	*Peatiness* – 7	*Availability* – 4

Colour – Mid-amber with old gold highlights. *Nose* – Full, medium-sweet and honeyed and nutty with a quite solid peatiness, quite dark, rich, oaky vanilla and notes of demerara sugar and mandarin oranges. *Palate* – Medium-dry, quite big-bodied, rich and creamy with a nutty oakiness and quite a solid peat note. *Finish* – Long, quite fruity and spicy with a dark peaty note. *Notes* – D.o.b. finished in a Port cask.

Sweetness – 6	Peatiness – 7	Availability – 9

Colour – Amber with pale gold highlights. *Nose* – Clean with quite good body, medium-dry, smokily peaty, slightly creamy with a light green touch. *Flavour* – Quite full-bodied, round with a hint of spice, smoky and creamy. *Finish* – Quite long, clean and fresh. *Notes* – D.o.b.

11 yrs, 1989, 59.8% abv

Sweetness – 7	Peatiness – 5	Availability – 2

Colour – Straw with yellow/lemon highlights. *Nose* – Quite full-bodied, medium-sweet and appealingly fruity – apples & peaches, with a solid peat character. *Palate* – Quite full-bodied, round, medium-sweet & softly chewy. *Finish* – Long, sweet, fruity & apple peel-perfumed. *Notes* – Blackadder bottling from cask no. 1467 May, 1989.

1978, 40% abv

Sweetness – 7	Peatiness – 7	Availability – 3

Colour – Amber with good yellow highlights. *Nose* – Quite full-bodied and medium-sweet with a quite chunky peatiness, a touch of citrus and an almost jammy note. *Flavour* – Rich and medium-sweet with quite solid peat and of good weight. *Finish* – Long and sweet with a note of cocoa to the peat. *Notes* – Gordon & MacPhail bottling.

17 yrs, 1976, 53.8% abv

Sweetness – 6	Peatiness – 7	Availability – 2

Colour – Pale to mid-amber with yellow/gold highlights. *Nose* - Quite full-bodied and medium-sweet with a dark nutty peatiness. *Flavour* – Medium-dry, round and quite smooth with good body, a rich oakiness and a firm smokiness. *Finish* – Long, clean and gently smoky with richness on the tail. *Notes* – Gordon & MacPhail bottling; cask nos. 3588–91 distilled 21 July 1976.

Craigellachie

CRAIGELLACHIE, BANFFSHIRE [S] EST. 1891

Built by the Craigellachie Distillery Co Ltd, a partnership formed by a group of blenders and whisky merchants. Rebuilt in 1964–5 and doubled to four stills. Sold to Bacardi during 1998.

Location – The distillery stands on the spur of a hill, overlooking the village of Craigellachie, the precipitous Rock of Craigellachie, the River Spey and Thomas Telford's elegant single-span iron bridge of 1815.

Notes – Sir Peter Mackie, founder of *White Horse* blended whisky, was one of its original owners. The workers in 1923 lived in tied cottages and tended their gardens carefully. The owners of the best-kept gardens received prizes annually from the *White Horse* board.

Water – A spring on Little Conval hill.

14 yrs, 43% abv

Sweetness – 8	Peatiness – 3	Availability – 6

Colour – Straw with lemon highlights. *Nose* – Fresh and cereally with a touch of greenness, a sherbet character, medium-sweet with good body. *Flavour* – Fresh, round, smooth, sweet and cereally. *Finish* – Long and sweet with a touch of spice and a hint of smokiness at the back. *Notes* – United Distillers bottling.

15 yrs, 46% abv

Sweetness – 7	Peatiness – 6	Availability – 2

Colour – Very pale, almost crystal clear, watery coloured. *Nose* – Pungent, peaty, burnt heather with a slight orange/citrus tang to the edge. *Flavour* – Heavy, pungent, peaty, but with an edge of sweetness. *Finish* – Good, spicy and long – reminiscent of Islay. *Notes* – Wm Cadenhead bottling.

Dailuaine

Founded by William Mackenzie, a farmer at Carron and Rinnachat, the business was amalgamated with Talisker on Skye and nearby Imperial in 1898 to form Dailuaine-Talisker Distilleries Ltd. Became part of DCL in 1925 and run by SMD since 1930. Rebuilt after a fire in 1917 and again in 1959–60 when it was increased from four to six stills. Now part of Diageo plc and licensed to UMGD. The old floor maltings were converted to a Saladin box system, the use of which was discontinued in 1983.

Location – Situated in a natural hollow by the Carron Burn with river meadows all round it on an unclassified road between the A95 and B9102 at Archiestown. It is to the south of the River Spey.

Notes – The name "Dailuaine" comes from the Gaelic words "dail uaine", meaning "green valley", an apt description of its location. Although electricity reached the Carron area in 1938, it was not introduced to Dailuaine until 1950. For some years from the late 1880s the distillery operated a rail link to the Spey Valley line at Carron Station, a few hundred yards away. The steam locomotive which once worked the line is preserved on the Strathspey Railway which runs from Aviemore to Boat of Garten. The Spey Valley line itself fell to the Beeching axe in 1967, but much of it is now given over to walkers as The Speyside Way. Like its near neighbour, *Cardhu*, *Dailuaine* is one of the principal malts used in the *Johnnie Walker* blends.

Water – The Bailliemullich Burn.

SPEYSIDE
SINGLE MALT *SCOTCH WHISKY*

DAILUAINE

is the GAELIC for "the green vale". The *distillery*, established
in 1852, lies in a hollow by the *CARRON BURN* in *BANFFSHIRE*. This
single Malt Scotch Whisky has a *full bodied fruity* nose and a *smoky* finish.
For more than a *hundred years* all *distillery supplies* were despatched by
rail. The *steam locomotive* "DAILUAINE NO.1" was in use
from 1939~1967 and is *preserved* on the *STRATHSPEY RAILWAY*.

AGED **16** YEARS

43% vol Distilled & Bottled in *SCOTLAND*. DAILUAINE DISTILLERY, Carron, Aberlour, Banffshire, *Scotland*. 70 cl

16 yrs, 43% abv

Sweetness – 5	Peatiness – 7	Availability – 6

Colour – Deep, full amber with bronze highlights. *Nose* – Quite full and sherried, a nutty, rubbery and damp oak character, medium-dry, slightly spirity. *Flavour* – Full-bodied, nutty, rubbery, medium-dry with a touch of tannin and a hint of richness. *Finish* – Long, dark and quite smooth with a touch of peat. *Notes* – D.o.b.

23 yrs, 46% abv

Sweetness – 4	Peatiness – 6	Availability – 2

Colour – Very pale straw with a slight green tinge. *Nose* – Slightly medicinal, sweet with a gentle smokiness. *Flavour* – Very sweet, rich, peppery, fruity and spicy. *Finish* – Fine, smooth and with a nice sweetness. *Notes* – Wm Cadenhead bottling.

1971, 40% abv

Sweetness – 3	Peatiness – 6	Availability – 3

Colour – Straw/amber with lemon/gold highlights. *Nose* – Quite dry with a rich fruitiness at the back. *Flavour* – Not quite dry, softly smoky and quite big-bodied with an oaky fullness. *Finish* – Smooth with good smoky length, but no real pungency. *Notes* – Gordon & MacPhail bottling.

1974, 40% abv

Sweetness – 5	Peatiness – 6	Availability – 3

Colour – Amber with good yellow highlights. *Nose* – Soft, round, medium-bodied, medium-sweet and quite delicately peated with a slight note of toffee. *Flavour* – Quite soft and rich with good body, delicate peat and medium-sweet. *Finish* – Long, quite fresh and clean. *Notes* – Gordon & MacPhail bottling.

Dallas Dhu

FORRES, MORAY [H] [V]   EST. 1899

Originally to be called Dallasmore in 1898, the plans for the new distillery, designed by local Elgin architect Charles Doig, caused much correspondence in the local paper, the *Forres Gazette*. This included some verses from a local councillor. The fillings were eventually advertised as Dallas Dhu in November 1899, when it came on stream. One of several distilleries on the estate of the local laird, Alexander Edward, who in 1900 sold the distillery to the proprietors of *Roderick Dhu*, a whisky brand popular at the turn of the last century. The still house was burned down on 9 April 1939 and it did not reopen until 1947. It closed in 1983 and the licence was cancelled in 1992.

Location – Built in a hollow to the east of an unclassified road which forks south of the A940 on the southern outskirts of Forres.

Notes – The distillery buildings were handed over by Scottish Malt Distillers to the Historic Buildings and Monuments department of the Scottish Executive which now run them as a model example of a distillery on the tourist trail. It is still possible to obtain special bottlings from old casks, although supplies of the whisky are dwindling. Dallas Dhu is a perfectly preserved example of what a small Highland distillery would have been like at the turn of the century. Had its water supply been more plentiful, it is most likely that the distillery would have been one of the ones chosen for expansion in recent years. As it is, its single pair of old stills has been preserved, as have all the old plant and machinery and the fine old distillery buildings.

Water – The Altyre Burn (known locally as the Scourie Burn).

The Cooper's Choice
Single Malt Scotch Whisky
DISTILLED AT
DALLAS DHU DISTILLERY
DISTILLED
1978
AGED 18 YEARS
BOTTLED
1997
THE VINTAGE MALT WHISKY CO. LTD, GLASGOW G61 3RW
DISTILLED AND BOTTLED IN SCOTLAND
750 ml
PRODUCT OF SCOTLAND
43%Alc./Vol.

18 yrs, 1978, 43% abv

Sweetness – 4	Peatiness – 6	Availability – 2

Colour – Amber with yellow highlights. **Nose** – Quite full-bodied, slightly spirity and medium-dry with a dark, burnt stick peaty character. **Flavour** – Smooth, slightly chewy and medium-dry with good body. **Finish** – Long, smoky and gently chewy. **Notes** – A *Cooper's Choice* bottling from The Vintage Malt Whisky Co.

18 yrs, 1974, 60.8% abv

Sweetness – 4	Peatiness – 3	Availability – 1

Colour – Mid-amber with gold highlights. **Nose** – Medium-bodied, nutty and malty, medium-dry with an edge of richness and a touch of lanolin. **Flavour** – Medium-dry, gently peaty, oaky tannins and a woody character. **Finish** – Quite dry, almost astringently tannic and spirity. **Notes** – Signatory bottling.

24 yrs, 60.6% abv

Sweetness – 4	Peatiness – 4	Availability – 2

Colour – Pale amber with pale gold/lemon highlights. **Nose** – Medium-dry, slightly peppery with oaky vanilla. **Flavour** – Oaky, quite full, round and medium-dry. **Finish** – Chewy, spirity and gently oaky. **Notes** – D.o.b.

1978, 59.7% abv

Sweetness – 4	Peatiness – 6	Availability – 2

Colour – Amber with pale gold highlights. **Nose** – Mature, slightly musty, oak, medium-dry; ripe apple & peach comes out with water. **Palate** – Quite big-bodied, round & gently chewy with sweet vanilla oak & a quite solid peat character. **Finish** – Long, medium-sweet, round & very smooth with a little touch of greenness on the end. **Notes** – Signatory bottling.

1974, 40% abv

Sweetness – 6	Peatiness – 4	Availability – 2

Colour – Straw/amber with yellow/gold highlights. **Nose** – Quite full, gently peated, oaky vanilla and a slight greenness. **Flavour** – Round, smooth, medium-sweet with a touch of nuttiness. **Finish** – Almost dry, oaky. **Notes** – Gordon & MacPhail bottling.

1971, 40% abv

Sweetness – 3	Peatiness – 6	Availability – 2

Colour – Amber with old gold highlights. **Nose** – Quite rich, medium-sweet and appley with a smokiness at back. **Flavour** – Medium-dry, rich, quite fresh, clean and peaty with an appley richness. **Finish** – Clean, gently smoky, of medium length with a richness on the tail. **Notes** – Gordon & MacPhail bottling.

Dalmore

Alexander Matheson was a partner in the Hong Kong firm Jardine Matheson & Co, traders in everything from tea to opium and, of course, whisky. In 1839, the very year of the first Opium War between China and Britain, Matheson purchased Ardross farm, on the shore of the Cromarty Firth and opened a distillery. Whisky production at Dalmore was taken over by the Mackenzie family, who were able to buy the distillery and land as a result of the 1886 Crofters Act. Much of the whisky went to supply long-standing customers and friends, James Whyte and Charles Mackay, who owned the popular blend of *Whyte & Mackay*. The two businesses eventually merged in 1960. *Whyte & Mackay* is now owned by JBB (Greater Europe) plc, which is itself owned by Jim Beam Bourbon.

Location – Situated just off the A9, the distillery is in a beautiful position overlooking the Cromarty Firth to the Black Isle.

Notes – The distillery was well sited by its founders in the middle of a fine barley growing district. Its handsome offices are panelled with carved oak taken from a nearby shooting lodge. During the First World War, it was used by the US Navy as a base for manufacturing deep-sea mines and was burned down as the result of a fire. Production resumed again in 1922. Doubled from four to eight stills in 1966. Two of the stills in use today date from 1874.

Water – The River Alness which flows from Loch Morie.

12 yrs, 40% abv

Sweetness – 6	Peatiness – 6	Availability – 8

Colour – Full, deep amber with good gold highlights. **Nose** – Fresh, clean, slightly sweet and delicately oaked with a grapey/mandarin orange fruitiness and a floral note. **Palate** – Very good body, with a solid masculine note, a touch of sweetness and an elegantly-knit peaty character. **Finish** – Smooth, almost dry, lightly malty and very distinguished. **Notes** – D.o.b.

21 yrs, 43% abv

Sweetness – 6	Peatiness – 5	Availability – 6

Colour – Mid-amber with gold highlights. **Nose** – Fresh, soft oak character, medium-dry, quite full-bodied and yet delicate with a slight citrus note. **Palate** – Full-bodied, medium-sweet and rich with a slight oaky unctuousness, a floral note and zesty tangerine. **Finish** – Long, elegant, a hint of chocolate and citrus, with the final smokiness. **Notes** – D.o.b. Bourbon cask aged.

11 yrs, 1989, 57.2% abv

Sweetness – 6	Peatiness – 6	Availability – 1

Colour – Deep, dark amber with ruby-tinted bronze highlights. **Nose** – Quite full, unctuous, soft and rich with quite a green peat note and a liquorice character. **Palate** – Big-bodied, medium-dry, rich, round with an unctuous honey touch. **Finish** – Long, rich and nutty with a nice thump of sweetness. **Notes** – Adelphi bottling.

1978, 60.5% abv

Sweetness – 6	Peatiness – 5	Availability – 2

Colour – Quite pale straw with pale lemon highlights. **Nose** – Medium-bodied, fresh, clean and slightly green with an aroma of fennel, medium-dry with a slight mashy/malty character. **Flavour** – Medium-bodied, fresh, medium-dry with a ripe greenness, slightly chewy with a delicate peatiness. **Finish** – Long, fresh and clean with a slight hedgerow character. **Notes** – Scotch Malt Whisky Society bottling: cask no.13.14, bottled January 1994.

30 yrs, 1963, 54.5% abv

Sweetness – 6	Peatiness – 5	Availability – 2

Colour – Straw with pale yellow highlights. **Nose** – Quite full-bodied, round, medium-sweet and smooth with a rich liquorice/aniseed aroma. **Flavour** – Big-bodied, medium-sweet and round with a tangy touch of spice, pleasantly chewy tannins and gently peated. **Finish** – Long and gently chewy with a tang of aniseed. **Notes** – Wm Cadenhead bottling.

1990, 59.5% abv

Sweetness – 6	Peatiness – 6	Availability – 1

Colour – Very pale, watery straw with pale yellow highlights. *Nose* – Medium-bodied, medium-sweet and soft with quite a rich oatmeal character, a little citrus note on the tail and a slightly green peatiness. *Palate* – Medium-sweet and soft with good body, rich with quite a solid peaty character and creamily smooth. *Finish* – Long, quite elegant and gently smoky. *Notes* – Blackadder Raw Cask bottling.

52 yrs, 1939, 51.5% abv

Sweetness – 6	Peatiness – 3	Availability – 0

Colour – Full, rich amber. *Nose* – Enormous! Soft, gentle and smooth, a dark nuttiness, a slight delicate smokiness, very complex and with a liquorice character at the back. *Flavour* – Very full, still quite a fresh, green flavour, reminiscent of hedgerows. *Finish* – Long, powerful and very distinguished. *Notes* – A cask sample supplied by Whyte & Mackay for a tasting at Christie's in Glasgow.

DALMORE STILLMAN'S DRAM, 30 yrs, 45% abv

Sweetness – 6	Peatiness – 5	Availability – 4

Colour – Quite full amber with old gold highlights. *Nose* – Big-bodied, elegant, rich, dark and medium-dry with a slight malic note. *Palate* – Medium-dry, with an oaky-oily unctuousness, quite big-bodied and silkily smooth. *Finish* – Very long, elegant and rich with complex notes of chocolate & Cooper's Olde English marmalade. *Notes* – D.o.b.

Dalwhinnie

Originally called Strathspey distillery, the company went into voluntary liquidation the year after it opened. Its name was changed c.1900, when it was purchased from the liquidator by the Dalwhinnie Distillery Co The distillery was then sold at auction for £1,250 in 1905 to Cook & Bernheimer of New York and Baltimore, who, in turn, sold it to Macdonald Greenlees of Edinburgh in 1919. Macdonald Greenlees joined DCL in 1926 and SMD took over its management in 1930. Badly damaged by fire in 1934, it reopened in 1938. The distillery is now owned by Diageo plc and licensed to James Buchanan & Co Ltd. Two stills.

Location – The distillery is situated next to the main railway line at the junction of the A9 (Inverness to the north, Perth to the south) and the A889 to Fort William.

Notes – "Dalwhinnie" derives from the Gaelic word meaning "meeting place". At 326 m (1,073 ft) above sea-level, Dalwhinnie is Scotland's highest distillery. The distillery was located to take advantage of plentiful supplies of local peat, the railway line and the abundant supply of pure Highland water from the Lochan an Doire-Uaine. The distillery is Station 0582 of the Meteorological Office and it is the manager's duty to take daily readings of maximum and minimum temperatures, the number of hours of sunshine, wind speed and snow depth. Now readily available as one of UDV's *Classic Malts*, Dalwhinnie was previously better known for its role as one of the main building blocks of the *Buchanan* blends.

Water – Lochan an Doire-Uaine.

15 yrs, 43% abv

Sweetness – 7	Peatiness – 5	Availability – 8

Colour – Straw/golden, honey-like. *Nose* – Quite aromatic, with a light peatiness and medium-sweet. *Flavour* – Round and sweet with a honey-like richness. *Finish* – Good, slightly sweet richness and excellent length. *Notes* – D.o.b.

8 yrs, 40% abv

Sweetness – 6	Peatiness – 7	Availability – 0

Colour – Light straw with golden highlights. *Nose* – Quite light, spirity and aromatic. *Flavour* – Round, but light, medium-sweet. *Finish* – Quite good, if a little spirity. *Notes* – DCL bottling (pre-Guinness).

1970, 40% abv

Sweetness – 5	Peatiness – 6	Availability – 2

Colour – Quite full amber with old gold highlights. *Nose* – Medium to full-bodied with a freshly hung wallpaper character, medium-dry and quite darkly smoky with a light nuttiness. *Flavour* – Big-bodied with a dark nuttiness, quite full tannins and medium-dry. *Finish* – Long, quite spicy and chewy with good richness. *Notes* – Gordon & MacPhail bottling.

27 yrs, 1966, 45.5% abv

Sweetness – 5	Peatiness – 4	Availability – 1

Colour – Pale amber with pale gold highlights. *Nose* – Quite full-bodied, medium-sweet and oaky with an aroma of wet cement, a slight burnt wood character and a touch of mint. *Flavour* – Quite good body, fairly dominant wood, slightly chewy and medium-dry. *Finish* – Of reasonable length, with a burnt wood tang and a chewy tail. *Notes* – Wm Cadenhead bottling, bottled October 1993.

Deanston

DOUNE, PERTHSHIRE [H] EST. 1965

Founded by the Deanston Distillery Co Ltd and sold to Invergordon Distillers in 1972. Silent from 1982 until sold to Burn Stewart Distillers in 1990. Four stills.

Location – Situated on the south bank of the River Teith within two miles of the centre of Doune village.

Notes – Burn Stewart have decided to use only unpeated barley in the production of Deanston, the company believing there to be sufficient peat for their purposes in the waters of the River Teith. Part of the buildings originally housed a textile mill. This was established in 1748 and was designed by Richard Arkwright of Spinning Jenny fame. Like the distillery, the mill also required good water supplies. The River Teith, as well as supplying all the process water, drives generators which provide all the distillery's electrical power needs – who also export power to the National Grid. The distillery complex includes attractive historic warehouses, many underground, in which are housed 45,000 casks of maturing whisky. The film *Monty Python and the Holy Grail* was shot at nearby Doune Castle.

Water – The River Teith.

12 yrs, 40% abv

Sweetness – 5	Peatiness – 6	Availability – 6

Colour – Amber with pale yellow highlights. *Nose* – Quite light, medium-sweet and gently peated with notes of caramel, toffee & cappuccino. *Palate* – Medium-dry, round, smooth, of good body, delicately peated and creamy with a toffee flavour. *Finish* – Long, quite rich and creamy with a coffee tang. *Notes* – D.o.b.

17 yrs, 40% abv

Sweetness – 7	Peatiness – 3	Availability – 4

Colour – Amber with yellow highlights. *Nose* – Quite full, fresh & sweet with a slight green edge, medium-peated with quite unctuous creamy oak and notes of banana & coconut. *Palate* – Medium-sweet, quite full-bodied with a nice caress of peat and a toffeeyed richness. *Finish* – Long, sweet, showing citrus & coconut. *Notes* – D.o.b.

21 yrs, 40% abv

Sweetness – 4	Peatiness – 6	Availability – 3

Colour – Full amber with old gold highlights. *Nose* – Light & quite delicate, medium-sweet with notes of honey, chocolate & vanilla, toffee and a hint of tobacco. *Palate* – Medium-dry, of good body, slightly chewy, smooth & rich with flavours of cocoa & toffee. *Finish* – Long, elegant & softly chewy with a smoky toffee character. *Notes* – D.o.b.

25 yrs, 40% abv

Sweetness – 4	Peatiness – 6	Availability – 3

Colour – Quite deep amber with bronze highlights. *Nose* – Soft, round, quite light & delicate, a light hazelnut character & sweet vanilla. *Palate* – Medium-dry, smooth, quite creamy with a firm, but delicate peaty note at the back & very gently chewy. *Finish* – Long, creamily smooth with notes of toffee & coffee. *Notes* – D.o.b.

1977, 55.8% abv

Sweetness – 4	Peatiness – 3	Availability – 2

Colour – Straw/very pale amber with lemon/yellow highlights. *Nose* – Fresh and medium-sweet, round with a slight cereal note, lightly peated. *Flavour* – Medium-dry and round with a gentle smokiness and light oaky tannins. *Finish* – Fresh, quite zingy, lightly smoky and a hint of coffee. *Notes* – Wm Cadenhead bottling.

Dufftown

Converted from a former meal mill in 1896 by the Dufftown-Glenlivet Distillery Co and acquired in 1897 by P. MacKenzie & Co, also owners of Blair Athol distillery, Pitlochry. Purchased by Perth blenders Arthur Bell & Sons in 1933. Originally with two stills extended to four in 1974 and six in 1979. Owned by United Distillers since 1985 and licensed to UMGD from 1992. Now a part of Diageo plc.

Location – Situated in the Dullan Glen on the outskirts of Dufftown near the 6th-century Mortlach parish church.

Notes – From Dufftown, which has always been a source of good whisky. It is said that Rome was built on seven hills, but Dufftown was built on seven stills. Dufftown was the sixth distillery to be established in Dufftown and the fourth in the 1890s. The original water mill at Dufftown is still in working order. Dufftown, like the malt from its sister distillery, Blair Athol, plays an important role as one of the principal constituents of the Bell's blends.

Water – Jock's Well in the Conval Hills.

HIGHLAND
SINGLE MALT *SCOTCH WHISKY*

DUFFTOWN

distillery was established near *Dufftown* at the end of the (19th The *bright flash* of the KINGFISHER can often be seen over the *DULLAN RIVER*, which flows past the *old stone buildings* of the *distillery* on its way *north* to the *SPEY*. This *single HIGHLAND MALT WHISKY* is typically *SPEYSIDE* in character with a *delicate, fragrant*, almost *flowery* aroma and taste which *lingers* on the *palate*.

A G E D **15** Y E A R S

43% vol Distilled & Bottled in *SCOTLAND* DUFFTOWN DISTILLERY, Dufftown, Keith, Banffshire, *Scotland* 70 cl

15 yrs, 43% abv

Sweetness – 8	Peatiness – 3	Availability – 6

Colour – Pale amber with lemon/gold highlights. *Nose* – Medium-bodied, medium-sweet, quite rich and fruity with a slight floral note. *Flavour* – Medium-sweet and fresh, quite rich and delicately peated with a nice sweetness. *Finish* – Clean and gently smoky with the good sweetness lasting. *Notes* – D.o.b.

10 yrs, 40% abv

Sweetness – 8	Peatiness – 4	Availability – 0

Colour – Straw/golden. *Nose* – Light with hints of burnt rubber and a floweriness in the background. *Flavour* – Medium-sweet, smooth and slightly fruity. *Finish* – Lasts well, with good richness, but the rubberiness lingers. *Notes* – Arthur Bell Distillers bottling.

12 yrs, 1980, 43% abv

Sweetness – 7	Peatiness – 4	Availability – 1

Colour – Very pale watery straw with pale lemon highlights. *Nose* – Quite big-bodied, fresh, young and cerealy, green herby and mashy. *Flavour* – Medium-dry, quite full-bodied, fresh and spicy with a richness at the back. *Finish* – Long, slightly vegetal and medium-sweet. *Notes* – Blackadder International bottling.

16 yrs, 1980, 55.7% abv

Sweetness – 7	Peatiness – 3	Availability – 2

Colour – Amber with old gold highlights. *Nose* – Quite full-bodied with a dark, nutty, earthy peaty character, medium-sweet, quite rich and with a peppery touch. *Flavour* – Medium-dry, quite big-bodied, nutty, very rich and quite delicately peated. *Finish* – Long and medium-sweet with a delicate lightness and a hint of tablet. *Notes* – Signatory bottling from butt no. 3786 distilled 10 April 1980.

Edradour

Founded on land rented from the Duke of Atholl, Edradour appears little changed by the passing of time. The distillery has gone through several interesting changes of ownership, the most notable of which was becoming a subsidiary of William Whitely & Co, which it remained for most of the 20th century. It is now owned by Campbell Distillers, a subsidiary of the French company Pernod Ricard, who have invested substantially in the development of both the distillery and its single malt.

Location – Situated on the A924, just outside the village of Moulin, at the foot of a steep hill; a collection of old farmstead-like buildings, past which tumbles a fast-flowing burn. An idyllic setting.

Notes – Scotland's smallest distillery whose actual output is only enough spirit to fill 40 casks per week. The last remaining of the once numerous Perthshire "farm" distilleries and the last actually distilling by hand. It is run by just three people. The output of single malt is just 2,000 cases a year, the balance being kept as "top dressing" principally for the *House of Lords* blend. Also previously known as *Glenforres*, which name is now given to a vatting of several single malts, of which the Edradour is one. An excellent visitor centre.

Water – A spring on Ben Vrackie

10 yrs, 40% abv

Sweetness – 9	Peatiness – 3	Availability – 7

Colour – Richly gold, gloriously viscous. *Nose* – Sweet, almondy aroma with a slight fruitiness. *Flavour* – A smooth, malty taste with a hint of dryness. *Finish* – A buttery aftertaste and creamily smooth. *Notes* – D.o.b.

Fettercairn

The Fettercairn distillery originally stood two miles further up the mountain in the heart of a smuggling district, but this was abandoned in 1824 when the present building, converted from a former cornmill, was opened. It was rebuilt in 1887–90 after a fire. Silent 1926–39, when acquired by a subsidiary of National Distillers of America. Extended from two to four stills in 1966. Now owned by JBB (Greater Europe) who market their own bottlings as *Old Fettercairn*.

Location – Situated just off the B974 close to the River Esk on the outskirts of Fettercairn, the distillery rests at the foot of the Cairngorm mountains.

Notes – According to one contemporary account at the turn of the 19th century, the village of Fettercairn was home to 50 weavers, 10 millers, seven shopkeepers, five flaxdressers and one surgeon. There were also numerous distillers who practised their illicit trade on the remote slopes of the nearby Cairngorm Mountains, but these, not surprisingly, did not admit to their trade. In 1829, one John Gladstone bought the nearby Fasque estate. He was the father of William Ewart Gladstone, one of Britain's most illustrious prime ministers and probably the best friend the whisky industry ever had amongst their number. He introduced several reforms crucial to the industry, the most important of which was in 1853 when he abolished the crippling Malt Tax. Another was to permit the selling of bottled whisky to the public. Extensive warehouses contain some 25,000 casks of whisky in differing stages of maturity.

Water – Springs in the nearby Cairngorm Mountains.

Sweetness – 4	Peatiness – 4	Availability – 0

Colour – Palish straw/golden with yellow edges. *Nose* – Light and fresh, delicately peated. *Flavour* – Slightly dry, leafy and smooth with good body. *Finish* – Clean with a subtle smokiness. *Notes* – D.o.b.

10 *yrs*, 40% *abv*

Sweetness – 4	Peatiness – 4	Availability – 6

Colour – Straw with good gold highlights. *Nose* – Quite full, dryish with notes of oaky vanilla and malty. *Flavour* – Dry, spicy, of medium weight, creamy and smooth. *Finish* – Dry, long and chewy. *Notes* – D.o.b.

1980, 43% *abv*

Sweetness – 3	Peatiness – 6	Availability – 2

Colour – Quite deep amber with ruby-bronze highlights. *Nose* – Quite big and nutty with a dark, deep burnt character, a hint of rubber and quite gently peated. *Flavour* – Good body, round and well-peated with a slight burnt character, medium-dry with oaky tannins. *Finish* – Long and smoky with a touch of richness and spicy with an almost salty tail. *Notes* – Signatory bottling.

Glen Albyn

Founded by James Sutherland, the then Provost of Inverness on the ruins of the Muirtown brewery which had catered for the thirst of the men who built the Caledonian Canal. Rebuilt in 1884 after being used as a flour mill following a period of disuse. Acquired in 1972 by DCL from Mackinlay & Birnie Ltd, a company owned by 14 members of the Mackinlay family of the Leith distillers and 11 members of the local Birnie family, John Birnie having been the manager and distiller in 1892. Managed by SMD until its demolition in 1988, distilling having ceased in 1983. When operational it had two stills.

Location – Glen Albyn was situated on the east side of the A9 to the north of Inverness. It faced Glen Mhor distillery across the Great North Road where it crosses the Caledonian Canal.

Notes – The distillery was closed between 1917 and 1919 and used as a US Naval base for the manufacture of mines. For a long time supplies were delivered by sea. Demolished in 1988, along with Glen Mhor, to make way for a supermarket development. Prior to 1745, Inverness had been the chief malting town in Scotland.

Water – Loch Ness.

1972, 40% *abv*

Sweetness – 7	Peatiness – 5	Availability – 4

Colour – Amber with yellow highlights and a green tinge. *Nose* – Quite good body, medium-sweet, ripe and fruity, a slight buttery toffee character with a nice dark smokiness. *Flavour* – Medium-sweet, rich and cerealy with an almost hop-like flavour, good body and delicately peated. *Finish* – Clean, quite rich and of good length. *Notes* – Gordon & MacPhail bottling.

Sweetness – 7	Peatiness – 2	Availability – 0

Colour – Very pale straw with lemon highlights. *Nose* – Light, fresh, fruity and medium-dry. *Flavour* – Medium-sweet, quite full-bodied and round. *Finish* – Of good length, fresh with a lingering sweetness. *Notes* – Master of Malt bottling, cask no. 294.

1963, 40% abv

Sweetness – 7	Peatiness – 4	Availability – 1

Colour – Peaty gold with greenish tinges. *Nose* – Quite sweet, creamy and fruity with hints of almonds. *Flavour* – Sweet, nutty and creamy. *Finish* – Fine, long and delicately sweet. *Notes* – Gordon & MacPhail bottling.

1965, 40% abv

Sweetness – 7	Peatiness – 4	Availability – 1

Colour – Full amber with gold highlights. *Nose* – Medium-sweet, rich, lanolin and peppery characters with an almost raisiny fruitiness. *Flavour* – Rich, oaky, of medium weight and quite smooth. *Finish* – Peppery, oaky and dry. *Notes* – Gordon & MacPhail bottling.

Glenallachie

Built in 1967–8 by Mackinlay McPherson Ltd, a subsidiary company of Scottish & Newcastle Breweries Ltd. Sold to Invergordon Distillers in 1985 along with its then sister distillery, Isle of Jura. Closed in 1987 and reopened again in 1989 after being purchased by Campbell Distillers, a subsidiary of the French company Pernod Ricard. Four stills.

Location – The distillery nestles at the foot of Ben Rinnes, a short way from the A95.

Notes – Campbell Distillers also own Aberlour and Edradour distilleries. One of three distilleries designed by Delme Evans, the other two being Jura and Tullibardine.

Water – Springs near Ben Rinnes.

12 yrs, 40% abv

Sweetness – 7	Peatiness – 4	Availability – 0

Colour – Pale, soft golden. *Nose* – Full and delightfully leafy. *Flavour* – Full-bodied, lightly peated, slightly sweet. *Finish* – Elegant and smooth. *Notes* – Invergordon bottling.

11 yrs, 1985, 43% abv

Sweetness – 7	Peatiness – 3	Availability – 2

Colour – Very pale straw with pale lemon highlights. *Nose* – Medium-bodied, quite fresh with a slight youthful mashy character, lightly peated with a sweet apple note. *Flavour* – Medium-sweet, quite smooth and lightly peated with a touch of spice. *Finish* – Lingeringly sweet with hints of smoke and vanilla tablet on the tail. *Notes* – Signatory bottling from cask nos. 4072–4.

Glenburgie

ALVES, NR FORRES, MORAY   [H]   EST. 1829

Founded on this site as Kilnflat by William Paul, the grandfather of Dr Listen Paul, a celebrated London surgeon of the latter part of the 19th century. Silent from 1927 to 1935. Controlled by Hiram Walker from 1930, and purchased outright by them in 1936. Now part of Allied Domecq and operated by Allied Distillers Ltd. Two stills.

Location – Sited in a valley to the south of the A95 some five miles to the east of Forres.

Notes – The distillery did once have two short-necked Lomond stills which produced a heavier malt known as *Glencraig. Glenburgie* is one of the main malts associated with Ballantine's blended whisky. An earlier distillery, possibly founded in 1810, was once on this site.

Water – Local springs.

1948, 40% abv

Sweetness – 5	*Peatiness* – 6	*Availability* – 1

Colour – Deep amber with bronze highlights. *Nose* – Very big, dark and powerful, with characters of linseed and soft oak with a slightly green touch, medium-dry, with a slight "burnt" character and a pleasant spiritiness. *Flavour* – Big, rich and smoky with a not too dominant oakiness, the "burnt" character again and quite big tannins. *Finish* – Long, quite elegant, slightly chewy and gently smoky. *Notes* – Bottled in 1995 as part of Gordon & MacPhail's *Centenary Reserve* series.

1960, 40% *abv*

Sweetness – 7	Peatiness – 5	Availability – 2

Colour – Pale straw with good yellow highlights. *Nose* – Woody, slightly sweet and floral. *Flavour* – Medium-sweet, slightly spicy, oaky, quite heavy. *Finish* – Oaky, of reasonable length. *Notes* – Gordon & MacPhail bottling.

1966, 57.6% *abv*

Sweetness – 7	Peatiness – 5	Availability – 3

Colour – Quite deep amber with old gold highlights. *Nose* – Big-bodied, unctuous, creamy oak and medium-sweet with a light peat note. *Flavour* – Rich and round, with sweet oaky vanilla, medium-sweet and quite delicately peated. *Finish* – Long with gently chewy tannins and a slight hint of coffee on the tail. *Notes* – Gordon & MacPhail bottling from cask no. 3410 distilled 31 March 1996 and 11690 distilled 15 November 1966.

GLENCRAIG, 1970, 40% *abv*

Sweetness – 3	Peatiness – 1	Availability – 2

Colour – Mid amber with yellow/gold highlights and a tinge of green. *Nose* – Light, fresh, fruity, medium-sweet with a greenness. *Flavour* – Light, clean, medium-dry, very lightly peated with a fresh greenness. *Finish* – Clean and fresh. *Notes* - Produced from the Lomond stills and bottled as *Glencraig* by Gordon & MacPhail.

Glencadam

BRECHIN, ANGUS [H] EST. 1825

Said to have been founded in 1825, the distillery passed through a number of owners until purchased by Hiram Walker in 1954. Now part of Allied Domecq and operated by Allied Distillers Ltd. Two stills.

Location – Situated half a mile to the east of the town of Brechin in the cleft of a hill. It is also about half a mile from the River Esk.

Notes – Presently available only through the independent bottlers. Some of the make goes into *Stewart's Cream of the Barley* blended Scotch whisky.

Water – Springs in the Unthank Hills.

1974, 40% abv

Sweetness – 7	Peatiness – 4	Availability – 4

Colour – Straw/amber with gold/lemon highlights. *Nose* – Rich, medium-sweet, woody, spirity with a touch of linseed and greenness. *Flavour* – Medium-bodied, quite rich, soft oak, quite simple and lightly peated. *Finish* – Light with a touch of spice. *Notes* – Gordon & MacPhail bottling.

12 yrs, 1984, 43% abv

Sweetness – 6	Peatiness – 4	Availability – 1

Colour – Quite deep amber with old gold highlights. *Nose* – Full-bodied, dark, burnt and rich brazil-nutty, quite delicately peated with unctuous vanillin. *Flavour* – Big, dark and full-bodied, rich and round with notes of oaky vanilla. *Finish* – Long and dark with touches of vanilla and spice. *Notes* – Blackadder International bottling from sherry butt no. 5786, distilled 6 November 1984.

Glendronach

FORGUE, NR HUNTLY, ABERDEENSHIRE [H] [V] EST. 1826

Glendronach's founder, James Allardes, was a frequent guest of the 5th Duke of Gordon who was largely responsible for the Excise Act of 1823 which was instrumental in creating the modern malt whisky industry. The distillery has had various owners over the years, including Captain Charles Grant, younger son of William Grant of Glenfiddich fame, who purchased it from the Crown in 1920. It remained in that branch of the Grant family until 1960, when George Grey Grant sold it to Wm Teacher & Sons Ltd. Extended from two to four stills in 1966–7. Now part of Allied Domecq and operated by Allied Distillers Ltd.

Location – Situated straddling the Dronach Burn in the valley of Forgue, which supplies the cooling water. The distillery is set amongst tall trees, in which an established colony of rooks is said to bring luck.

Notes – Distilling was undoubtedly carried out in the area in the days before legal distilling came to Glendronach and the noisy rooks would have proved a useful ally to warn of approaching strangers – especially excise officers. Built in the form of a square and covering four acres, Glendronach is one of the few distilleries where barley is still malted on a malting floor, providing about 15% of the distillery's requirement. It also has coal-fired stills. Glendronach is one of the most important constituents of *Teacher's Highland Cream* Scotch whisky.

Water –"The Source" – a spring four miles east of the distillery.

Sweetness – 7	Peatiness – 4	Availability – 6

Colour – Deep amber with ruby-tinted bronze highlights. *Nose* – Full-bodied, rich, quite creamy, nutty & medium-sweet with lovely soft, sweet vanilla, notes of dried fruits – raisins, prunes & apricots & a slight fresh citrus touch. *Palate* – Full, round, smooth, medium-sweet, rich, creamy & quite delicately peated. *Finish* – Long, sweet & quite ethereal with characters of sweetmeal biscuits, toffee & hazelnuts. *Notes* – D.o.b. '100% matured in sherry casks'.

TRADITIONAL, 12 *yrs*, 40% *abv*

Sweetness – 5	Peatiness – 6	Availability – 6

Colour – Straw with golden highlights. *Nose* – Quite full, medium-sweet, rich, soft, almost honeyed with a slight oily note. *Flavour* – Medium-dry, quite rich, full and smooth with a touch of spice, buttery and delicately smoky. *Finish* – Soft, smooth and long with some smokiness on the tail. *Notes* – Caledonian Distillers bottling.

SHERRY CASK, 18 *yrs*, 43% *abv*

Sweetness – 6	Peatiness – 3	Availability – 1

Colour – Deep amber with mahogany highlights. *Nose* – Full, dark oak, nutty, medium-dry with a slight richness. *Flavour* – Big-bodied, smooth, rich, oaky, nutty and medium-dry. *Finish* – Long, dark, oaky with a toasted nutty character. *Notes* – D.o.b. Very little remains available.

9 *yrs*, 1987, 58.5% *abv*

Sweetness – 4	Peatiness – 7	Availability – 2

Colour – Amber with old gold highlights. *Nose* – Full-bodied, rich and medium-dry with a fresh peatiness and a peanut/popcorn character. *Flavour* – Full, medium-dry and rich with a dark nutty smokiness. *Finish* – Long, chewy and smoky. *Notes* – Signatory bottling from butt no. 57, distilled 29 May 1987.

ONLY MATURED IN SHERRY CASKS, BUTTS & PUNCHEONS

Glendullan

DUFFTOWN, BANFFSHIRE [S] EST. 1897

The last distillery to be built in Dufftown in the 19th century and the distillery which prompted the "Dufftown is built on seven stills" line. The location was chosen not just for its beauty, but also for its practical convenience. It was sited to take advantage of water power and was also able to share neighbouring Mortlach's private railway siding. Two stills. Acquired by DCL in 1926 and managed by SMD, latterly UMGD, from 1930, the licensees are Macdonald Greenlees & Co Ltd. Rebuilt 1962. An additional distillery with six stills was built on the field between "Old Glendullan" and the employees' homes in 1971–2. The distance between the two units was defined as "a short one when the weather's good and a long one when it isn't". The old distillery was closed in 1985 and is used as UMGD's maintenance workshops. Now part of Diageo plc.

Location – Close by the junction of the A941 and A920.

Notes – Glendullan's process water comes from the River Fiddich. *Glendullan* was a favourite whisky of King Edward VIII and plays an important role in the *Old Parr* blend.

Water – Springs in the Conval Hills.

12 yrs, 43% abv

Sweetness – 8	*Peatiness* – 4	*Availability* – 6

Colour – Pale straw with a touch of green and lemon/yellow highlights. *Nose* – Quite full, rich appley, slightly spirity with a hint of cereals and lightly peated. *Flavour* – Medium-dry, rich, sweet oaky vanilla, a touch of greenness, spirity and malty. *Finish* – Long, smooth, oaky with a delicately smoky tail. *Notes* – D.o.b.

12 yrs, 43% abv

Sweetness – 5	Peatiness – 3	Availability – 0

Colour – Pale golden with a slightly greenish edge. *Nose* – Full and fruity with a distinctly sweet oaky hint. *Flavour* – Full, round, warm, sweet and spicy with a slight flavour of coffee/toffee. *Finish* – Long and lingering, sweet and memorable. *Notes* – DCL (pre-Guinness) bottling.

10 yrs, 1983, 43% abv

Sweetness – 8	Peatiness – 3	Availability – 1

Colour – Very pale watery straw with a pale lemon tinge. *Nose* – Sweet, fruity, quite full-bodied, a touch mashy, quite fresh and delicately peated. *Flavour* – Quite sweet, fresh with good body and a nice fruity touch. *Finish* – Quite fresh, of good length with a firm touch of dry tannin. *Notes* – Blackadder International bottling

Glen Elgin

LONGMORN, ELGIN, MORAY [S] EST. 1898

Built between 1898 and 1900 by a partnership of William Simpson, a former manager of Glenfarclas, and James Carle, the local agent for the North of Scotland Bank. Production began on 1 May 1900. Acquired by SMD in 1930. Extended from two to six stills when rebuilt in 1964. The distiller's licence is held by *White Horse* Distillers Ltd. Now part of Diageo plc.

Location – Situated on the A941, the main Elgin to Rothes road.

Notes – A very compact distillery, due to a shortage of capital when it was built. The architect, Charles Doig of Elgin, said at the time that Glen Elgin would be the last to be built on Speyside for more than sixty years. He was right! The next was Glen Keith in 1957. *Glen Elgin* is an important constituent in the *White Horse* blend.

Water – Springs near Millbuies Loch.

12 yrs, 43% abv

Sweetness – 8	Peatiness – 4	Availability – 1

Colour – Pale gold with peaty depths. *Nose* – Sweet, slightly green with fine, soft oak and hints of honey. *Flavour* – Soft, pleasantly sweet, smooth and round with honey coming through on the palate. *Finish* – Smooth, fruity and distinguished. *Notes* – DCL (pre-Guinness bottling). A more recent version is now available, apparently still 12 years old, but with no age statement on the label.

26 yrs, 1974, 57.3% abv

Sweetness – 8	Peatiness – 4	Availability – 2

Colour – Quite pale amber with pale gold highlights. *Nose* – Quite full, soft, sweet, rich, honeyed, with a touch of beeswax & perfume, fruit notes of citrus, orange, ripe melon & delicately peated. *Finish* – Long, with notes of ripe apples & peaches & gloriously rich on the tail. *Notes* – Adelphi bottling from cask no. 3.

Glenesk

HILLSIDE, BY MONTROSE, ANGUS [H] EST. 1897

Glenesk distillery was first known as *Highland Esk* when converted from a former flax-spinning mill in 1897 by Septimus Parsonage & Co and James Isles of Dundee. Its name was changed to *North Esk* in 1899 when acquired by J. F. Caille Heddle. Closed during the First World War. Reopened in 1938, and re-equipped by new owners Associated Scottish Distillers Ltd to produce grain whisky under the name Montrose Distillery. Acquired by DCL in 1954 and operated off and on by SGD until 1964, when it was transferred to SMD and converted back to a malt distillery. A large drum maltings was built in 1968. Renamed Glenesk in 1980.

Location – Two miles north of Montrose, half a mile west of the A92 on the south bank of the River Esk.

Notes – *Glenesk* has also been known as *Hillside*, which is the name United Distillers bottles under in its *Rare Malts* series. Now closed and unlikely to reopen, however the maltings are in full production for UDV. *Glenesk* was traditionally important to the blend *VAT 69*.

Water – The river North Esk.

17 yrs, 61.8% abv

Sweetness – 4	Peatiness – 6	Availability – 1

Colour – Quite full amber with old gold highlights. *Nose* – Quite full, dark & smoky, quite fresh, creamy & malty with a hint of toffee and a slightly green vegetal note. *Palate* – Medium-sweet and quite full-bodied with a zingy, fresh green note and a good peatiness. *Finish* – Long, fresh and hedgerow-like. *Notes* – Cadenhead bottling.

25 yrs, 1970, 60.1% abv

Sweetness – 3	Peatiness – 7	Availability – 1

Colour – Pale straw with pale yellow highlights. *Nose* – Medium-dry, quite rich with a lemon sherbet touch, firm peatiness at the back and a slight cereal note on the end. *Flavour* – Quite good body and medium-dry with chewy tannins and a burnt peat character. *Finish* – Long with a dry cereal note and a chewy burnt smokiness. *Notes* – D.o.b.

Glenfarclas

Founded by Robert Hay, a tenant farmer at Rechlerich farm, it is said that the plant used was taken from Dandaleith Distillery, near Craigellachie. It came into the family ownership of the Grant family when Hay died in 1865 and John Grant took over the tenancy. It was let to John Smith until 1870, when he left to run his new Cragganmore distillery. The running of the distillery was then taken over by John Grant himself and it has been run by successive generations of the Grant family ever since. The present John Grant is the fifth generation to be in charge, while his father George Grant sits as Chairman of the company. Extended from two to four stills in 1960 and to six in 1976.

Location – South of the A95, almost midway between Grantown-on-Spey and Craigellachie, lying in quite desolate moorland at the foot of Ben Rinnes.

Notes – Glenfarclas means "valley of the green grass". The whisky ages very well. "Whisky Tom" Dewar waxed most lyrical of a 30-year-old he tasted in 1912, although George Grant considers the 15-year-old to be perfection – all a matter of personal taste. Glenfarclas has been the pioneer of cask strength whiskies, the company's *Glenfarclas 105*, bottled at 60% abv, long setting the bench mark for such whiskies and having a loyal following worldwide. *Glenfarclas* used to be casked in a variety of casks, but all new Glenfarclas spirit is now aged in 100% sherrywood at the distillery. Glenfarclas has an excellent reception centre.

Water – Springs on Ben Rinnes.

10 yrs, 40% abv

Sweetness – 9	Peatiness – 5	Availability – 9

Colour – Straw with good gold highlights. *Nose* – Slightly rubbery, delicately light and sweet, leafy oak with a slight tang of coffee. *Flavour* – Sweet, malty, full, rich and round. *Finish* – Slightly spicy, long and characterful. *Notes* – D.o.b.

15 yrs, 46% abv

Sweetness – 9	Peatiness – 4	Availability – 6

Colour – Gold/peaty with very bright rich golden highlights. *Nose* – Full, rich and sweet, with a luscious, unctuous oily-oak character and delicately peated. *Flavour* – Sweet, rich and creamy, very intense, full bodied and smooth with hints of burnt peat. *Finish* – Gloriously sweet, gently smoky – long and distinguished. *Notes* – D.o.b.

19 yrs, 57% abv

Sweetness – 8	Peatiness – 4	Availability – 2

Colour – Amber with pale gold highlights. *Nose* – Quite full-bodied, sweet, with a slightly unctuous creaminess, buttery with oaky vanilla & notes of apples, raisins, demerara sugar & coffee. *Palate* – Quite full-bodied, soft, round & sweet, with vanilla flavours & gently chewy tannins. *Finish* – Long, quite chewy & toffeeyed. *Notes* – Cadenhead bottling.

21 yrs, 43% abv

Sweetness – 9	Peatiness – 4	Availability – 3

Colour – Quite dark amber with rich gold highlights. *Nose* – Full, rich, sweet vanilla oak with hints of mint. *Flavour* – Rich, big, full-bodied, delicately smoky. *Finish* – Lightly smoky, rich and long-lasting. *Notes* – D.o.b.

25 yrs, 43% abv

Sweetness – 9	Peatiness – 5	Availability – 4

Colour – Amber with old gold highlights. *Nose* – Full, ripe, sweet and round, finely peated with aromas of orange marmalade, honey, coffee and sherry nuttiness. *Flavour* – Full-flavoured, smooth, sweet with oaky vanilla tannins and coffee and toffee flavours. *Finish* – Fresh with a smoky nuttiness and long lasting. *Notes* – D.o.b.

30 yrs, 43% abv

Sweetness – 6	Peatiness – 4	Availability – 2

Colour – Quite full amber with old gold highlights. *Nose* – Big-bodied, medium-sweet, mature and quite fresh, intense and very rich with notes of lemon/honey cough linctus, mandarin oranges, citrus oil and honeyed oak. *Palate* – Big-bodied, almost dry, but with a good rich edge, gently oakily chewy, a velvety smooth unctuousness and citrus character. *Finish* – Long, quite delicately perfumed and complex – honey, beeswax & chocolate. *Notes* – D.o.b. Possibly the driest of Glenfarclas's bottlings.

40 yrs, 43% abv

Sweetness – 8	Peatiness – 4	Availability – 0

Colour – Quite deep, dark amber with dark bronze/ruby highlights. *Nose* – Quite full-bodied, rich and quite buttery with a hint of liquorice and good background peat, slight honey, clove and dried apricot notes, a dark walnut character, a hint of turmeric and a creamy toffee note. *Palate* – Medium-sweet, quite malty, a good fresh greenness, a touch of spice and a nice, delicate peatiness. *Finish* – Long, fresh, very good oak integration, liquorice and very complex with a lovely malty tail. *Notes* – D.o.b. Bottle no. 56 of 600.

GLENFARCLAS 105, No age statement, 60% abv

Sweetness – 7	Peatiness – 6	Availability – 7

Colour – Deep, peaty amber with gold highlights. *Nose* – Very spirity, slightly astringent, slightly sweet. *Flavour* – Spirity, malty, a little oily-oak character, quite austere. *Finish* – Long, flavoursome and, surprisingly, quite dry. *Notes* – D.o.b.

Glenfiddich

DUFFTOWN, BANFFSHIRE [S] [V] EST. 1887

W hen Alfred Barnard published his *Whisky Distilleries of the United Kingdom* in 1887, the home of the world's best-selling malt was only just being built. Owned by William Grant & Sons Ltd, it today boasts no fewer than 28 stills: 10 wash and 18 spirit. No mean achievement for a distillery founded with £120 capital and using second-hand equipment from Cardow distillery; but such has been the success of the family enterprise founded by William Grant of Glenfiddich, the son of a soldier who had served under Wellington.

Location – Situated near the junction of the A941 and the B975 to the north of the centre of Dufftown.

Notes – One of only two malt whiskies to be bottled at the distillery (the other being *Springbank*). The first distillery in Scotland to open a visitor centre, Glenfiddich now attracts 125,000 visitors a year. It welcomed its one millionth visitor, Mr Ronald Pederson from Albany in New York State, on 4 August 1987.

Water –The Robbie Dhu springs

12 yrs, 40% abv

Sweetness – 8	Peatiness – 5	Availability – 10

Colour – Straw/amber with pale gold highlights. *Nose* – Fresh, clean and softly malty with a delicately fresh peatiness, medium-sweet and fresh with fruity notes of apples & peaches. *Palate* – Quite full-bodied, smooth & fruity with a firm smoky peat character, obvious apples and a touch of cocoa & vanilla. *Finish* – Long, fresh, rich, smooth and quite creamy, cocoa & apples. *Notes* – D.o.b.

GLENFIDDICH EXCELLENCE, 18 *yrs*, 43% *abv*

Sweetness – 8	*Peatiness* – 4	*Availability* – 2

Colour – Straw with pale gold highlights. *Nose* – Fresh, medium-bodied and round, notes of citrus and a grapey character, a slight bubble-gummy sweetness, lanolin character and lightly peated. *Flavour* – Soft, smooth, medium-sweet and round with an unctuous lanolin oakiness. *Finish* – Clean, surprisingly dry, but rich, with a fresh, light peatiness. *Notes* – D.o.b.

GLENFIDDICH ANCIENT RESERVE, 18 *yrs*, 43% *abv*

Sweetness – 8	*Peatiness* – 3	*Availability* – 4

Colour – Straw with greeny/gold highlights. *Nose* – Rich, medium-sweet, grapey, quite soft and with a slight tang of coffee. *Flavour* – Medium-sweet, spicy, slightly peppery with a slight green leafiness. *Finish* – Good, smooth and long with hints of coffee. *Notes* – D.o.b.

GLENFIDDICH WEDGWOOD DECANTER, 21 *yrs*, 43% *abv*

Sweetness – 9	*Peatiness* – 5	*Availability* – 1

Colour – Quite pale straw with good yellow/gold highlights. *Nose* – Fresh, malty, medium-dry and slightly grapey. *Flavour* – Soft, warm, grapily fruity, quite big-bodied, spicy and medium-sweet. *Finish* – Herby, long, sweet and smooth with a soft maltiness at the end. *Notes* – D.o.b.

GLENFIDDICH CASK STRENGTH, No age statement, 51% *abv*

Sweetness – 8	*Peatiness* – 6	*Availability* – 4

Colour – Straw with pale gold highlights. *Nose* – Fresh, medium-sweet and quite full-bodied with a quite soft peat character and fruity notes of lemon and apple. *Flavour* – Medium-sweet, smooth, round, medium-bodied with a gentle peatiness. *Finish* – Long and fresh with a good smoky backbone. *Notes* – D.o.b.

GLENFIDDICH SOLERA RESERVE, 15 *yrs*, 40% *abv*

Sweetness – 7	*Peatiness* – 5	*Availability* – 6

Colour – Amber with pale gold highlights. *Nose* – Quite full-bodied and relatively solid with a slight dark nuttiness, medium-sweet, a touch of honey and rich orange/lime marmalade. *Palate* – Quite big, rich, medium-dry & a good, delicate peat character. *Finish* – Long, nutty, rich with a dark peat note and a touch of chocolate orange. *Notes* – D.o.b.

Glen Flagler

MOFFAT, BY AIRDRIE, LANARKSHIRE [L] EST. 1965

Founded within the Moffat grain distillery complex by Inver House Distillers, at the time a subsidiary of Publicker Industries of Philadelphia. The distillery was closed in 1985 and the pot stills dismantled at this time. Inver House was bought from its American parent by its UK directors in 1988. Six stills.

Location – At Moffat Mills on the eastern outskirts of Airdrie

Notes – The distillery complex was converted from Moffat Mills paper mill. Originally known as Garnheath.

Water – Lilly Loch.

Vintage 1970
Single Lowland Malt Scotch Whisky
Matured in oak casks for 23 years
Distilled at the Glenflagler Distillery
on 6.10.70   *Bottled 5.94*
Cask nos. 1260 + 7861   *Bottle no.*   of 350
This whisky has been selected, produced and bottled in Scotland for and under the sole responsibility of Signatory Vintage Scotch Whisky Co. Ltd. Edinburgh EH6 Scotland
5cl   50.1%vol

23 yrs, 1970, 50.1% abv

Sweetness – 3	Peatiness – 2	Availability – 1

Colour – Pale to mid-amber with yellow highlights. *Nose* – Fresh, quite light and delicate, malty, nutty, a dark oaky character and medium-dry. *Flavour* – Medium-dry, a touch of spice, quite fresh and round with good body and a malic apple touch. *Finish* – Quite long and round, medium-sweet and fresh. *Notes* – Signatory bottling – distilled 6 October 1970.

Glen Garioch

Established by one Thomas Simpson, the first spirit was announced on 1 December 1785 in the *Aberdeen Journal*. Glen Garioch is one of Scotland's oldest distilleries. In two centuries, ownership has passed through various hands, including SMD who acquired it in 1943. It was closed by SMD in 1968 and sold to Stanley P. Morrison, who extended it from two to three stills in 1973. Now operated by Morrison Bowmore Distillers, who are wholly owned by Japanese company Suntory. Glen Garioch closed in October 1995.

Location – The distillery is situated in Old Meldrum village on the Banff to Aberdeen road, close by the historic Meldrum House.

Notes – Garioch is pronounced "Geerie". Waste heat was used to grow tomatoes. The Garioch valley, an 18 mile or so stretch of highly fertile land is known as the granary of Aberdeenshire. Glen Garioch was indeed a canny place to build a distillery. Other dates have been given elsewhere for the opening of this distillery, but the *Aberdeen Journal* announcement of December 1785 clearly pre-dates them. This source refers to a "licensed distillery", making it Scotland's longest licensed on the same site. Glen Garioch is housed in a very attractive cluster of old buildings with the pagoda heads of the floor maltings adding to its appeal. The floor maltings supplied about half of the distillery's requirements, the rest being bought in from outside maltsters. Pitsligo Moss peat was used for the malt drying, which was finished by gas-firing. In 1982 Glen Garioch was the first distillery in Scotland to convert its stills to gas-firing.

Water – Springs on Percock Hill.

8 yrs, 43% abv

Sweetness – 4	Peatiness – 5	Availability – 2

Colour – Straw/pale amber with lemon/yellow highlights. **Nose** – Fresh and clean, slightly perfumed, malty and medium-dry. **Flavour** – Medium-dry, perfumed, fresh and quite rich. **Finish** – A spirity youthfulness with a lingering flavour of violets. **Notes** – D.o.b.

10 yrs, 40% abv

Sweetness – 4	Peatiness – 5	Availability – 6

Colour – Bright gold. **Nose** – Delicately peated, flowery and smoky. **Flavour** – Peaty, dry and slightly pungent. **Finish** – Good, smooth and delicate. **Notes** – D.o.b.

12 yrs, 40% abv

Sweetness – 4	Peatiness – 5	Availability – 6

Colour – Mid-amber with gold/green highlights. **Nose** – Medium-bodied, delicately peated and floral (almost violets), dry with a slight edge of sweetness. **Flavour** – Medium-dry, slightly spicy, floral and fresh with good body. **Finish** – Quite long, spicy and tangy with a green edge. **Notes** – D.o.b.

15 yrs, 43% abv

Sweetness – 3	Peatiness 6	Availability – 6

Colour – Straw/light amber with yellow/gold highlights. **Nose** – Medium-bodied, malty, round with a smoky peatiness. **Flavour** – Quite big-bodied and smooth with a rich edge and smoky character. **Finish** – Long, almost pungent, a gentle heathery smokiness and slightly chewy. **Notes** – D.o.b.

21 yrs, 43% abv

Sweetness – 4	Peatiness – 5	Availability – 5

Colour – Pale with yellow/green highlights. **Nose** – Medium-sweet and quite smoky. **Flavour** – Full-bodied, rich, medium-dry, and delicately peated. **Finish** – Smoky, slightly spicy and quite long with touches of oak. **Notes** – D.o.b.

1984, 40% abv

Sweetness – 4	Peatiness – 5	Availability – 3

Colour – Straw/amber with yellow/gold highlights. **Nose** – Medium-bodied with a lemon/citrus note, floral peaty and a heathery perfumed character. **Flavour** – Quite soft and round, a touch perfumed and a gentle smokiness. **Finish** – Good with a touch of heather and spice. **Notes** – D.o.b.

Glenglassaugh

Founded by the Glenglassaugh Distillery Company. Acquired by the Highland Distilleries Co Ltd in the 1890s. Glenglassaugh was silent from 1907 to 1931 and again from 1936 until it was extensively rebuilt 1959–60. Closed again in 1986, but reopened. Since closed again. Two stills.

Location – Sited on the slope of a steep hillside in the Glassaugh Glen close to the sea approximately two miles west of Portsoy.

Notes – During the period 1907 to 1960, Glenglassaugh only produced for a handful of years in all. When rebuilt, the distillery managed to double its output simply by doubling the size of its stills.

Water – The Glassaugh spring

1983, 40% *abv*

Sweetness – 5	Peatiness – 4	Availability – 4

Colour – Mid-amber with gold highlights. **Nose** – Quite full, smoky with an oily-oaky character, medium-dry. **Flavour** – Medium-dry with good richness in the middle, smooth and round with good body. **Finish** – Long, medium-dry and rich with a nice spiciness. **Notes** – Gordon & MacPhail bottling.

13 yrs, 1977, 59.8% *abv*

Sweetness – 8	Peatiness – 4	Availability – 2

Colour – Straw/pale amber with yellow/gold highlights. **Nose** – Quite full-bodied, fresh and clean with a touch of cereal and green apple, medium-sweet with a hint of perfume. **Flavour** – Fresh, green, medium-peated and medium-sweet. **Finish** – Long and fresh, sweet with a touch of spice and a soft peaty backdrop. **Notes** – Wm Cadenhead bottling distilled November 1977.

Glengoyne

O riginally known as Burnfoot, Glengoyne has been owned by Lang
Brothers since 1876, that company becoming a part of the Robertson
& Baxter group in 1965. Rebuilt in 1966/67 and extended from two to
three stills.

Location – About twelve or so miles from the centre of Glasgow and about
seven from Loch Lomond, Glengoyne nestles in a truly delightful setting
at the foot of Dumgoyne Hill, at the north west end of the Campsie Hills.

Notes – The distillery is sited on the Highland Line, but, as its water supply
comes from north of the Line, it is classified as a Highland malt. The West
Highland Way, the long-distance footpath which runs from Glasgow to
Fort William runs past the distillery. Although first licensed in 1833, the
distillery is believed to be somewhat older. The make was triple distilled in
Victorian times, but is now double distilled. The make is reduced using
natural spring water. Not far from the distillery is the hollow tree in which
Rob Roy MacGregor, immortalised by Sir Walter Scott – and Hollywood –
is reputed to have hidden while fleeing from the English King's men. The
malt used to produce *Glengoyne* is unpeated. This, coupled with the lack
of peat in its source water, makes *Glengoyne* the least peated of all Scottish
malts. The excise officer at Glengoyne at the turn of the century was Arthur
Tedder, who later became the Chief Inspector of Excise and was knighted.
His son, who had grown up at Glengoyne, was eventually to become Air
Chief Marshal of the Royal Air Force. When later he was made a baron,
he chose as his title Baron Tedder of Glenguin, the old spelling of
Glengoyne. The distillery has an excellent visitor centre which sits at the
bottom of the 50 foot waterfall which cascades down the side of Dumgoyne
Hill.

Water – A burn which falls down Dumgoyne Hill and is known locally as
"the Distillery Burn".

10 yrs, 40% abv

Sweetness – 5	Peatiness – 0	Availability – 9

Colour – Pale straw with lemony gold highlights. *Nose* – Round, fresh and medium-sweet, quite light and rich with a slight floral note and a touch of greenness at the back. *Flavour* – Round, smooth, creamy, medium-dry, fresh and clean with good body. *Finish* – Quite long with a smooth, buttery vanilla character and a touch of greenness on the tail. *Notes* – D.o.b.

12 yrs, 40% abv

Sweetness – 5	Peatiness – 0	Availability – 4

Colour – Pale straw with lemony gold highlights. *Nose* – Medium-bodied, round and fresh, medium-dry with a sweet-oily oak character and hints of buttery toffee. *Flavour* – Medium-dry, round, smooth and clean, fresh and medium-bodied with a touch of the toffee character. *Finish* – Long and fresh, buttery, smooth and clean with a touch of oaky vanilla. *Notes* – D.o.b. available in export markets.

17 yrs, 43% abv

Sweetness – 6	Peatiness – 0	Availability – 5

Colour – Pale peaty with yellow/golden highlights. *Nose* – Rich, sweet oak, light fruit and toffee with an almost liquorice-like character. *Flavour* – Soft, rich and smooth with sweet oaky vanilla. *Finish* – Spicy, malty and of nice length, quite chewy. *Notes* – D.o.b.

25 yrs, 1969, 47% abv

Sweetness – 6	Peatiness – 0	Availability – 3

Colour – Straw/mid-amber with gold/yellow highlights. *Nose* – Fresh, clean, quite full-bodied and rich with a good unctuous oaky underlay, a hazelnut character, a touch of tarry rope and green apple fruit. *Flavour* – Quite fresh with a good malty character and a touch of chocolate, firm oaky tannins. *Finish* – Medium-dry and rich, quite spicy with a note of liquorice on the tail. *Notes* – D.o.b.

25 yrs, 1970, 48.5% abv

Sweetness – 7	Peatiness – 0	Availability – 1

Colour – Straw/pale amber with gold/yellow highlights. *Nose* – Quite full, round and soft with a delicate ripeness and a lush fruitiness, a slight note of charred oak and and almost Christmas cake richness. *Flavour* – Medium-dry, rich, soft and round with a smooth oakiness and a lush, fat texture. *Finish* – Long and clean with a rich, fruity note. *Notes* – Bottled as *Glengoyne Vintage 1970*, only 1200 bottles were produced.

1985, 59.1% *abv*

Sweetness – 6	*Peatiness* – 0	*Availability* – 1

Colour – Deep amber with old gold highlights. *Nose* – Full-bodied, medium-dry, rich and fruity, unctously oily with just a hint of nuttiness, a toffee sweetness and a herby note. *Flavour* – Medium-sweet, smooth, round, quite full-bodied and nutty. *Finish* – Long, very gently chewy and quite complex. *Notes* – D.o.b. from cask no. 104 distilled during February 1985 – only available at the distillery.

1985, 57.8% *abv*

Sweetness – 7	*Peatiness* – 0	*Availability* – 1

Colour – Deep amber with bronze highlights and a ruby hue. *Nose* – Full and warm with a dark nuttiness – Brazil nuts – rich, medium-sweet and with a mahogany character. *Flavour* – Big-bodied with nice chewy tannins, medium-sweet and nutty. *Finish* – Powerful, gently chewy and very long. *Notes* – D.o.b. from cask no. 103 distilled during February,1985 – only available at the distillery.

21 *yrs*, 43% *abv*

Sweetness – 6	*Peatiness* – 0	*Availability* – 4

Colour – Deep amber with old gold highlights. *Nose* – Round, dark and medium-dry, fruity, richly nutty with unctuous oaky vanilla and notes of mint and toffee. *Flavour* – Full-bodied, medium-sweet, rich round and velvety smooth. *Finish* – Long, clean, and sweet with a slight hint of mint on the tail. *Notes* – D.o.b.

Glen Grant

Founded by the brothers James and John Grant who had previously been distillers at nearby Aberlour. Amalgamated with George & J.G. Smith of The Glenlivet in 1953. Owned by the Seagram Company of Canada since 1977. Purchased by Pernod Ricard in 2001. Extended from four to six stills in 1973 and to eight in 1977.

Location – At the northern end of Rothes.

Notes – The Glen Grant stills are direct-fired gas and all have purifiers fitted, which are said to add extra finesse to the style of spirit produced. It is not generally recognised that *Glen Grant* is the world's second-best-selling single malt, thanks to its dominant position in Italy, where, as a 5-years-old, it has around 70% of the considerable single malt market. It is also Italy's best-selling whisky. A supply of over-proof *Glen Grant* is kept in a whisky safe built into the rock at the burnside above the distillery. It is reached through the Glen Grant gardens. Taste it cut with water from the burn if you get the chance. Glen Grant was the first distillery to be established in Rothes, and the first industrial building in the north of Scotland to have electric lighting. Although a best-seller through its younger ages, *Glen Grant* ages particularly well.

Water – The Glen Grant Burn.

5 yrs, 40% abv

Sweetness – 4	*Peatiness* – 4	*Availability* – 4

Colour – Light gold/copper. *Nose* – Light, somewhat hard and astringent. *Flavour* – Drier than most Speyside malts, spirity, slightly peppery. *Finish* – Reasonable length with a strange heathery perfumed tang. *Notes* – D.o.b.

12 yrs, 43% abv

Sweetness – 6	Peatiness – 4	Availability – 2

Colour – Straw/gold with amber highlights. *Nose* – Light, sweet, slightly fruity with an astringent character. *Flavour* – Light, medium-sweet, spirity and creamy. *Finish* – Dry, slightly astringent and lingering. *Notes* – D.o.b.

15 yrs, 40% abv

Sweetness – 6	Peatiness – 4	Availability – 5

Colour – Peaty/gold with good highlights. *Nose* – Sweet, lightish, nutty and with a slight fruitiness. *Flavour* – Medium-sweet, nutty, smooth, slightly smoky. *Finish* – The smokiness comes through on the finish, which is smooth and mellow. *Notes* – Gordon & MacPhail bottling.

18 yrs, 46% abv

Sweetness – 5	Peatiness – 4	Availability – 4

Colour – Full amber with gold highlights. *Nose* – Full, quite rich, slightly green and a little austere, soft oaky vanilla with a little smokiness at the back and hints of apricots and apples. *Flavour* – Medium-dry, quite full, round and rich with a touch of toffee and maltiness. *Finish* – Long and rich with a nice edge of greenness. *Notes* – Wm Cadenhead bottling.

21 yrs, 40% abv

Sweetness – 5	Peatiness – 4	Availability – 3

Colour – Amber with good gold highlights. *Nose* – Fruity, slightly astringent with a note of green wood. *Flavour* – Medium-sweet, peppery and oaky. *Finish* – Smooth, well-balanced, dry, of medium length with good oaky vanilla. *Notes* – Gordon & MacPhail bottling.

31 yrs, 1969, 53.9% abv

Sweetness – 6	Peatiness – 4	Availability – 2

Colour – Very deep amber with ruby-tinted bronze highlights. *Nose* – Quite big-bodied, with sweet oak and a slight hedgerow greenness, a burnt mahogany aroma, almost cough linctus and rich toffee/coffee/burnt Christmas cake. *Palate* – Big-bodied, medium-dry, medium-peated, with chewy tannins & quite imposing. *Finish* – Long, chewy with a touch of spice & chocolate & good sweetness on the end. *Notes* – Adelphi bottling from cask no. 1772.

31 yrs, 1965, 58.4% abv

Sweetness – 6	Peatiness – 4	Availability – 1

Colour – Pale amber with pale gold highlights. *Nose* – Quite full-bodied, sweet and rich with a slightly green, nutty peaty character, smooth with a note of honeyed beeswax. *Flavour* – Full and medium-sweet with chewy oaky tannins. *Finish* – Long with characters of vanilla and oak. *Notes* – Signatory bottling for the USA from cask no. 5849 distilled 1 November 1965.

Glen Keith

KEITH, BANFFSHIRE [S] EST. 1957

Originally part of an oat mill of uncertain age, it was converted into a distillery by Chivas Brothers Ltd, a subsidiary of The Seagram Company of Canada, between 1957 and 1960. It was originally designed for triple distillation, but converted to the more normal double distillation in 1970. Bought by Pernod Ricard in 2001.

Location – By the Linn Pool near the centre of Keith.

Notes – The first distillery to be founded in Scotland since the boom years of the late 19th century. It was also the first distillery in Scotland to have a gas-fired still and the first to use a micro-processor to control the whole operation.

Water – The Balloch Hill springs.

Before 1983, 43% *abv*

Sweetness – 6	Peatiness – 3	Availability – 6

Colour – Pale amber with lemon highlights. *Nose* – Medium-bodied and medium-sweet with firm peat and soft rich lanolin, a touch mashy and an unctuous oakiness. *Flavour* – Medium-sweet, soft oak, rich, creamy and smooth. *Finish* – Rich and smooth with a slight toffee touch. *Notes* – D.o.b.

22 yrs, 1967, 45.6% *abv*

Sweetness – 7	Peatiness – 3	Availability – 1

Colour – Bright straw with gold/green highlights. *Nose* – Quite full, rich, oily, nutty and oaky with a slight citrus note. *Flavour* – Rich, medium-sweet, gently peated and with an oily creaminess. *inish* – Long and sweet with a touch of vanilla. *Notes* – Wm Cadenhead bottling.

Glenkinchie

PENCAITLAND, EAST LOTHIAN [L] [V] EST. 1837

E stablished by John and George Rate, Glenkinchie was disused between 1853 and 1880, when it was revived by the Glen Kinchie Distillery Co Owned by SMD since 1914, Glenkinchie was one of the founding distilleries in SMD, and licensed to John Haig & Co. Now a part of Diageo plc. Two stills.

Location – Due south of Pencaitland, the distillery is in a hollow in the hills and, although the chimney can be seen from some distance, the road end could easily be missed as the sign was traditionally overgrown.

Notes – The distillery has a unique museum of distilling which was originated around 1968 by Alistair Munro, a former manager, the work being continued by his successors. This includes an enormous model of a Highland malt distillery which was built to a scale of one-sixth of actual size for the Empire Exhibition in 1924–5. Glenkinchie has also been known as Kinchie and is probably also the same distillery as Milton of which records exist of being operated by John and George Rate from 1825 to 1834. *Glenkinchie* has long been an important malt to the *Haig* blend.

Water – Reservoirs in the Lammermuir Hills.

10 yrs, 43% abv

Sweetness – 2	Peatiness – 5	Availability – 7

Colour – Pale straw/golden with yellow highlights. *Nose* – Fresh, dry, pleasantly peated and slightly spirity. *Flavour* – Dry, malty, quite spicy, full and smooth. *Finish* – Long, lingering, delicately smoky and quite rich. *Notes* – D.o.b.

GLENKINCHIE DISTILLER'S EDITION, 1986, 43% abv

Sweetness – 4	Peatiness – 5	Availability – 6

Colour – Honey-amber with old gold highlights. *Nose* – Sweet, rich, herby with a slight edge of toffee & honey & a winey note. *Palate* – Medium-dry, very rich, nutty, full-bodied, round & smooth. *Finish* – Long, clean, delicately peated, very fresh & creamy on the tail. *Notes* – D.o.b. Double-matured, finished in an Amontillado cask.

The Glenlivet

MINMORE, BALLINDALLOCH, BANFFSHIRE [S] [V] EST. 1824

George Smith established his distillery in 1824 at Upper Drummin farm, being the first distiller in the Highlands to take out a licence after the passing of the Excise Act of 1823. In 1858, after the original distillery had been destroyed by fire, a new one was built at Minmore on land obtained from the Duke of Gordon. The Glenlivet was amalgamated with J & J Grant of Glen Grant in 1953 and later with Longmorn-Glenlivet Distilleries Ltd in 1970. The enlarged Glenlivet group of companies was purchased by the Seagram Company of Canada in 1977. Eight stills. Sold to Pernod Ricard in 2001.

Location – Situated on the slopes of the Braes of Glenlivet, the local hills.

Notes – The very district of Glenlivet is rich in history. It was here that, in 1594, the King's army under the Earl of Huntly defeated the Covenanters commanded by the Duke of Argyll. The real name of the very English-sounding Smiths was Gow. They had been supporters of the Jacobites and Bonnie Prince Charlie, but after his defeat at Culloden in 1746, the family apparently changed their name to avoid the oppression which followed. Although many others have laid claim to the "Glenlivet" appellation, following legal action taken by the Glenlivet distillery's then owners in the 1880s, there is only one whisky which can rightly be called *The Glenlivet*. So famous had the name Glenlivet already become by then that the wags of the day christened it "the longest glen in Scotland". Such was the reputation for quality that The Glenlivet had gained, that whiskies that had not even been distilled anywhere near the Livet glen were claiming its provenance on their labels.

Water – Josie's Well.

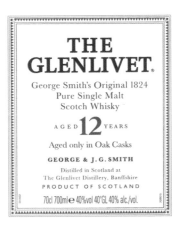

12 yrs, 40% abv

Sweetness – 8	Peatiness – 4	Availability – 10

Colour – Straw with a definite greenness to its edge. *Nose* – Leafy, floral, slightly malty, very fragrant. *Flavour* – Sherry cask on palate with typical honeyed shortbread-sweet flavour. *Finish* – Good length. *Notes* – D.o.b.

12 yrs, 40% abv

Sweetness – 3	Peatiness – 6	Availability – 4

Colour – Amber with gold highlights and a dark tinge. *Nose* – Slightly dumb, floral, violet character and medium-dry. *Flavour* – Quite dry with quite big oaky tannins, a slight touch of richness and quite full-bodied. *Finish* – Long with quite chewy dry tannins and an earthy peatiness. *Notes* – Gordon & MacPhail bottling.

15 yrs, 57% abv

Sweetness – 8	Peatiness – 6	Availability – 4

Colour – Amber with old gold highlights. *Nose* – Quite full, sweet, rich and malty. *Flavour* – Rich, Full-bodied and round with a touch of tannin, malty and quite sweet. *Finish* – Big-bodied, spicy, gently tannic, warm. *Notes* – Gordon & MacPhail bottling.

18 yrs, 43% abv

Sweetness – 6	Peatiness – 5	Availability – 3

Colour – Quite deep amber with bronze highlights. *Nose* – Quite full-bodied, medium-sweet with a dark, soft nuttiness, a good, peaty character with a lightly honeyed, almost Christmas cake richness and a gentle peaty fruitiness. *Flavour* – Big-bodied, smooth, round, soft, rich and medium-sweet, slightly toffeeyed and gently peated. *Finish* – Rich with a touch of spice, a light, elegant smoky touch to the tail and surprisingly dry. *Notes* – D.o.b.

21 yrs, 40% abv

Sweetness – 6	Peatiness – 7	Availability – 4

Colour – Full amber with good gold highlights. *Nose* – Sweet and fruity (peaches) with touches of oaky vanilla. *Flavour* – Smooth, medium-sweet, round and full-bodied, gently malty. *Finish* – Long and toffee-like. *Notes* – Gordon & MacPhail bottling.

1976, 57.7% abv

Sweetness – 7	Peatiness – 4	Availability – 2

Colour – Deep amber with old gold highlights. *Nose* – Round, rich & medium-sweet with smooth, sweet vanilla & shortbread aromas. *Palate* – Medium-sweet, quite intense & gently chewy with rich butterscotch & a medium weight of peat. *Finish* – Long, toffeeyed & gently chewy with a tail of creamy coffee. *Notes* – Signatory bottling.

THE GLENLIVET AMERICAN OAK FINISH, 12 yrs, 40% abv

Sweetness – 8	Peatiness – 4	Availability – 6

Colour – Amber with old gold highlights. *Nose* – Sweet, quite full-bodied, fresh & medium-peated with notes of rich shortbread & green apples. *Palate* – Medium-sweet, quite soft, round, gently peated of nice weight with touches of honey, toffee & butterscotch. *Finish* – Long, clean, quite ethereal & rich. *Notes* – D.o.b.

THE GLENLIVET FRENCH OAK FINISH, 12 yrs, 40% abv

Sweetness – 8	Peatiness – 4	Availability – 6

Colour – Mid-amber with old gold highlights. *Nose* – Sweet, round, quite fresh, rich & soft, with notes of banana & grapefruit. *Palate* – Soft, round, medium-sweet, rich & slightly unctuous, oily oaked, of good weight, gently peated & flavours of toffee/coffee; softer than the *American Oak Finish*. *Finish* – Long & quite ethereal with notes of cappuccino, tobacco & cocoa; more delicate & complex than the *American Oak Finish*. *Notes* – D.o.b.

THE GLENLIVET ARCHIVE, 21 yrs, 40% abv

Sweetness – 7	Peatiness – 4	Availability – 6

Colour – Mid-amber with bronze highlights. *Nose* – Quite full-bodied, round, slightly honeyed, mature vanilla with a nutty note & touches of beeswax, coconut & dried fruit. *Palate* – Medium-sweet, honeyed, beeswax, very gently chewy, toffee, butterscotch & with a slight edge of greenness to the peat. *Finish* – Long, surprisingly fresh, ethereal, elegant & softly chewy. *Notes* – D.o.b.

Glenlochy

FORT WILLIAM, INVERNESS-SHIRE [H] EST. 1898

Glenlochy was always very up-to-date. All the fittings in 1898 were "arranged throughout with a view to saving labour". A visitor reported, in 1907, that Glenlochy possessed "every modern facility for enabling it to be worked with a minimum of labour". Joseph Hobbs of Associated Scottish Distillers sold it in 1940. Eight years later, he established the Great Glen cattle ranch, an area of 54 square kilometres where beef cattle fend for themselves, as they do on the US prairies. The ranch is still in operation. Glenlochy was silent from 1917 to 1924 and again from 1926 to 1937. It was bought by DCL in 1953 when the unit was transferred to SMD. It had two stills.

Location – Situated within Fort William on the north bank of the River Nevis, to the west of the A82.

Notes – The distillery closed for good in 1983.

Water – The River Nevis.

22 yrs, 61.4% abv

Sweetness – 7	Peatiness – 4	Availability – 1

Colour Amber with pale old gold highlights. *Nose* – Quite light, fresh, rich and medium-sweet with notes of citrus and demerara sugar. *Palate* – Quite big-bodied, round, rich and smooth, medium-sweet with gently chewy tannins, quite delicately peated with coffee/cocoa characters and a touch of toffee. *Finish* – Long and quite tangy with an apple note, a touch of perfume and a good, soft peat note. *Notes* – Cadenhead bottling.

30 yrs, 1963, 52.2% abv

Sweetness – 3	Peatiness – 6	Availability – 1

Colour – Mid-amber with gold highlights. *Nose* – Light, quite fresh with a cooked apple character and quite dry. *Flavour* – Quite dry with a smoky oak and coffee character. *Finish* – Good length and delicately smoky. *Notes* – Signatory bottling.

Glenlossie

Built in 1876 by John Duff, tenant of the Fife Arms, Lhanbryde, and previously manager of the Glendronach distillery. A controlling interest was obtained by SMD in 1919 and the distillery was taken over completely by DCL in 1930. Extended from four to six stills in 1962. The make is important to John Haig's blends, the distillery being licensed to that company. Now part of Diageo plc.

Location – Sited at Thomshill on an unclassified road to the west of the A941, two miles south of Elgin.

Notes – A purifier has been installed between the lyne arm and the condenser on each of the three spirit stills. Electricity only replaced steam as late as 1960 as the means of power generation at the distillery. A fire at the distillery in 1929 caused some damage. One of the appliances that fought the blaze was the distillery's own engine. Dating from the 1860s and originally horse drawn, it can now be seen at Dallas Dhu. The site now houses two distilleries, the other being the much newer Mannochmore, built in 1971.

Water – The Bardon Burn.

SPEYSIDE
SINGLE MALT *SCOTCH WHISKY*

The three *spirit stills* at the

GLENLOSSIE

distillery have *purifiers* installed between the *lyne arm* and the *condenser*. This has a bearing on the *character* of the *single MALT SCOTCH WHISKY* produced which has a *fresh, grassy* aroma and a *smooth*, lingering flavour. Built in 1876 by *John Duff*, the *distillery* lies four miles *south* of ELGIN in *Morayshire*.

AGED **10** YEARS

43% vol   Distilled & Bottled in *SCOTLAND* GLENLOSSIE DISTILLERY. Elgin, Moray, *Scotland*   70 cl

10 yrs, 43% abv

Sweetness – 6	Peatiness – 3	Availability – 6

Colour – Quite pale straw with lemon yellow highlights. **Nose** – Fresh, cerealy and green, fragrant with a touch of perfume. **Flavour** – Fresh with a touch of oaky tannin, quite green and gently smoky, medium-dry with richness in the middle of the palate. **Finish** – Lasts quite well – clean, fresh and spicy. **Notes** – D.o.b.

17 yrs, 1981, 59.0% abv

Sweetness – 6	Peatiness – 6	Availability – 2

Colour – Full amber with bronze highlights. *Nose* – Big-bodied, dark & nutty – Brazil nuts – a touch of citrus & apple (Macintosh Red) & quite delicately peated. *Palate* – Round, smooth, medium-sweet, darkly peated & with gently chewy tannins. *Finish* – Long, quite ethereal, softly chewy & finally delicately smoky. *Notes* – Adelphi bottling from cask no. 1679.

CASK No 1679

ADELPHI DISTILLERY LIMITED

3 GLOUCESTER LANE, EDINBURGH EH3 6ED, SCOTLAND

FROM GLENLOSSIE, 17 YEARS OLD

59.0% vol

DISTILLED AT GLENLOSSIE DISTILLERY 1981
BOTTLED IN SCOTLAND 1998
SELECTED BY ADELPHI DISTILLERY LIMITED

70cl

16 yrs, 1980, 43% abv

Sweetness – 7	Peatiness – 5	Availability – 1

Colour – Pale straw with pale lemon highlights. *Nose* – Surprisingly fresh and youthful, quite full-bodied and clean with a note of mintiness, an edge of richness and a good, burnt peat character. *Flavour* – Medium-sweet, clean and fresh with good body and a creamy peatiness. *Finish* – Long and creamy with a slightly perfumed peatiness. *Notes* – Blackadder International bottling from cask no. 1365 distilled 7 March 1980.

1969, 40% abv

Sweetness – 7	Peatiness – 4	Availability – 2

Colour – Straw/amber with gold highlights. *Nose* – Medium-bodied, quite rich with a tang of gunpowder and a warm nuttiness. *Flavour* – Quite rich, medium-bodied, lightly peated with a nice sweet edge and a slightly oily texture. *Finish* – Of reasonable length, rich with a touch of greenness. *Notes* – Gordon & MacPhail bottling.

1968, 40% abv

Sweetness – 7	Peatiness – 4	Availability – 2

Colour – Palish gold with good bright highlights. *Nose* – Sweet, fruity, slightly musty, nutty. *Flavour* – Sweet, fruity, musty and spicy. *Finish* – Nice fruitiness, good length and with a nuttiness on the tail. *Notes* – Gordon & MacPhail bottling.

Glen Mhor

INVERNESS, INVERNESS-SHIRE [H] EST. 1892

Founded by ex-Provost John Birnie and James Mackinlay of Charles Mackinlay & Co, Glen Mhor began production on 8 December 1894. It became a part of DCL in 1972, John Walker & Co having long had a large shareholding in the company, from which date it was operated by SMD. Closed in 1983 and subsequently demolished to make way for a shopping complex.

Location – The distillery was situated at the north end of the Caledonian Canal where it intersects with the Great North Road (the A9) at the north west of Inverness, across the road from Glen Albyn.

Notes – The name Glen Mhor means "Great Glen". It was the first distillery in Scotland to introduce mechanical maltings. Glen Mhor, like its sister Glen Albyn, is alas no more.

Water – Loch Ness.

8 yrs, 57% abv

Sweetness – 4	Peatiness – 4	Availability – 2

Colour – Straw/amber with good gold highlights. *Nose* – Lightly peated with an edge of sweetness. *Flavour* – Medium-sweet, slightly woody and quite full-bodied. *Finish* – Spicy, creamy, long and almost leafy. *Notes* – Gordon & MacPhail bottling.

14 yrs, 1978, 43% abv

Sweetness – 4	Peatiness – 6	Availability – 0

Colour – Straw with lemon highlights. *Nose* – Medium-bodied and quite rich with an appley sweetness and a slight floral touch. *Flavour* – Quite dry and smooth with big, full, dark, nutty tannins. *Finish* – Long with a salty smokiness. *Notes* – Master of Malt bottling; cask nos. 4041/2 distilled 21 September 1978.

Glenmorangie

Converted from the Morangie Brewery of McKenzie & Gallie by William Mathieson. Rebuilt in 1887 and again in 1979, when it was extended from two to four stills. Glenmorangie has been owned by Macdonald & Muir (who were renamed Glenmorangie plc in 1996), the Leith blenders, since 1918.

Location – Sited on the Dornoch Firth on the A9 between Tain and Edderton, looking across the Firth towards the hills of Sutherland.

Notes – One of the smallest of all Highland distilleries. All of the make is used by the owners, none being made available as fillings. A noted feature of the distillery is that the stills have very tall necks, at 16 ft 10 ins (5.14m), the tallest in Scotland.

Water – Springs in the Tarlogie Hills above the distillery.

10 yrs, 40% abv

Sweetness – 4	Peatiness – 4	Availability – 10

Colour – Good light gold/pale straw. *Nose* – Fresh, medium-bodied, steely with floral notes and a touch of peat. *Flavour* – Light, fresh, slightly smoky with an oily creaminess. *Finish* – Sweet with good length. *Notes* – D.o.b.

18 yrs, 43%abv

Sweetness – 4	Peatiness – 4	Availability – 6

Colour – Honey-amber with good gold highlights. *Nose* – Fresh, salty, nutty (almonds), with an edge of sweetness, quite full and round. *Flavour* – Smooth, medium-dry, fresh, good nut-oily glycerine, quite full-bodied. *Finish* – Medium-dry, spicy, long and almost creamy. *Notes* – D.o.b.

10 yrs, 57.2% abv

Sweetness – 5	Peatiness – 4	Availability – 4

Colour – Amber with yellow highlights. *Nose* – Fresh, clean and medium-dry with floral and citrus notes, round and delicately peated with a light, sweet, vanilla tablet/toffee character. *Flavour* – Medium-sweet, smooth, round and delicately nutty (almonds) with good body. *Finish* – Long and fresh with a sweet oakiness. *Notes* – D.o.b. Bottled as *Glenmorangie 100° Proof.*

15 yrs, 43% abv

Sweetness – 4	Peatiness – 5	Availability – 6

Colour – Amber with old gold highlights and an edge of bronze. *Nose* – Quite full-bodied and honeyed with a really distinctive lemon curd tang, medium-dry and smooth with notes of vanilla, beeswax & apple blossom. *Palate* – Dry, round and smooth with a nice, chunky peatiness, good body and a slightly green citrus bite. *Finish* – Long, dry and complex, with notes of honey, vanilla & cocoa. *Notes* – D.o.b.

1963 (Bottled 1988), 43% abv

Sweetness – 4	Peatiness – 4	Availability – 1

Colour – Quite pale peaty/straw with gold and green highlights. *Nose* – Rich, full malty, oaky with sweet appley fruit. *Flavour* – Sweet, full spicy, quite green with a toffee-like richness. *Finish* – Long, spicy, caramelly and fine. *Notes* – D.o.b. Matured in a Bourbon cask, as all *Glenmorangie* is, for 22 years and "finished off" for the last year in an Oloroso sherry cask.

THE NATIVE ROSS-SHIRE GLENMORANGIE, 10 yrs, 1980, 57.6% abv

Sweetness – 4	Peatiness – 4	Availability – 1

Colour – Bright pale amber, yellow-gold highlights. *Nose* – A touch of sweetness, fresh, quite full, dried hay, lanolin and vanilla. *Flavour* – Quite rich, round, medium-dry oaky-vanilla, quite full, fat and soft. *Finish* – Fresh, clean, aromatic and quite long. *Notes* – D.o.b. Cask no. 4336; distilled 15.5.80; bottled 5.9.90. Branded as *The Native Ross-shire Glenmorangie.*

PORT FINISH GLENMORANGIE, No stated age, 56.5% abv

Sweetness – 4	Peatiness – 3	Availability – 1

Colour – Quite full amber with bronze highlights. *Nose* – Medium-bodied, quite fresh with a slightly green mint character and richness with notes of vanilla, butterscotch and toffee. *Flavour* – Medium-dry, rich, spicy, fresh, soft round and with good body. *Finish* – Rich, smooth, spicy and with a long chocolate-sweet tail with a fresh, green edge. *Notes* – D.o.b.

MADEIRA WOOD FINISH GLENMORANGIE
No age statement, 43% *abv*

Sweetness – 3	Peatiness – 3	Availability – 5

Colour – Pale amber with yellow/pale gold highlights. *Nose* – Quite full-bodied, but quite delicate, a dark winey character, fresh, rich and medium-sweet with a slight green citrus edge. *Flavour* – Sweet, rich and quite full with notes of vanilla and a gentle peatiness. *Finish* – Quite long and elegantly ethereal, rich with a dry note. *Notes* – D.o.b.

PORT WOOD FINISH GLENMORANGIE
No age statement, 43% *abv*

Sweetness – 4	Peatiness – 3	Availability – 5

Colour – Quite deep amber with ruby/bronze highlights and a purple hue. *Nose* – Medium-bodied and rich, with notes of mint, butterscotch and oaky vanilla. *Flavour* – Medium-dry with an edge of richness, of good weight and gently peated. *Finish* – Long, nutty and rich with a slight green edge. *Notes* – D.o.b.

SHERRY WOOD FINISH GLENMORANGIE
No age statement, 43% *abv*

Sweetness – 4	Peatiness – 3	Availability – 5

Colour – Amber with old gold highlights. *Nose* – Quite big-bodied, fresh and nutty, medium-sweet, round and quite rich with vanilla and a honeyed beeswax note. *Flavour* – Smooth, fresh and medium-dry, full-bodied and round with slightly chewy oaky tannins and a gentle, slightly green peatiness. *Finish* – Long, gently chewy and clean. *Notes* – D.o.b.

GLENMORANGIE FINO SHERRY WOOD FINISH, 43% *abv*

Sweetness – 5	Peatiness – 4	Availability – 4

Colour – Mid-amber with almost old gold highlights and a slight hint of lemon. *Nose* – Quite fresh, fruity, rich & full-bodied with hints of tangerine, apple & sweet vanilla, medium-sweet with a slight hint of dark peat at the back and spicy with a Christmas cake grapiness. *Palate* – Medium-dry, soft, sweet oaky vanilla, almost biscuity (digestives), spicy, delicate and with a subdued peatiness. *Finish* – Long, winey, elegant, biscuity and complex. *Notes* – D.o.b. Finished for 3 years in a Fino cask.

GLENMORANGIE COTE DE NUITS WOOD FINISH, 1975

Sweetness – 4	Peatiness – 6	Availability – 1

Colour – Quite full amber with a wonderful rosé, almost salmon pink hue and old gold/onion skin highlights. *Nose* – Rich, perfumed, delicate with almost a hazelnut note & a sensuous pinot noir aroma of strawberries, a fresh green note to the peat and bubble-gummy cherries. *Flavour* – Soft, medium-dry and gently chewy with vanilla oak tannins, good body and a hint of toffee & cherry fruit. *Finish* – Long, fruity, round and magnificently scented. *Notes* – D.o.b. finished in a Grand Cru Burgundy cask.

GLENMORANGIE CLARET WOOD FINISH, 43% *abv*

Sweetness – 6	Peatiness – 3	Availability – 1

Colour – Mid-amber with old gold highlights. *Nose* – Soft, quite delicate, but with good weight, medium-sweet, rich & unctuous with notes of vanilla, toffee, fudge & fruit cake. *Palate* – Round, rich, smooth, medium-sweet, toffeeyed & quite full-bodied. *Finish* – Long, rich and elegant with very gentle tannins. *Notes* – D.o.b. finished in a Premier Cru Bordeaux cask.

GLENMORANGIE COGNAC FINISH, 1985

Sweetness – 5	Peatiness – 3	Availability – 1

Colour – Mid-amber with pale old gold highlights. *Nose* – Fresh and youthful with a slightly green toffee apple character, the peat note is slightly darker with the addition of water. It is very sweet (for *Glenmorangie*) with notes of pear drops, acid drops and almost Fox's glacier mints. *Palate* – Dry with a quite burnt smoky character and a cooked, Madeira-like fruitiness, a Calvados-like apple note and a touch of spice. *Finish* – Lasts well, with notes of toffee/green coffee, a gently chewy note and a nice touch of oaky tannin. *Notes* – D.o.b. From a limited bottling of 850 bottles.

GLENMORANGIE DISTILLERY MANAGER'S CHOICE, 1983, 53.2% *abv*

Sweetness – 4	Peatiness – 4	Availability – 1

Colour – Mid-amber with gold highlights. *Nose* – Quite full, fresh, quite lightly peated, with grassy & hay characters and notes of nutty vanilla toffee, liquorice & a slight orange tang. *Palate* – Medium-dry, delicately peated, fresh and round with notes of rich, sweet creamy & buttery shortbread and a slight touch of toffee. *Finish* – Long, rich, smooth and flavoursome, with touches of toffee & coffee & a slight floral note on the tail. *Notes* – D.o.b. Bottled at (and can only be bought by a personal visit to) the distillery from cask no. 5340.

Glen Moray

ELGIN, MORAY [H] EST. 1897

Like its sister distillery, Glenmorangie, a former brewery, having been built in 1815. It was closed in 1910 and passed into the ownership of Macdonald & Muir, which is now known as Glenmorangie plc, in 1923. It was rebuilt in 1958, when it was converted from two to four stills.

Location – Situated in a hollow on the bank of the River Lossie, on the western outskirts of Elgin.

Notes – Close by the distillery is Gallowcrook Hill, which was, as its name implies, the scene of public hangings in days gone by. Some of the make goes into Macdonald & Muir's *Highland Queen* blend. The old steam engine that formerly powered the distillery is still in place.

Water – River Lossie.

12 yrs, 40% abv

Sweetness – 7	Peatiness – 3	Availability – 7

Colour – Pale gold. *Nose* – Clean, fresh, aromatic and slightly peppery. *Flavour* – Light, creamy, heathery and medium-sweet. *Finish* – Delicate, of reasonable length and soft. *Notes* – D.o.b.

16 yrs, 43% abv

Sweetness – 7	Peatiness – 2	Availability – 5

Colour – Amber with gold highlights. *Nose* – Fresh, medium-bodied with an appley character, sweet soft bubble-gummy vanilla, good richness and a hint of perfume. *Flavour* – Round with oaky tannins, quite a rich fruity character and good body. *Finish* – Smooth, spicy and medium-sweet with a rich chewy tail. *Notes* – D.o.b.

13 yrs, 1982, 56.0% *abv*

Sweetness – 6	*Peatiness* – 3	*Availability* – 1

Colour – Pale straw with pale yellow highlights. *Nose* – Medium-bodied, quite softly peated with an appley fruitiness, touches of perfume and oaky vanilla and a sherbetty freshness. *Flavour* – Medium-bodied and medium-sweet with a hint of perfumed peatiness. *Finish* – Quite fresh and clean with good length. *Notes* – Adelphi bottling.

27 yrs, 1962, 55.1% *abv*

Sweetness – 7	*Peatiness* – 3	*Availability* – 1

Colour – Rich, mid-dark amber with good gold highlights. *Nose* – Quite full-bodied, toffee & chocolate, medium-sweet, lightly peated with warm, oaky vanilla. *Flavour* – Medium-sweet, quite full-bodied, spicy, nutty, almost austere with oaky tannins. *Finish* – Smooth, medium-dry and quite firm with a smoky touch; it lingers well. *Notes* – Wm Cadenhead bottling.

No age statement, 40% *abv*

Sweetness – 6	*Peatiness* – 3	*Availability* – 6

Colour – Amber with yellow/lemon highlights. *Nose* – Quite fresh & full-bodied, round, smooth, buttery, malty & rich with notes of banana & creamy, toasty vanilla. *Palate* – Dry, but quite rich, round with a sweet edge to the vanilla, gently chewy oaky tannins and a soft peat character. *Finish* – Long, quite elegant & complex with a soft dryness. *Notes* – D.o.b. Mellowed in Chardonnay barrels.

GLEN MORAY MELLOWED IN WINE BARRELS, *12 yrs*, 40% *abv*

Sweetness – 6	*Peatiness* – 4	*Availability* – 6

Colour – Quite pale amber with yellow highlights tinged with lemon. *Nose* – Medium-bodied, medium-dry with a touch of honeyed oak, quite delicate, but chunky peat, a creamy toffee character opens up with water, as does a slight hazelnut note. *Palate* – Medium-dry, round, quite soft toffee & honey with a firm backbone of peat. *Finish* – Rich, smooth, honeyed & long. *Notes* – D.o.b. finished in Chenin Blanc casks.

Glen Rothes

Built by William Grant & Co Amalgamated in 1887 with the Islay Distillery Company (owners of Bunnahabhain distillery) to form The Highland Distilleries Ltd. Now licensed to Berry Bros. Enlarged in 1963 from four to six stills, and from six to ten in 1980.

Location – A short way up the glen formed by the Burn of Rothes which flows from the Mannoch Hills.

Notes – The first spirit ran from the stills in 1897 on the night of the Tay rail bridge disaster. The distillery experienced "one of the most disastrous distillery fires" on 15 May 1922 when no. 1 bonded warehouse was destroyed, along with 2,500 casks (800,000 litres of maturing spirit): a stream of burning whisky flowed out of the stricken building and into the burn. *Glenrothes*, as the make is usually known, is one of the malts at the heart of the *Famous Grouse* and *Cutty Sark* blends.

Water – Springs in the hills above the distillery.

15 yrs, 1979, 43% abv

Sweetness – 7	Peatiness – 3	Availability – 5

Colour – Mid-amber with gold highlights.   *Nose* – Rich, soft and round with an unctuous sweetness, a slight nutty character and a touch of fresh citrus. *Flavour* – Full-bodied, soft, round and medium-sweet with gentle tannins.   *Finish* – Long, quite fresh, delicately peated, rich and smooth.   *Notes* – D.o.b. The bottle, label and individual carton for this presentation was lauded and received many prizes in the 1994 industry awards.

8 yrs, 40% abv

Sweetness – 8	Peatiness – 3	Availability – 4

Colour – Full mid-amber with gold highlights. *Nose* – Full-bodied, quite spirity, rich, dark, lightly peated and medium-sweet. *Flavour* – Medium-sweet, very rich and toffee-like, light to medium-peated. *Finish* – Warm, sweet and of good length. *Notes* – Gordon & MacPhail bottling.

16 yrs, 46% abv

Sweetness – 8	Peatiness – 3	Availability – 2

Colour – Deep gold, quite peaty in depth. *Nose* – Fruity, sweet, slightly oaky. *Flavour* – Full-bodied, richly sweet, possibly a little woody. *Finish* – Long and complex with a dry tail. *Notes* – Wm Cadenhead bottling.

1978, 40% abv

Sweetness – 7	Peatiness – 4	Availability – 2

Colour – Straw/pale amber with yellow highlights. *Nose* – Light to medium-bodied, sweet, with a honeyed nuttiness, delicately peated and a little spirity. *Flavour* – Quite full-bodied, medium-sweet and quite smooth with a good smoky character. *Finish* – Good length, quite fresh, clean and rich. *Notes* – 1995 Gordon & MacPhail *Centenary Reserve* bottling.

19 yrs, 1974, 43% abv

Sweetness – 8	Peatiness – 3	Availability – 0

Colour – Pale straw with yellow/gold highlights. *Nose* – Soft, medium-sweet, caramel/toffee and malty with quite good body and a shortbread character. *Flavour* – Sweet, malty, soft with gentle tannins, sweet oaky vanilla and quite big-bodied. *Finish* – Sweet and rich vanilla with good length. *Notes* – Master of Malt bottling – cask no. 11810 distilled 9 July 1974.

27 yrs, 1966, 51.3% abv

Sweetness – 7	Peatiness – 3	Availability – 1

Colour – Very dark amber with an almost black heart and bronze/ruby highlights. *Nose* – Big-bodied, dark nutty oak with spirit at the back, almost a beeswax note, rich and medium-dry. *Flavour* – Big and dark with quite gentle tannins, full-bodied and smooth. *Finish* – Long, quite spirity and rich. *Notes* – Signatory bottling – butt no. 13512 distilled 3 November 1966.

Glen Scotia

Since it was founded as Scotia in 1832 by Stewart, Galbraith & Co, Glen Scotia has gone through many changes of ownership, the most recent being when Gibson International, who had owned it since 1987, went into receivership in 1994. It has two stills of classic swan neck design. The distillery and all maturing stocks were bought by Glen Catrine Bonded Warehouses Ltd in 1994. The distillery recommenced production in the spring of 1999 and remained in production during 2000, being now owned and operated by Loch Lomond Distillery Co Ltd, an associate company of Glen Catrine. The company advise that they remain open to offers for the sale of the distillery.

Location – In the centre of the town, at the junction of High Street with Saddell Street.

Notes – One of only two distilleries remaining in Campbeltown (the other being Springbank); somewhat fewer than the 19 which existed at the start of the economic recession of the 1920s and early '30s, during which time all were closed. Glen Scotia and Springbank were the only two to reopen. After £1,000,000 had been spent upgrading the distillery between 1979 and 1982, it was closed again until 1989 when it reopened, only to cease production late in 1994 following Gibson International's receivership. The distillery and all maturing stocks have since been purchased by Glen Catrine Bonded Warehouse Ltd. It is now back in production (spring 2001).

Water – The Crosshill Loch and two wells bored 80 feet down into the rocks below the distillery.

8 yrs, 40% abv

Sweetness – 8	*Peatiness* – 6	*Availability* – 2

Colour – Golden with hints of peaty water. *Nose* – Slightly peaty, complex, but delicate. *Flavour* – Lightish, smoky, richly sweet and slightly spirity. *Finish* – Soft and long. *Notes* – D.o.b.

14 yrs, 40% abv

Sweetness – 4	Peatiness – 3	Availability – 3

Colour – Straw with yellow/gold highlights. *Nose* – Clean, medium-bodied with a slight bubble-gummy sweetness, a touch of perfume and a hint of greenness. *Flavour* – Round, smooth and gentle, quite good body and medium-dry with the bubble-gummy note and a soft peatiness. *Finish* – Long, clean and slightly tangy with a hint of smokiness. *Notes* – D.o.b.

16 yrs, 1977, 57.6% abv

Sweetness – 5	Peatiness – 6	Availability – 2

Colour – Pale amber with yellow/gold highlights. *Nose* – Medium-bodied, fresh and off-dry with hints of Orange Pekoe tea and a light, earthy peatiness. *Flavour* – Quite rich, medium-dry with a touch of spice, gentle tannins, a firm peatiness and a flavour of tea. *Finish* – Quite tangy, softly smoky and of good length. *Notes* – Wm Cadenhead bottling

27 yrs, 1966, 51.5% abv

Sweetness – 4	Peatiness – 2	Availability – 2

Colour – Pale straw with yellow/lemon highlights. *Nose* – Fresh and medium-dry with a leafy greenness, a delicate nuttiness and a slight oaky unctuousness. *Flavour* – Medium-dry, fresh and clean with a good richness and an almost chocolatey maltiness. *Finish* – Clean, quite crisp and lightly tangy with good length and concentration. *Notes* – Signatory bottling – cask nos. 1271–2 distilled April 1966.

Glen Spey

Established by James Stuart & Co. Owned by W & A Gilbey since 22 September 1887 and now part of Diageo plc. Rebuilt in 1970 when it was extended from two to four stills.

Location – The distillery stands just below the ruins of Castle Rothes, the ancient seat of the Leslie family, the Earls of Rothes.

Notes – James Stuart & Co also once owned the Macallan distillery, a short distance away at Craigellachie. Like *Knockando, Glen Spey* is an important constituent of the J & B blends. The original unit covered an area of two acres, the distillery beginning life as an extension to a mill which was the company's original business as a grain merchant. The maturation warehouse was very innovative for its day – 10,000 square feet covered by two arched corrugated iron spans and supported by decorative iron pillars. Regrettably, on 10 January 1892, there was an exceptionally heavy snowfall and the roof collapsed under the weight of a covering of two feet of snow.

Water – The Doonie Burn.

8 yrs, 40% abv

Sweetness – 7	Peatiness – 3	Availability – 0

Colour – Pale amber with lemon highlights and a definite green tinge. *Nose* – Quite light and mashy, gently smoky with a greenness at the back. *Flavour* – Medium-sweet, fragrant, cerealy, spirity, quite fresh and smooth. *Finish* – Nice sweetness, spirity and spicy. *Notes* – D.o.b.

Glentauchers

MULBEN, BANFFSHIRE [S] EST. 1898

The foundation stone was laid on 29 May 1897, on one of the fields belonging to Tauchers Farm, and the first brew was made on 16 June 1898. One of the original owners was James Buchanan, later Lord Woolavington of *Black & White* fame. Merged with DCL in 1925, the distillery came under SMD's wing in 1930. Rebuilt in 1965–6 when it was increased from two to six stills. Closed in May 1983. Sold to Allied Distillers in 1989 and reopened. Now part of Allied Domecq and operated by Allied Distillers Ltd.

Location – On the A95, four miles west of Keith.

Notes – Experiments in the continuous distillation of malt whisky were carried out here around 1910.

Water – Springs in the local hills.

1979, 40% abv

Sweetness – 7	Peatiness – 3	Availability – 4

Colour – Light amber with gold highlights. *Nose* – Medium weight with good richness, nutty, medium-sweet with an aroma of dried apricots and delicately peated. *Flavour* – Nutty, oaky, medium-sweet with a touch of spice. *Finish* – Fresh, smooth, good length with a nice light nuttiness. *Notes* – Gordon & MacPhail bottling.

16 yrs, 1977, 63.8% abv

Sweetness – 5	Peatiness – 6	Availability – 4

Colour – Straw/pale amber with yellow highlights. *Nose* – Fresh, round and slightly green, medium-sweet with slight floral and aromatic notes. *Flavour* – Medium-sweet, round and quite full-bodied with a floral note and quite big tannins, gently smoky. *Finish* – Long, smooth and delicately smoky. *Notes* – Wm Cadenhead bottling.

Glenturret

Glenturret, previously called Hosh, is the second to take that name. It was renamed Glenturret in 1875, some 20 or so years after the nearby original distillery of that name closed. The distillery which, with two stills, is one of Scotland's smallest, was silent from 1923 to 1959. It was revived by James Fairlie who, with the later assistance of his son, Peter, established *Glenturret* as one of the world's most sought-after single malts and the Glenturret distillery as a superb tourist attraction.

Location – On the banks of the River Turret north west of Crieff on a secondary road which leads from the A85 round Crieff to Monzie and Gilmerton.

Notes – Now part of Highland Distillers Co plc. Although the present buildings were erected in 1775, illicit distilling took place at least as early as 1717. The Drummond Arms Hotel in Crieff was the building in which Prince Charles Edward Stuart (Bonnie Prince Charlie) held his stormy council of war on 3 February 1746. Apart from being possibly the oldest distillery in Scotland (see Littlemill) and certainly the oldest in the Highlands, Glenturret has another impressive claim to fame in the *Guinness Book of Records*. A legend even in her own lifetime, Towser, the distillery's rodent operative, was credited with catching a world-record 28,899 mice. Born at the distillery on 21 April 1963, Towser died on 20 March 1987, not far short of her 24th birthday – a very good age for a cat! As well as the mice, Towser was also more than a match for rats, baby rabbits and even pheasants.

Water – Loch Turret.

8 yrs, 40% abv

Sweetness – 6	Peatiness – 4	Availability – 1

Colour – Very pale straw with yellowy green highlights. *Nose* – Full, fruity, quite spirity, malty and dryish. *Flavour* – Lightweight, medium-dry, round, smooth and slightly nutty. *Finish* – Lightly spicy, grapey, of medium length. *Notes* – D.o.b.

10 yrs, 57.1% abv

Sweetness – 6	Peatiness – 4	Availability – 1

Colour – Very pale straw with pale yellow/green highlights. *Nose* – Full-bodied, slightly sweet, floral and slightly meaty. *Flavour* – Quite full-bodied, round, smooth, creamy, slightly meaty and medium-dry. *Finish* – Smooth, dry and quite long with soft edges. *Notes* – D.o.b.

12 yrs, 40% abv

Sweetness – 7	Peatiness – 3	Availability – 6

Colour – Straw/amber with good greeny gold highlights. *Nose* – Rich and sherried with oaky vanilla, medium-sweet. *Flavour* – Rich, medium-sweet, sweet oaky vanilla, full-bodied and smooth. *Finish* – Long and sherried. *Notes* – D.o.b.

15 yrs, 40% abv

Sweetness – 7	Peatiness – 3	Availability – 4

Colour – Golden/copper coloured with good yellow highlights. *Nose* – Big-bodied, full, spicy and medium-sweet with oaky vanilla and characters of liquorice, citrus and mint. *Flavour* – Full, rich, sweet and slightly peppery with hints of mint and liquorice – very complex. *Finish* – Smooth, spicy, long and memorable. *Notes* – D.o.b.

18 yrs, 40% abv

Sweetness – 7	Peatiness – 3	Availability – 4

Colour – Straw/amber with yellow/gold highlights. *Nose* – Rich, medium-bodied and slightly perfumed with characters of honey, toffee and green coffee. *Flavour* – Round, smooth, medium-sweet with a slight apple and coffee tang. *Finish* – Smooth, sweet and rich with a slight tang of fennel. *Notes* – D.o.b.

21 yrs, 40% abv

Sweetness – 7	Peatiness – 3	Availability – 1

Colour – Light mid-amber with old gold highlights. *Nose* – Rich and quite full-bodied, a greenness and liquorice/aniseed, medium-sweet. *Flavour* – Medium-sweet, lightly peated, rich aniseed and creamily smooth with a touch of oaky vanilla. *Finish* – Fresh, clean and long with a touch of sweetness. *Notes* – D.o.b.

25 yrs, 43% abv

Sweetness – 6	Peatiness – 3	Availability – 1

Colour – Straw with yellow/gold highlights. *Nose* – Quite fresh, medium-bodied and medium-sweet, a slight oaky oiliness and a nice citrus character. *Flavour* – Quite full-bodied and sweet with touches of vanilla and tannin. *Finish* – Long and sweet, tannic and quite fresh. *Notes* – D.o.b.

17 yrs, 1980, 53.7% abv

Sweetness – 8	Peatiness – 4	Availability – 2

Colour – Pale amber with yellow/lemon highlights. *Nose* – Sweet and fresh with an almost lemon citrus note, medium-bodied and quite lightly peated. *Flavour* – Sweet and rich with a quite soft peatiness, smooth and gentle. *Finish* – Long and lingering with smoky peat coming through on the finish. *Notes* – Blackadder International bottling from cask no. 4906 distilled 7 April 1980.

1968, 40% abv

Sweetness – 6	Peatiness – 3	Availability – 1

Colour – Straw with yellow/lemon highlights. *Nose* – Medium-sweet, grapey and rich with slight chocolate and nutty characters, caramel toffee and bubble-gummy notes. *Flavour* – Medium-sweet, quite good body, rich and smooth with a coffee/toffee tang. *Finish* – Long, tangy with a coffee/toffee note, quite rich and clean. *Notes* – D.o.b.

1968, 40% abv

Sweetness – 7	Peatiness – 3	Availability – 2

Colour – Pale straw with good greeny-gold highlights. *Nose* – Rich oaky vanilla, malty, medium-sweet and delicate. *Flavour* – Rich, soft, round with hints of smokiness and medium-sweet. *Finish* – Smooth, pleasantly soft and with reasonable length. *Notes* – D.o.b.

1966, 40% abv

Sweetness – 6	Peatiness – 3	Availability – 1

Colour – Pale to mid-amber with gold highlights. *Nose* – Rich and quite full-bodied, medium-sweet oaky vanilla with a tang of orange and delicately peated. *Flavour* – Medium-dry, quite full-bodied, oaky, spicy with characters of liquorice and vanilla, quite round. *Finish* – Quite long and complex, with rich liquorice/aniseed and a tail of oaky tannin. *Notes* – D.o.b.

5,000 DAYS
5,000 days old, 40% abv

Sweetness – 6	Peatiness – 3	Availability – 2

Colour – Pale amber with yellow highlights. *Nose* – Good body, fresh with a slight floral note, lightly peated and a hint of tablet. *Flavour* – Soft, smooth, quite sweet, coffee flavour and lightly smoky. *Finish* – Medium-sweet, quite soft and of good length. *Notes* – D.o.b. in miniatures.

10,000 DAYS
10,000 days old, 40% abv

Sweetness – 6	Peatiness – 4	Availability – 1

Colour – Mid-amber with yellow/gold highlights. *Nose* – Quite full, sweet, rich and fruity with a touch of greenness, an oaky lanolin character and a hint of green coffee. *Flavour* – Good body, quite zesty, fresh and medium-dry with a slight greenness. *Finish* – Clean, of good length with a touch of coffee. *Notes* – D.o.b. in miniatures.

Glenugie

PETERHEAD, ABERDEENSHIRE [H] EST. 1831

Built by Donald McLeod & Co, Glenugie passed through the hands of a number of different owners. More recently, in 1970, it was owned by a company called Long John International, which was purchased by Whitbread & Co Ltd in 1975, who were also at the time owners of Laphroaig distillery. Unlike many distilleries which were originally breweries, Glenugie was converted into a brewery for a while before being turned back to distilling. Two stills.

Location – About three miles south of Peterhead, Glenugie sits close to the sea, below the A92.

Notes – The distillery buildings, with their cast-iron frames, are of an unusual and interesting design. Closed in 1983, the buildings have since been sold for use other than distilling.

Water – Springs in the local hills.

1966, 40% *abv*

Sweetness – 7	*Peatiness* – 4	*Availability* – 2

Colour – Quite full amber with old gold highlights. *Nose* – Full and rich, quite sweet and delicately peated with a ripe fruitiness. *Flavour* – Medium-sweet, rich and oaky with a green tang. *Finish* – Clean and lightly smoky with oaky characters. *Notes* – Gordon & MacPhail bottling.

Glenury

Built to provide a market for barley in a period of agricultural depression by Barclay, McDonald & Co It was closed from 1925 to 1937, having been sold for £7,500 to Joseph Hobbs the preceding year. He, in turn, sold it to Associated Scottish Distilleries Ltd in 1938 for £18,500. Glenury acted as the "control office" for all of ASD's distilleries and the site was landscaped and roads were built into the unit. ASD was bought by DCL in 1953 and Glenury was worked from that date by SMD. The licensees were John Gillon & Co Ltd. Glenury was extensively rebuilt from 1965–6, at which time it was doubled from two to four stills. Glenury was closed in 1985. Its licence was cancelled in 1992 and the site sold for development.

Location – On the north bank of the Cowie Water, on the northern outskirts of Stonehaven.

Notes – The water supply was also that of the town of Stonehaven. Glenury's founder, Captain Robert Barclay, was the local member of Parliament. Through influence he was given permission by King William IV to call his whisky "Royal".

Water – The Cowie Water.

Vintage 1978
Single Highland Malt Scotch Whisky
Matured in oak casks for 15 years
Distilled at the Glenury Royal Distillery
on 22.11.78   *Bottled 23.11.93*
Cask no. 9770   *Bottle no.   of 290*
This whisky has been selected, produced and bottled in Scotland for and under the sole responsibility of Signatory Vintage Scotch Whisky Co., Ltd. Edinburgh EH6 Scotland
70cl   62.3%vol

15 yrs, 1978, 62.3% abv

Sweetness – 4	*Peatiness* – 2	*Availability* – 2

Colour – Very pale with hints of watery-green and lemon-green highlights. *Nose* – Quite full-bodied, malty and almost dry with an apple hint and fresh lanolin characters. *Flavour* – Medium-dry, round and smooth with a touch of spice and greenness; gentle tannins and lightly peated. *Finish* – Long, smooth and quite sweet *Notes* – Signatory bottling from cask no. 9770.

12 yrs, 40% abv

Sweetness – 2	Peatiness – 7	Availability – 2

Colour – Mid-amber with gold highlights. *Nose* – Medium-bodied, quite dry, dark and smoky with a dry burnt character. *Flavour* – Dry, peaty, quite smooth and fragrant with a slight floral character at the back. *Finish* – Long, smoky and quite fresh. *Notes* – Gordon & MacPhail bottling.

12 yrs, 40% abv

Sweetness – 3	Peatiness – 6	Availability – 0

Colour – Gold/copper. *Nose* – Light, spirity, malty and quite dry. *Flavour* – Light, medium-dry and slightly smoky. *Finish* – Smoky, but quite short. *Notes* – DCL (pre-Guinness) bottling.

14 yrs, 1978, 43% abv

Sweetness – 6	Peatiness – 3	Availability – 1

Colour – Very pale straw with pale lemon highlights. *Nose* – Light and fresh, medium-dry with a touch of richness and an appley character. *Flavour* – Medium-sweet, good body, a slightly green character with good richness. *Finish* – Lasts well: good, rich and delicate with a dry tail. *Notes* – Blackadder International bottling.

15 yrs, 1978, 62.3% abv

Sweetness – 7	Peatiness – 7	Availability – 1

Colour – Very pale watery straw with pale yellow highlights. *Nose* – Medium-dry and fresh with a mashy/cerealy character, a slight citrus tang and a light dark smokiness. *Flavour* – Rich and medium-sweet with a good under-pinning of peat and dry, oaky tannins. *Finish* – Long, quite chewy, rich and lingering. *Notes* – Master of Malt bottling.

Highland Park

KIRKWALL, ORKNEY [H] [V] EST. 1798

Said to have been founded by David Robertson, Highland Park is Scotland's most northerly distillery. It had several different owners, before coming into the hands of James Grant and family in the late 1800s. Enlarged from two to four stills in 1898 and operated by James Grant & Co until 1935, when the company was purchased by the Highland Distilleries Co Ltd.

Location – Sited on a hillside overlooking Scapa Flow to the south and Kirkwall to the north.

Notes – The distillery is built on the spot where the legendary 18th-century smuggler Magnus Eunson's bothy stood. A local minister as well as a distiller, he apparently kept a stock of whisky under his pulpit. Hearing that his church was about to be searched by the excisemen, he had the kegs removed to the manse where they were shrouded in white cloth. A coffin lid was placed next to the cloth and Eunson and his "mourners" knelt in prayer. The whispered word "smallpox" quickly ended any idea of a search by the excisemen.

Water – From springs below the level of the distillery. The water has to be pumped uphill!

12 yrs, 40% abv

Sweetness – 2	*Peatiness* – 7	*Availability* – 9

Colour – Pale straw with pale yellow depths. *Nose* – Pleasantly peaty, dryish and with a hint of smokiness. *Flavour* – Well balanced and almost dry. *Finish* – Long, distinguished and lightly smoky. *Notes* – D.o.b.

HIGHLAND
PARK
SINGLE MALT SCOTCH WHISKY
ORKNEY ISLANDS
25

25 yrs, 53.5% abv

Sweetness – 4	Peatiness – 6	Availability – 4

Colour – Quite deep amber with bronze highlights. *Nose* – Full-bodied, round, vanilla & nuttiness (Brazil nuts) with quite a dark, soft peat note and characters of rich toffee, citrus & beeswax. *Palate* – Soft & round, with smooth, creamy peat, medium-dry & flavours of vanilla & coffee. *Finish* – Long, quite fresh & gently chewy with lingering coffee/chocolate & tobacco, very complex. *Notes* – D.o.b.

1989, 58% abv

Sweetness – 5	Peatiness – 6	Availability – 2

Colour – Very pale straw with pale lemon/yellow highlights. *Nose* – Fresh, clean and medium-dry with a slightly meaty character, a smooth peatiness and an almost fruity note. *Flavour* – Medium-sweet with good body, a gentle edge of tannin and rich with a smooth peaty character. *Finish* – Long and gently smoky with a rich sweetness. *Notes* – Clydesdale Original bottling.

10 yrs, 1989, 40% abv

Sweetness – 5	Peatiness – 6	Availability – 2

Colour – Quite pale amber with yellow highlights. *Nose* – Medium-dry, quite full-bodied, fresh & softly malty with slightly fruity notes of lemon & apple. *Palate* – Round, rich, quite creamy & medium-dry with a touch of spice, quite a delicate peat note & very good balance. *Finish* – Long, rich & honeyed with a toffee apple character. *Notes* – Hart Brothers bottling.

THE

Clydesdale

ORIGINAL SCOTCH
WHISKY COMPANY LTD

THIS SUPERIOR EXAMPLE OF
original single Highland malt whisky
WAS PRODUCED IN SCOTLAND AT THE
HIGHLAND PARK
DISTILLERY
USING THE SKILLS AND
EXPERTISE HANDED DOWN
over generations of distilling

DISTILLED 1ST MARCH 1989
BOTTLED SEPTEMBER 1997
FROM SHERRY OAK CASK NO. 10034

70CL   PRODUCE OF SCOTLAND   58% vol

1988, 46% *abv*

Sweetness – 5	Peatiness – 6	Availability – 2

Colour – Straw with pale lemon highlights. *Nose* – Quite big-bodied, creamy & medium-dry with a slightly fresh green hedgerow peaty character. *Palate* – Big-bodied, smooth & medium-dry. *Finish* – Long, fresh, quite tangy, rich & creamy. *Notes* – Murray McDavid bottling.

10 *yrs*, 1983, 58.6% *abv*

Sweetness – 2	Peatiness – 7	Availability – 3

Colour – Pale amber with yellow/gold highlights. *Nose* – Fresh, creamy and delicately smoky with a slightly green apple touch. *Flavour* – Smooth, gently smoky, fruity and floral, medium-dry with a creamy richness. *Finish* – Quite big, long and fragrant, almost chewy and gently smoky. *Notes* – Gordon & MacPhail bottling. Distilled 14 April 1983.

19 *yrs*, 1977, 43% *abv*

Sweetness – 3	Peatiness – 5	Availability – 2

Colour – Very pale, watery straw with pale lemon highlights. *Nose* – Fresh, clean and medium-sweet with a note of rich mint, round with a delicate peatiness. *Flavour* – Fresh, quite dry and smooth with good body. *Finish* – Long, elegant and ethereal. *Notes* – Signatory bottling from cask nos. 5778/9 distilled 29 December 1977.

PRODUCT OF SCOTLAND
RARE VINTAGE BOTTLING

FORTIS ET FIDELIS

HART BROTHERS
Finest Collection

SINGLE MALT SCOTCH WHISKY

70cl ℮   AGED **10** YEARS   40%vol

DISTILLED AT
HIGHLAND PARK DISTILLERY
ORKNEY ISLES SCOTLAND

BOTTLED 1999 IN SCOTLAND
BY HART BROTHERS LIMITED

18 yrs, 1975, 52.1% abv

Sweetness – 2	Peatiness – 6	Availability – 2

Colour – Pale amber with beige highlights. *Nose* – Quite good body, round with a touch of perfume and a cereal character, medium-dry, delicate creamy peatiness. *Flavour* – Quite dry, round, creamily smooth, delicately peated with oaky tannins and a hint of treacle. *Finish* – Quite big, delicately smoky, elegant and long. *Notes* – Signatory bottling.

21 yrs, 1972, 56.5% abv

Sweetness – 4	Peatiness – 6	Availability – 2

Colour – Very deep amber with dark bronze highlights. *Nose* – Big-bodied, full, dark and nutty (Brazil nuts) with a burnt oak character and almost dry. *Flavour* – Big, dark and medium-sweet with a creamy peatiness, a salty tang and big tannins. *Finish* – Long, chewy, nutty and medium-sweet. *Notes* – Wm Cadenhead bottling.

1970, 40% abv

Sweetness – 3	Peatiness – 7	Availability – 4

Colour – Quite deep amber with bronze highlights. *Nose* – Full-bodied, fresh, rich and round with a peaty saltiness, medium-dry with a dark oaky, almost burnt Christmas cake character. *Flavour* – Big-bodied, smooth with quite gentle tannins, medium-dry and smokily peaty. *Finish* – Full, rich, salty, long and tangy. *Notes* – Gordon & MacPhail *Centenary Reserve* bottled 1995.

Imperial

CARRON, MORAY [S] EST. 1881

Built by Thomas Mackenzie in 1897, ownership was transferred to Dailuaine-Talisker Distilleries the following year. It closed in 1899 and was silent until 1919. Became a part of DCL in 1925 and closed again. Reopened under the control of SMD when rebuilt in 1955. Doubled to four stills in 1965. Closed again in 1985 and sold to Allied Lyons in May, 1989, when it was reopened. Now part of Allied Domecq and operated by Allied Distillers Ltd.

Location – On an unclassified road between the A95 and B9102, some two miles south west of Aberlour in a hollow on the banks of the Spey and next to the former Carron station.

Notes – The distillery was designed by architect Charles Doig of Elgin of red Aberdeen bricks within a framework of iron beams and frames. One of the malt kilns was surmounted by an enormous imperial crown which flashed and glittered in the sun. The crown, which by then had rusted, was taken down in 1955. It was one of the distilleries where experimentation on the technique of drying distillery effluent for use as cattle feed was pioneered.

Water – The Ballintomb Burn.

1979, 40% *abv*

Sweetness – 6	*Peatiness* – 7	*Availability* – 4

Colour – Amber with yellow/gold highlights. *Nose* – Quite full-bodied, medium-dry with a clean green freshness and a good peatiness. *Flavour* – Medium-sweet with a green edge, quite rich dark chocolatey and a firm peatiness. *Finish* – Clean, long, medium-sweet and delicately smokey. *Notes* – Gordon & MacPhail bottling.

12 yrs, 65% abv

Sweetness – 7	Peatiness – 6	Availability – 3

Colour – Slightly hazy, pale straw/yellow. *Nose* – Full, sweetish, malty and spirity. *Flavour* – Quite sweet, smooth, almost creamy, lightly smoky. *Finish* – Long, quite spicy, strong and quite scented, strangely chocolatey. *Notes* – James MacArthur bottling.

14 yrs, 1979, 64.9% abv

Sweetness – 6	Peatiness – 5	Availability – 4

Colour – Very pale straw with yellow/lemon highlights. *Nose* – Warm, with an unusual spiritiness, very fruity and medium-sweet. *Flavour* – Warm, soft, smooth, woody and tangy, medium-sweet and gently smoky. *Finish* – Quite long, fresh and gently smoky. *Notes* – Wm Cadenhead bottling.

1970, 40% abv

Sweetness – 6	Peatiness – 7	Availability – 2

Colour – Bright amber with good gold highlights. *Nose* – Medium-peaty, medium-sweet, oaky, lightly mashy with green fruit at the back. *Flavour* – Almost medium-dry, quite full-bodied, peaty, smooth and oily-creamy. *Finish* – Smooth, quite long, a touch smoky and with a peanut character. *Notes* – Gordon & MacPhail bottling.

HOGMANAY DRAM
16 yrs, 1976, 43% abv

Sweetness – 5	Peatiness – 7	Availability – 0

Colour – Very pale straw with a green tinge. *Nose* – Quite full, smoky, aromatic and medium-dry with a green fruitiness. *Flavour* – Slightly off-dry, smoky and full-bodied. *Finish* – Long, smoky and smooth. *Notes* – Master of Malt *Hogmanay Dram 1992* cask no. 7559.

Inchgower

BUCKIE, BANFFSHIRE [H] EST. 1871

Built by Alexander Wilson and Co as "The great distillery of Inchgower" to replace Tochineal, which had become outdated and cramped. The company celebrated its centenary on 12 July 1922. It was purchased by Buckie Town Council for £1,000 in 1936 and sold on to Arthur Bell & Sons in 1938, reputedly for £4,000. Doubled to four stills in 1966. Now part of Diageo plc.

Location – On the north side of the A98 between Fochabers and Buckie.

Notes – A farm on the hill above the distillery was once the home of a noted local smuggler by the name of Macpherson. His still, well hidden at the back of the hill, was only discovered when some stray Highland cattle dislodged a large piece of turf, thus exposing the still to the farmer driving his cattle home. Sad to say for Macpherson, the farmer was quick to tip off the excisemen and claim his reward.

Water – Springs in the Menduff Hills.

14 yrs, 43% abv

Sweetness – 7	Peatiness – 3	Availability – 6

Colour – Straw with lemon yellow highlights. *Nose* – Medium-sweet, good richness with vanilla and a greenness at the back. *Flavour* – Smooth, creamy vanilla, medium-sweet with a fresh greenness. *Finish* – Long, clean and fresh with a hint of coffee on the tail. *Notes* – D.o.b.

12 yrs, 40% abv

Sweetness – 8	Peatiness – 6	Availability – 0

Colour – Pale golden/straw. *Nose* – Slightly sweet and peaty. *Flavour* – Rich, sweet and full-bodied with a delicate peatiness. *Finish* – Distinguished, long and delicately sweet. *Notes* – Arthur Bell (pre-Guinness) bottling.

13 yrs, 43% abv

Sweetness – 7	Peatiness – 3	Availability – 1

Colour – Pale amber/straw with lemon highlights. *Nose* – Quite good body, fresh, quite sweet, gently peated and gently nutty. *Flavour* – Clean, quite zingy, medium-sweet, fruity and rich with good body. *Finish* – Quite long, fresh and clean. *Notes* – Master of Malt bottling.

1966, 61.6% abv

Sweetness – 7	Peatiness – 4	Availability – 1

Colour – Mid-amber with old gold highlights. *Nose* – Sweet with an aroma of unctuous oily oak, almost buttery and quite a fresh, ripe green fruitiness. *Flavour* – Medium-sweet with good body, chewy oaky tannins and a smooth, slight toffee note. *Finish* – Rich toffee, good length with a touch of menthol. *Notes* – Scotch Malt Whisky Society bottling; cask no. 16.5; bottled May 1994.

Inverleven

Inverleven was built in 1938 by Hiram Walker & Sons, Scotland, within the site of the Dumbarton grain distillery complex. Licensed to George Ballantine & Son Ltd. Now part of Allied Domecq, but closed in 1991.

Location – Next to the River Clyde in the centre of Dumbarton.

Notes – Two pot stills (which have now been removed) for malt whisky production at Dumbarton. There was also a third Lomond-type still which produced a heavier style of spirit known as *Lomond*.

Water – Loch Lomond.

INVERLEVEN, 1979, 40% *abv*

Sweetness – 6	Peatiness – 1	Availability – 4

Colour – Mid-amber with gold highlights. *Nose* – Quite light and cerealy with a touch of apple fruit, medium-dry with an edge of richness. *Flavour* – Medium-sweet with good richness and a smooth, creamy character. *Finish* – Long, spicy, quite sweet and tangy. *Notes* – Gordon & MacPhail bottling – followed by 1984.

LOMOND, 30 *yrs*, 60% approx. *abv*

Sweetness – 2	Peatiness – 3	Availability – 0

Colour – Pale straw/amber with yellowy green highlights. *Nose* – Quite full-bodied, good richness and still with a touch of greenness. *Flavour* – Full, spirity, dry, but with a richness at the back, the greenness of the aroma is still present. *Finish* – Long, quite light and spicy. *Notes* – A *Lomond* cask sample supplied by Whyte & Mackay for a tasting tutored by Richard Paterson held at Christie's, Glasgow.

Isle of Arran

Harold Currie had a dream, when he retired as managing director of Chivas Brothers, to create his own distillery. He found a site at Lochranza in the north of the island of Arran and built a modern distillery with the architectural appearance and feel of much older buildings. Very small, it dovetails perfectly with the rest of the island which has been described as "Scotland in miniature".

Location – Immediately to the east of the village of Lochranza in the north of the island.

Notes – The only distillery on the Isle of Arran – the last (legal) distillery, at Lagg in the south, closed in 1837. The manager, Gordon Mitchell, has a number of ducks which swim in the water-cooling pond. There are also a pair of golden eagles which nest on the crags above the distillery and caused the initial building works to stop while they tended to their young. Whilst waiting for their own spirit to be ready for sale, the company are marketing a range of whiskies, including vatted and single malts under their own labels.

Water – Loch na Davie.

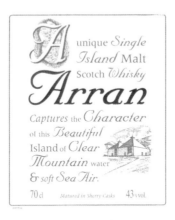

3 yrs, 43% abv

Sweetness – 7	*Peatiness* – 5	*Availability* – 3

Colour – Straw with pale yellow highlights. *Nose* – Fresh, sweet rich & malty with a touch of citrus & a slight hedgerow greenness, an apple fruitiness and a gentle, but solid peat note. *Palate* – Quite sweet, rich, fresh and gently peated with good body. *Finish* – Long, sweet with quite a solid backbone, gloriously rich with a nice fresh, green touch on the tail. *Notes* – D.o.b.

Isle of Jura

CRAIGHOUSE, ISLE OF JURA, ARGYLL   [H] [V]   EST. 1810

After passing through several different owners in its early years, Jura blossomed in the late 1800s when it came into the hands of Messrs James Ferguson & Sons in 1875, being rebuilt at a cost of £25,000. However, it closed in the early 1900s because, it is said, of an argument over the rent, after which the distiller upped and went, taking his still and equipment with him. Jura was abandoned until the late 1950s when a rebuilding programme was begun. The first spirit for more than 50 years flowed in 1963. Enlarged from two to four stills in 1978. Now owned by Invergordon Distillers plc, which in turn was taken over by JBB (Greater Europe) plc in 1994.

Location – Across from Islay on the leeward east coast of Jura, on a bay where a string of islands forms a natural breakwater.

Notes – Records are said to trace distilling on Jura as far back as 1502. After the distillery had been rebuilt in the 1870s it gained a reputation for being one of the most efficient in Scotland. However it was once discovered that the spent wash from the stills was finding its way into a local cattle trough. The effect on the animals, it is said, was most interesting.

Water – Loch a' Bhaile Mhargaidh (Market Loch).

10 *yrs*, 40% *abv*		
Sweetness – 3	Peatiness – 7	Availability – 9

Colour – Amber with pale gold highlights. *Nose* – Medium-bodied, fresh & delicately peated with a rich touch of fresh greenness to the peat and a slight toffee note. *Palate* – Quite big-bodied, rich, warm & round with quite a solid fresh peatiness. *Finish* – Long, rich, round & quite fresh with a nice belt of peat on the tail. *Notes* – D.o.b.

16 yrs, 40% abv

Sweetness – 4	Peatiness – 6	Availability – 4

Colour – Amber with pale old gold highlights. *Nose* – Quite full-bodied, rich & quite buttery with floral notes of honey, citrus & a herbal (oregano) touch, the peat has an edge of liquorice. *Palate* – Quite full and rich with flavours of vanilla & toffee & a good belt of dry peat. *Finish* – Long, spicy and rich with a touch of liquorice & rich toffee on the tail. *Notes* – D.o.b.

21 yrs, 40% abv

Sweetness – 3	Peatiness – 6	Availability – 3

Colour – Amber with old gold highlights. *Nose* – Rich, round, creamy, quite full & gently tarry with notes of tobacco, melon & citrus and, on the end, dry paper. *Palate* – Soft, smooth, rich & gently chewy with a definite fresh peppermint leaf character. *Finish* – Long, minty, very fresh & complex. *Notes* – D.o.b.

ISLE OF JURA 'STILLMAN'S DRAM', 33 yrs, 43% abv

Sweetness – 3	Peatiness – 6	Availability – 2

Colour – Full amber with bronze highlights. *Nose* – Quite big-bodied, round medium-dry, quite creamy & rich, showing vanilla, toffee, beeswax, slight honey & marzipan characters. *Palate* – Big-bodied, quite solid, dark vanilla nuttiness, gently chewy & slightly tarry. *Finish* – Long, very rich, smooth & quite ethereal. *Notes* – D.o.b.

Killyloch

TOWERS ROAD, AIRDRIE, LANARKSHIRE [L] EST. 1965

Killyloch was a second still at Moffat distillery which produced a malt for blending purposes only (see Glen Flagler). The whisky was supposed to be named *Lillyloch*, from the water source on the outskirts of Airdrie, but at the time of filling, it was discovered that the cask stencil had been mis-spelt. As the whisky was intended for blending purposes only, it was decided to leave the name as Killyloch.

Location – Within the Glen Flagler complex at Moffat distillery.

Notes – Prior to June 1994, its make had never been bottled as a single malt.

Water – Lillyloch.

22 yrs, 1972, 52.6% abv

Sweetness – 4	Peatiness – 2	Availability – 0

Colour – Pale mid-amber with lemon/gold highlights. *Nose* – Medium-bodied, cerealy, a fairly harsh spirit character and a slightly green, almost leafy, dry and with a creamy oiliness. *Flavour* – Medium-dry, soft with good richness, a touch of spice and medium-bodied with gentle tannins. *Finish* – Medium-length with good sweetness, a light smokiness and a fresh green note. *Notes* – Signatory bottling, distilled 21 March 1972 and bottled June 1994.

Kinclaith

MOFFAT STREET, GLASGOW [L] EST. 1957

Built 1957–8 by Strathclyde & Long John Distilleries Ltd, at that time a subsidiary of the US company Seager Evans & Co Ltd. Sold to Whitbread & Co Ltd in 1975 and dismantled in 1976 to make way for an enlarged Strathclyde grain distillery. Two stills.

Location – In the centre of Glasgow within the Strathclyde Grain Distilling complex.

Notes – The last of Glasgow's once numerous malt whisky distilleries.

Water – The local Glasgow water supply, which comes from Loch Katrine.

20 yrs, 46% abv

Sweetness – 6	Peatiness – 3	Availability – 1

Colour – Very pale straw with yellow/green highlights. *Nose* – Quite sweet oak, rich and full-bodied. *Flavour* – Creamy, smooth and medium-sweet. *Finish* – Peppery and spicy with a dry, clean tail. *Notes* – Wm Cadenhead bottling.

1966, 40% abv

Sweetness – 6	Peatiness – 3	Availability – 2

Colour – Amber with old gold highlights. *Nose* – Medium-bodied, lightly peated and medium-sweet with a leather and shoe wax aroma. *Flavour* – Medium-sweet and quite full-bodied with gentle oaky tannins and a leathery smokiness. *Finish* – Long, rich and creamy with dry tannins and almost chewy. *Notes* – Gordon & MacPhail bottling – followed by 1967.

Knockando

Built by the Knockando-Glenlivet Distillery Co Owned by J Thomson & Co from 1900 to 1903. Acquired by W & A Gilbey in 1904. Now managed by Justerini & Brooks, a subsidiary of Diageo plc.

Location – South of the B9102 between Knockando and Archiestown, sited on the banks of the River Spey.

Notes – Much of the make is used in the *J & B* blend. An individual feature of the malt is that its bottle states both its year of distillation and date of bottling. If you believe that whisky, like wine, has vintage years, then *Knockando* is worthy of close study. Knockando is "cnoc an dhu" in Gaelic which means "little black hillock".

Water – The Cardnach Spring.

1982, 43% *abv*

Sweetness – 7	Peatiness – 3	Availability – 7

Colour – Straw with yellow/lemon highlights. *Nose* – Medium-bodied, medium-sweet and leafy with rich unctuous oaky vanilla notes, an almost grapey fruitiness and delicately peated. *Flavour* – Good body, quite sweet and fresh with gentle tannins and peatiness. *Finish* – Long, smooth and sweet with a slightly chewy tail and hints of green coffee. *Notes* – D.o.b. in 1996.

KNOCKANDO EXTRA RESERVE, 21 *yrs*, 43% *abv*

Sweetness – 7	Peatiness – 3	Availability – 1

Colour – Straw, lightly peaty with pale greeny-gold highlights. *Nose* – Lightly peated, medium-dry, rich and leafy with pleasantly oaky vanilla. *Flavour* – Medium weight, slightly green, medium-sweet and round. *Finish* – Smooth, not quite medium-sweet, delicately spicy and quite long. *Notes* – D.o.b. in 1995.

Knockdhu

Knockdhu, as the distillery is known, was the first to be built by the DCL, being licensed to John Haig & Co Closed in 1983. Sold late 1988 to the Knockdhu Distillery Company Ltd, a subsidiary of Inver House Distillers plc and reopened in 1989. Two stills.

Location – West of the B9022, seven miles north of Huntly.

Notes – Built of local grey granite by Gordon & Macbey, architects of Elgin. The water supply, owned by the company, is piped from Knock Hill and is also supplied to the villagers of Knock. The distillery was occupied by a unit of the Indian Army from 1940 to 1945. As Inver House want to avoid confusion with, or suggestion of another malt, the single malt from Knockdhu is now marketed under the Gaelic name *An Cnoc*.

Water – A spring on the southern slopes of Knock Hill.

12 yrs, 43% abv

Sweetness – 6	Peatiness – 7	Availability – 4

Colour – Straw/amber with gold highlights. *Nose* – Fresh, medium-bodied, malty and medium-sweet with a touch of greenness. *Flavour* – Sweet, round, quite full-bodied and lightly peated. *Finish* – Long, smooth and sweet with a green smokiness. *Notes* – Inver House bottling as *An Cnoc*.

21 yrs, 57.7% abv

Sweetness – 7	Peatiness – 3	Availability – 2

Colour – Pale amber with gold highlights. *Nose* – Quite full-bodied and medium-sweet, a quite creamy vanilla touch with notes of leafy apple . *Palate* – Medium-sweet, quite rich & gently chewy with quite a delicate peatiness and hints of toffee & coffee. *Finish* – Long, toffeeyed and pop corn, fresh. *Notes* – D.o.b.

Ladyburn

GIRVAN, AYRSHIRE [L] EST. 1966

Opened in 1966 by William Grant & Sons Ltd, Ladyburn has not produced any spirit since 1976. Four stills.

Location – Ladyburn is part of the complex which includes the Girvan grain distillery.

Notes – William Grant & Sons are also the proud owners of the Speyside malts *Glenfiddich* and *The Balvenie*, but *Ladyburn* is much harder to come by, as it is only occasionally released through the independent bottlers. None is available from the owners although there is a rumour that William Grant & Sons have 30 casks laid down for future bottling.

Water – Penwapple reservoir.

PURE MALT SCOTCH WHISKY
from
LADYBURN
Distillery

Proprietors: William Grant & Sons Ltd.

75 cl

Bottled by Wm. Cadenhead,
18 Golden Square, Aberdeen
Scotland

46% vol

20 yrs, 46% abv

Sweetness – 4	Peatiness – 4	Availability – 1

Colour – Pale straw with lemon/gold highlights. *Nose* – Malty, lightly peated, leafy and slightly rich with an oily character. *Flavour* – Almost dry, smooth, round, soft and peaty; quite simple, but with good body. *Finish* – Slightly smoky, a touch of spice and of reasonable length. *Notes* – Wm Cadenhead bottling.

Lagavulin

Originally two legal distilleries were set up on the site; the first in 1816 was Lagavulin, founded by John Johnson. The second, the following year, was established by Archibald Campbell and is believed to have been known as Kildalton. In Alfred Barnard's report on his visit of 1887, he stated that the make was "principally sold in Glasgow, England and the Colonies". Lagavulin has long been important to *White Horse* blended whisky, becoming part of DCL in 1927 and managed by SMD from 1930. Rebuilt in 1962 when the stills from Malt Mill (see below) were incorporated. Four stills. Now part of Diageo plc.

Location – Occupying a site of six acres, Lagavulin stands at the head of a small bay. The ruins of Dunyvaig Castle are next door.

Notes – "Lagganmhouillin", or Lagavulin, means "mill in the valley". Distilling on the site is thought to date from as early as 1742 when there were ten small bothies there. One of UDV's *Classic Malts* portfolio. Mackie & Co, owners at the turn of the century, were also the agents for neighbouring *Laphroaig*. When they lost the agency in 1907, they built a new distillery within the Lagavulin complex to produce a similar style of whisky. Called Malt Mill, it had its own maltings which had a haircloth-floored kiln fired only with open peat fires. The Lagavulin mash tun was utilised, but there were two independent wash backs and two pear-shaped stills. Malt Mill closed in 1960 and the stills were incorporated in Lagavulin.

Water – The Solan Lochs.

16 yrs, 43% abv

Sweetness – 3	Peatiness – 10	Availability – 10

Colour – Deep amber with rich gold highlights. *Nose* – Distinctive, pungent, burnt heather, very peaty and full-bodied. *Flavour* – Big, peaty, dry, very smooth and powerfully complex. *Finish* – Long and smoky with an almost burnt character, very persistent. *Notes* – D.o.b.

15 yrs, 1980, 63.3% abv

Sweetness – 3	*Peatiness* – 8	*Availability* – 1

Colour – Deep amber with bronze highlights and a ruby hue. *Nose* – Full-bodied, dark, powerful and pungent (but its inherent character is partly masked by the influence of the Oloroso cask), rubber/liquorice and burnt heather roots. *Flavour* – Big-bodied, pungently smoky, with good richness and quite gentle, tarry tannins. *Finish* – Long, dark, smoky and tangy. *Notes* – Scotch Malt Whisky Society bottling as cask no. 111.1.

LAGAVULIN DISTILLER'S EDITION, 1979, 43% abv

Sweetness – 1	*Peatiness* – 9	*Availability* – 6

Colour – Deep amber with bronze highlights. *Nose* – Dark, dry, quite powerful and tarry with a burnt stick and dried seaweed character. *Palate* – Dry, full-bodied, powerful, tangy, seashore characters combined with wood fire. *Finish* – Long, good richness, a slight hint of sweetness & vanilla, but overwhelmingly peaty. *Notes* – D.o.b. finished in an Pedro Ximinez cask.

15 yrs, 1978, 64.4% abv

Sweetness – 5	*Peatiness* – 9	*Availability* – 2

Colour – Pale amber with a greenish tinge and yellow highlights. *Nose* – Full and pungent with ozone, burnt heather and a rich, slightly creamily unctuous character. *Flavour* – Seaweed with great richness and quite big tannins, quite sweet, powerful and pungent. *Finish* – Long, lingering, smoky and rich. *Notes* – Wm Cadenhead bottling.

Laphroaig

NEAR PORT ELLEN, ISLAY, ARGYLL   [I] [V]   EST. 1815

Said to have been founded by Donald and Alex Johnston. Originally a
farm distillery, records show distilling took place on the site in 1812.
By 1815, when the forerunner of today's distillery opened, distilling had
overtaken farming in importance to the Johnston family. Laphroaig
remained in the Johnston family until 1954, when the then proprietor,
Ian Hunter, bequeathed it to Bessie Williamson. At this time she was
company secretary, having worked in the business for many years, and
she went on to become a most important and respected figure in the Scotch
whisky industry before she retired as managing director in 1972. Miss
Williamson sold Laphroaig to Long John Distillers Ltd, part of the Seager
Evans group, between 1962 and 1967 and the business is now part of
Allied Domecq and operated by Allied Distillers Ltd. Enlarged from two to
four stills in 1923, to six in 1968–9 and to seven in 1974.

Location – Situated on a small bay, frequented by otters, swans and a
heron, it has been greatly influenced by the sea throughout its history.

Notes – Generally accepted as being the most individually flavoured of all
single malts. Although Laphroaig, like all the distilleries on the island, is
built on the coast, it has always been maintained that it is not only the
sea air, but also the peat which accounts for the distinctiveness of the
make. The peat used by the distillery has a high proportion of moss in its
content and this is said to give *Laphroaig* its particular flavour. Laphroaig
has its own floor maltings. Part of the site occupied by the modern
Laphroaig distillery includes that of the old Ardenistle distillery (1837–
c. 1848).

Water – The Kilbride Dam.

LAPHROAIG®

SINGLE ISLAY MALT
SCOTCH WHISKY

10
Years Old

The most richly flavoured of
all Scotch whiskies
ESTABLISHED
1815

DISTILLED AND BOTTLED IN SCOTLAND BY

D. JOHNSTON & CO., (LAPHROAIG), LAPHROAIG DISTILLERY, ISLE OF ISLAY.

40%vol   IMPORTADOR WENCESLAO PAZ MARTINEZ
DOMICILIO C HADDU S/N R.S. NUM 40.1.125 ML   **70cl**

L00205

Sweetness – 2	Peatiness – 10	Availability – 10

Colour – Palish amber with slightly greenish tones. *Nose* – Dry, heavy and peaty with a heathery smokiness. *Flavour* – Full of character, very peaty and smoky with iodine/medicinal notes. *Finish* – Lingering, smoky, smooth and unique. *Notes* – D.o.b.

10 yrs, 57.3% abv

Sweetness – 2	Peatiness – 10	Availability – 6

Colour – Amber with gold highlights. *Nose* – Big, full-bodied and powerful with a dark, burnt heather peaty character, an ozone/wrack medicinal note and a slight hint of richness. *Flavour* – Smooth and big-bodied with a chewy tarriness, smoky and dry, but with an edge of richness. *Finish* – Long, tangy, smoky and slightly chewy, powerful and complex. *Notes* – D.o.b. as *Original Cask Strength Laphroaig – Straight from the Wood.*

15 yrs, 43% abv

Sweetness – 2	Peatiness – 10	Availability – 6

Colour – Amber/peaty with good gold highlights. *Nose* – Peaty, full and medicinal with a slightly fruity edge. *Flavour* – Soft, smoky, round and smooth with a slightly sweet middle to the palate. *Finish* – Long, smoky and refined. *Notes* – D.o.b.

LAPHROAIG®

AGED **15** YEARS

SINGLE *ISLAY* MALT
SCOTCH WHISKY

"The most richly flavoured of all Scotch Whiskies"

EST'D **1815** EST'D

DISTILLED AND BOTTLED IN SCOTLAND BY
D. JOHNSTON & CO.,(LAPHROAIG), LAPHROAIG DISTILLERY, ISLE OF ISLAY

UNI–HANDELSGESELLSCHAFT MBH
D66119 SAARBRUCKEN

L0114A   0.71e   43%vol   L00108

1976, 43% abv

Sweetness – 1	Peatiness – 10	Availability – 1

Colour –Amber with old gold highlights. *Nose* – Full-bodied, dark & pungent – an earthy coal dust/sea weed character to the peat and notes of heather blossom/violets & citrus oil. *Palate* – Big, dry, pungent and smoky with a nice edge of richness, vanilla, quite chewy tannins and violets. *Finish* – Long and quite elegant with a heathery softness in the middle and tangy poundings of the sea. *Notes* – D.o.b. Only available at the distillery.

ISLAY FROM LAPHROAIG, 1990, 45% abv

Sweetness – 1	Peatiness – 10	Availability – 1

Colour – Very pale gold with pale yellow highlights. *Nose* – Quite big-bodied and powerful with a dark, pungent peat character, liquorice, dry & smoky, archetypally medicinal – hospital wards & bandages. *Palate* – Dry, rich and smoky with quite solid tannins and hints of seaweed. *Finish* – Long, smoky, medicinally healthy and alcoholic. *Notes* – Blackadder bottling.

LEAPFROG, 1987, 46% abv

Sweetness – 1	Peatiness – 10	Availability – 2

Colour – Straw with yellow highlights. *Nose* – Big-bodied, pungent, dry & malty with a full-bodied peat character & aromas of corn flakes. *Palate* – Powerful & sea-tainted, heather peaty, dry & rich. *Finish* – Very long, softly perfumed, rich & intense. *Notes* – Murray McDavid bottling.

Linkwood

ELGIN, MORAY [S] EST. 1821

Built by Peter Brown in 1821 and named after the estate on which it was built. The *Elgin Courant* of 10 April 1874 reported that the old buildings of Linkwood distillery were being pulled down and that new, more extensive buildings were being erected. By 1887 Linkwood had a 2,000 gallon wash still and a 1,850 gallon spirit still and was producing 50,000 gallons a year. It was bought by SMD in 1933 and rebuilt twice more: in 1962 and again in 1971, when a second distillery unit was built alongside the original extending it from two to six stills. Now part of Diageo plc.

Location – On the A941 south of Elgin and on the River Lossie.

Notes – A very picturesque distillery with a reservoir of water for cooling purposes, which is inhabited by swans, alongside the buildings. It is surrounded by woodlands, hence the name. Roderick Mackenzie, who was manager from 1945 to 1963, believed that the character of the spirit depended not just on the vessels in which it was made, but also on everything in its immediate environment. He is reputed not to have permitted the removal even of spiders' webs in case the character of the whisky were to alter as a result.

Water – Springs near Millbuies Loch.

SPEYSIDE
SINGLE MALT
SCOTCH WHISKY

LINKWOOD

distillery stands on the *River Lossie*,
close to *ELGIN* in *Speyside*. The *distillery*
has retained its *traditional atmosphere*
since its *establishment* in 1821.
Great care has always
been taken to *safeguard* the
character of the *whisky* which has
remained the same through the
years. Linkwood is one of the
FINEST Single Malt Scotch Whiskies
available - *full bodied* with a *hint* of
sweetness and a *slightly smoky aroma*.

YEARS **12** OLD

43% vol   Distilled & Bottled in SCOTLAND
LINKWOOD DISTILLERY
Elgin, Moray, Scotland   70 cl

12 yrs, 43% abv

Sweetness – 7	Peatiness – 5	Availability – 6

Colour – Straw/amber with lemon highlights. *Nose* – Medium to full-bodied, medium-sweet with an appley character and a soft smokiness at the back. *Flavour* – Good weight, medium-sweet, fruity and lightly smoky. *Finish* – Long and spicy with a nice edge of sweetness. *Notes* – D.o.b.

15 yrs, 40% abv

Sweetness – 7	Peatiness – 5	Availability – 4

Colour – Quite full mid-amber with a tinge of green and gold highlights. *Nose* – Quite full-bodied, musty apples and oak with a fresh smokiness. *Flavour* – Medium-sweet and full-bodied with a touch of spice and oaky vanilla. *Finish* – Smooth and appley with a dry smoky finish. *Notes* – Gordon & MacPhail bottling.

21 yrs, 40% abv

Sweetness – 8	Peatiness – 6	Availability – 3

Colour – Quite deep amber with bronze highlights. *Nose* – Smooth, dark and nutty with a touch of demerara sugar, medium-sweet and rich with a musty apple aroma. *Flavour* – Sweet, quite full-bodied and smooth with a delicate, but firm, peatiness. *Finish* – Long and sweet with just a hint of smokiness on the tail. *Notes* – Gordon & MacPhail bottling.

17 yrs, 1982, 64.2% abv

Sweetness – 7	Peatiness – 5	Availability – 2

Colour – Pale amber with yellow highlights. *Nose* – Medium-sweet, medium-bodied, quite peachy, malty & citrus-charactered, apple & a touch of vanilla with a little perfume on the tail. *Palate* – Big-bodied, rich, sweet, appley with a soft peat character. *Finish* – Long, fresh, appley with a touch of bubble-gummy fruitiness. *Notes* – Adelphi bottling from cask no. 4592.

1979, 14 yrs, 58.5% abv

Sweetness – 3	Peatiness – 6	Availability – 2

Colour – Deep, treacly amber with deep bronze/ruby highlights. *Nose* – Big-bodied, burnt wood peatiness, a dark nuttiness, medium-dry with the soft aroma of one of Leith's old tea warehouses. *Flavour* – Big, burnt and almost dry with chewy tannins. *Finish* – Soft, rich, long, chewy and off-dry. *Notes* – Wm Cadenhead bottling.

Littlemill

BOWLING, DUNBARTONSHIRE [L] EST. 1772

The distillery has had numerous owners over its two centuries of operation, although its origins are somewhat obscure. Littlemill could be Scotland's oldest distillery. It is possible that whisky was distilled on the site as long ago as the 14th century, when the Colquhouns built Dunglas Castle to guard the crossing of the Clyde. About 1750, George Buchanan, a wealthy maltster from Glasgow bought Littlemill when he purchased the Auchterlonie estate and in 1772 he had to build houses for the excise officers. Annual production in 1821 is recorded as 20,000 gallons. Rebuilt in 1875, Littlemill used triple distillation until the 1930s. The distillery closed in 1984 and was reopened by Gibson International in 1989. Following that company's failure late in 1994, Littlemill is now owned by Loch Lomond Distillery Co Ltd, but is again closed and it is doubtful whether it will ever distil again. All the distillery equipment has been removed.

Location – Between the main road, the A82 and the River Clyde at the foot of the Kilpatrick Hills, 12 miles from Glasgow city centre towards Dumbarton.

Notes – Although strictly speaking a Lowland distillery, this is another which takes its water supply from north of the Highland Line. The stills are of a most unusual design.

Water – A spring in the Kilpatrick Hills.

PRODUCT OF SCOTLAND

LITTLEMILL

Established 1772

SINGLE LOWLAND MALT
SCOTCH WHISKY

DISTILLED AND BOTTLED IN SCOTLAND BY
LITTLEMILL DISTILLERY CO.LTD.
BOWLING, DUNBARTONSHIRE, SCOTLAND

70cl ℮   40%vol

8 yrs, 40% abv

Sweetness – 6	Peatiness – 1	Availability – 5

Colour – Straw with yellow/gold highlights. *Nose* – Quite young, slightly mashy with an unpeated green, new-mown grassiness, medium-dry and with quite good body. *Flavour* – Fresh, quite mashy, medium-sweet and clean with good body. *Finish* – Quite rich and clean, of good length with just a suggestion of darkness at the end. *Notes* – D.o.b.

Loch Lomond

Built in 1965–6 by the Littlemill Distillery Co Ltd. Barton Distilling (Scotland) operated it from 1971 until closure in 1984. It was bought by Glen Catrine Bonded Warehouse Ltd in 1986 and reopened in 1987. Now operated by a sister company, Loch Lomond Distillery Co Ltd. It has three sets of stills, two sets with traditional bulbous base, but with a rectifying column instead of a swan's neck, and one pair of traditional pot stills.

Location – Alexandria is at the southern end of Loch Lomond on the A82 Glasgow to Fort William road.

Notes – They produce no fewer than seven different malts, three of which are marketed as singles, the remaining four used solely for blending. There is also a continuous still producing grain whisky (which has recently been lauded as the finest grain spirit in Scotland) on the site.

Water – Loch Lomond.

No age statement, 40% *abv*

Sweetness – 7	*Peatiness* – 4	*Availability* – 4

Colour – Amber with pale gold highlights. *Nose* – Quite full-bodied, malty, round & medium-dry with a quite soft, fresh, green peatiness & a hedgerow character. *Palate* – Quite sweet, round, smooth, quite delicately peated & fresh. *Finish* – Long, rich, clean. *Notes* – D.o.b.

OLD RHOSDHU, 10 yrs, 40% abv

Sweetness – 6	Peatiness – 4	Availability – 4

Colour – Amber with pale gold highlights. *Nose* – Fresh, medium-dry and youthful with a cereal note and quite gentle dark peat. *Palate* – Medium-sweet with a touch of richness, of good body, with delicate peat and a cereal note. *Finish* – Long with a slight burnt note. *Notes* – D.o.b.

OLD RHOSDHU, 9 yrs, 1985, 60.5% abv

Sweetness – 6	Peatiness – 4	Availability – 2

Colour – Straw with lemon yellow highlights. *Nose* – Quite full, young, spirity and mashy, a dry earthy smokiness with just an edge of sweetness. *Palate* – Medium-sweet, mashy and vegetal, medium-bodied. *Finish* – Sweet, cerealy, of medium length and with a burnt toffee tail. *Notes* – Wm Cadenhead bottling.

INCHMURRIN, 10 yrs, 40% abv

Sweetness – 4	Peatiness – 6	Availability – 4

Colour – Amber with old gold highlights. *Nose* – Youthful, fresh, mashy, rich and medium-dry with a good weight of peat. *Palate* – Quite sweet and fresh with good weight and a nice green note to the peat character. *Finish* – Long, clean and rich. *Notes* – D.o.b.

INCHMURRIN, 9 yrs, 1985, 64% abv

Sweetness – 4	Peatiness – 3	Availability – 2

Colour – Pale watery straw with lemon highlights. *Nose* – Young, mashy, vegetal and dry with just a hint of sweetness at the back. *Palate* – Medium-sweet, vegetal and mashy with a citrus note, slightly harsh and austere. *Finish* – Earthy, quite short and spirity. *Notes* – Wm Cadenhead bottling, distilled March 1985.

Lochside

MONTROSE, ANGUS   [H]   EST. 1957

Established on the site of Deuchar's brewery in 1957 by Joseph Hobbs, formerly of Associated Scottish Distillers, as a grain and malt distillery and blending and bottling plant. It was to be run by Hobbs under the operational company, MacNab Distilleries Ltd. It was sold to Destilerias y Crianza de Whisky SA of Madrid in November 1973. Originally four pot stills and one Coffey (grain) still, the latter was closed in 1970.

Location –At the north end of Montrose, at the junction of the Aberdeen to Dundee road (the A92) and the A935 from Montrose to Brechin.

Notes – All of the make used to be bottled at the distillery by MacNab Distilleries. A small loch once existed opposite the distillery, hence the name. The stills ceased production in the mid-1980s and the plant is now closed. The buildings are in the process of being redeveloped.

Water – A bore well beneath the distillery.

10 yrs, 40% abv

Sweetness – 3	Peatiness – 5	Availability – 1

Colour – Light straw with gold highlights. *Nose* – Quite light, floral, leafy and slightly sweet. *Flavour* – Medium-dry, round and spicy, of medium weight. *Finish* – Leafy with hints of coffee, quite smooth. *Notes* – D.o.b.

1981, 46% abv

Sweetness – 4	Peatiness – 6	Availability – 2

Colour – Amber with gold highlights. *Nose* – Fresh, clean, slightly green, medium-bodied, malty, a medium-weight peat, leafy, hayfield character. *Palate* – Medium-dry, round, smooth, unctuous & gently chewy with a quite solid peat note. *Finish* – Long & dark with creamy vanilla & a touch of spice. *Notes* – Murray McDavid bottling

Longmorn

NEAR ELGIN, MORAY   [S]   EST. 1894

Built by the Longmorn Distillery Company, which was amalgamated with The Glenlivet and Glen Grant Distilleries and Hill, Thomson & Co Ltd to form The Glenlivet Distilleries Ltd. Bought by the Seagram Company of Canada in 1977 and sold to Pernod Ricard in 2001. Extended from four to six stills in 1972 and eight in 1974.

Location – On the A941 Elgin to Rothes and Craigellachie road.

Notes – Professor R J S McDowall considered *Longmorn* to be one of the four finest malts. The name Longmorn comes from the Gaelic "Llanmorgund" meaning "place of the holy man", the distillery reputedly being on the site of an ancient abbey. The distillery houses an old steam engine which is occasionally used and it also has a disused water wheel. This malt is much favoured by blenders as a "top dressing" for their blends.

Water – Local springs.

15 yrs, 45% abv

Sweetness – 6	*Peatiness* – 4	*Availability* – 6

Colour – Mid-amber with gold highlights. *Nose* – Rich, full-bodied with soft oak and a cooked apples/grapey fruitiness, slightly peppery. *Flavour* – Quite full-bodied, round, soft and smooth, medium-sweet with a delicate edge of smokiness and gentle tannins. *Finish* – Rich, smooth and elegant with just a touch of smokiness. *Notes* – D.o.b.

12 yrs, 40% abv

Sweetness – 6	Peatiness – 5	Availability – 4

Colour – Amber with old gold highlights. *Nose* – Medium-bodied, a light sweet smokiness, a touch of creamy toffee and an almost menthol character. *Flavour* – Medium-dry, round, slightly creamy and smooth with a dark nuttiness. *Finish* – Long and nutty with a slight fragrant smokiness and a floral tail. *Notes* – Gordon & MacPhail bottling.

12 yrs, 58.6% abv

Sweetness – 8	Peatiness – 3	Availability – 1

Colour – Pale/mid-amber with pale yellow/gold highlights. *Nose* – Sweet, unctuous banana fruitiness with quite good body and delicately peated. *Flavour* – Sweet, round, soft and full-flavoured, gently tannic with a good, clean chocolatey peatiness. *Finish* – Long, sweet, rich and lingering with a smooth oaky vanilla background. *Notes* – Blackadder International Limited Editions bottling.

30 yrs, 50% abv

Sweetness – 7	Peatiness – 5	Availability – 2

Colour – Mid-amber with old gold highlights. *Nose* – Full, round, medium-sweet with creamy, sweet vanilla, rich, round, quite soft with an apple fruitiness & a delicate pungency. *Palate* – Quite big-bodied and sweet with quite a dry oak character, and a well-integrated burnt stick peat character. *Finish* – Long and complex; a creosote pungency, a touch of spice and peach. *Notes* – Douglas Laing bottling.

Longrow

CAMPBELTOWN, ARGYLL [C] EST. 1973

Longrow is a particular type of malt produced occasionally from one of the stills within Springbank distillery.

Location – In the centre of Campbeltown.

Notes – Although the current brand was introduced only in 1973, the name was originally given to a distillery that once stood next door to Springbank, said to have been founded in 1824. It had closed by 1896. The old Longrow distillery site is now Springbank's car park. Very little *Longrow* has ever been released but this is now slowly changing.

Water – Crosshill Loch and a spring on the premises.

10 yrs, 46% abv

Sweetness – 4	Peatiness – 7	Availability – 2

Colour – Amber with gold highlights. *Nose* – Big-bodied, fresh and smoky with a fresh, green peatiness, creamy, rich & medium-sweet. *Palate* – Big, quite pungent & smoky, yet soft with a liquorice character & medium-dry. *Finish* – Long, tangy and peaty, finishing with a note of cocoa. *Notes* – D.o.b.

25 yrs, 46% abv

Sweetness – 3	Peatiness – 7	Availability – 2

Colour – Amber with pale old gold highlights. *Nose* – Quite big-bodied, fresh and rich with a slightly green edge to a quite heavy peat character. *Palate* – Medium-dry, quite full-bodied, round and creamily smooth with flavours of vanilla & honey & a solid peatiness. *Finish* – Long, fresh & quite pungent with a green edge. *Notes* – D.o.b.

LONGROW SHERRY, 10 yrs, 46% abv

Sweetness – 4	Peatiness – 7	Availability – 2

Colour – Amber with old gold highlights. *Nose* – Surprisingly delicate, nutty & darkly peaty with a touch of richness & hints of beeswax & citrus. *Palate* – Quite delicate, soft, medium-dry & of good body with a nice dollop of peat. *Finish* – Long, rich, round & warmly nutty. *Notes* – D.o.b.

The Macallan

Until the bridge at Craigellachie was built by Thomas Telford in 1814, the ford across the Spey at Easter Elchies was one of the few on the river. It was much used by cattle drovers, and whisky distilled at the old farm distillery which preceded the licensed distillery was a popular feature of the river crossing for them. The licensed distillery was founded by Alexander Reid in 1824. Macallan, although now a public limited company, was until recently controlled by the successors of Roderick Kemp who purchased it in 1892. The distillery was extended in the early 1950s and again in 1959, but the demand for *Macallan* fillings was such that it was doubled from six to twelve stills in 1965, increased to eighteen in 1974 and to twenty-one in 1975. The stills are small. Operational control passed to Highland Distilleries plc in 1996. The family interests were bought out by a partnership of Highland Distillers and Suntory, both of which have held Macallan shareholdings for some time. Highland Distillers are now the majority shareholders, with 75% of the equity.

Location – On a hillside overlooking the Spey with the old Easter Elchies house now magnificently refurbished as corporate offices.

Notes – The company's own bottlings are sold as *The Macallan*. The makers of *The Macallan* have championed the use of sherry casks for maturing whisky and have helped to reverse the trend away from their use. All The Macallan's make is now aged in various types of sherry wood. Old vintages of *The Macallan* are much sought after and very valuable. One bottle was bought for £12,000 in 1997.

Water – From bore holes.

Sweetness – 8	Peatiness – 4	Availability – 8

Colour – Light amber with yellow-gold highlights. *Nose* – Sweet, quite full-bodied, round and fresh, with green spiciness, peppery and with a note of coriander. *Palate* – Medium-sweet, quite rich and smoky with a medium peat character and notes of coffee, unctuous vanilla and toffee. *Finish* – Long, quite fresh and creamy with a toffee sweetness. *Notes* – D.o.b.

10 yrs, 40% abv

Sweetness – 7	Peatiness – 4	Availability – 10

Colour – Mid-amber with old gold highlights. *Nose* – Full, sherried, nutty and rich with notes of honey & dried fruits – banana, pears & apricots and a hint of demerara sugar. *Palate* – Sweet, full-bodied & rich with good peat integration. *Finish* – Long and sherried with sweet vanilla notes. *Notes* – D.o.b.

MACALLAN 100 PROOF, 10 yrs, 57% abv

Sweetness – 8	Peatiness – 4	Availability – 10

Colour – Mid-amber with old gold highlights. *Nose* – Medium-bodied, very rich, sweeter & more delicate that the 40% bottling, almost syrupy, with hints of ripe pears, citrus & almonds. *Palate* – Sweet, full-bodied and rich, possibly more elegant & subtle than the 40% bottling. *Finish* – Long, quite complex and sherried with creamy vanilla notes. *Notes* – D.o.b.

12 yrs, 43% abv

Sweetness – 7	Peatiness – 4	Availability – 8

Colour – Mid-amber with gold highlights. *Nose* – Medium-sweet, medium-bodied, rich and heather honeyed with an almond nuttiness and notes of apple, peach and a little citrus. *Palate* – Quite big-bodied, medium-sweet, honey, a quite delicate peatiness with a slightly green edge and a nutty chewiness. *Finish* – Long, rich and nutty. *Notes* – D.o.b.

25 yrs, 43% abv

Sweetness – 7	Peatiness – 5	Availability – 4

Colour – Full amber with deep old gold highlights. *Nose* – Quite full-bodied, a medium-sweet, rich fruitiness, soft, oaky vanilla and a creamy, almost menthol note. *Palate* – Medium-dry, soft and gentle, with quite rich, gently chewy tannins and an edge of sweet oak. *Finish* – Long, medium-sweet and quite dry with a rich, chocolatey peat note. *Notes* – D.o.b.

30 yrs, 43% abv

Sweetness – 5	Peatiness – 6	Availability – 2

Colour – Deep amber with ruby-tinted bronze highlights. *Nose* – Full round and honeyed, medium-sweet with citrus, a slightly unctuous vanilla & beeswax notes. *Palate* – Big-bodied, medium-dry and chewily tannic with beeswax, honey, dried apple, orange and quite a solid peat note. *Finish* – Dry and quite chewy with a dark peat note. *Notes* D.o.b.

15 yrs, 1984, 43% abv

Sweetness – 7	Peatiness – 4	Availability – 9

Colour –Mid-amber with a hint of bronze to the highlights. *Nose* – Quite full-bodied and medium-sweet with an unctuously-honeyed, delicate green edge and a dark fruitiness with notes of dried apricot, mango, sultanas & banana. *Palate* – Sweet with a creamy peatiness, gently chewy tannins and a fresh, slight green edge. *Finish* – Long, complex, medium-sweet and elegant. *Notes* – D.o.b.

18 yrs, 1982, 43% abv

Sweetness – 7	Peatiness – 4	Availability – 10

Colour – Amber with old gold highlights. *Nose* – Big-bodied, rich, fresh, sweet and sherried with notes of honey and apple and darkly peaty. *Palate* – Quite full-bodied, sherried and medium-sweet with a honeyed character, gently chewy with quite a delicate peatiness, darkly smoky and quite elegant. *Finish* – Long, elegant, richly smoky, sherried and toffeeyed. *Notes* – D.o.b.

20 yrs, 1974, 53.9% abv

Sweetness – 5	Peatiness – 6	Availability – 2

Colour – Deep amber with old gold highlights. *Nose* – Full-bodied, dark and nutty, medium-sweet with an edge of richness and a sooty, burnt peat character. *Flavour* – Medium-sweet, rich, soft and very smooth with gentle tannins. *Finish* – Nutty and peaty with a touch of spiciness. *Notes* – Wm Cadenhead bottling.

18 yrs, 1971, 43% abv

Sweetness – 8	Peatiness – 3	Availability – 2

Colour – Rich amber with good gold highlights. *Nose* – Medium-sweet, quite full-bodied and with a slight oily nuttiness. *Flavour* – Medium-dry, nutty, round and medium-bodied. *Finish* – Clean and fresh with a nice touch of richness and slightly smoky. *Notes* – D.o.b.

18 yrs, 1967, 43% abv

Sweetness – 6	Peatiness – 3	Availability – 1

Colour – Rich and deeply golden. *Nose* – Rich, sherry-sweet with oaky-vanilla. *Flavour* – Sweet and round, rich, velvety smooth and less spirity than the 10 years old. *Finish* – Long, sweet and very distinguished. *Notes* – D.o.b.

1948, 46.6% abv

Sweetness – 5	Peatiness – 6	Availability – 1

Colour – Full, dark amber with old gold highlights. *Nose* – Quite full and dark with a slightly earthy note to the peat, medium-dry, elegant & quite ethereal. *Palate* – Medium-dry with chewy tannins, good richness & quite full-bodied with hints of clove & cinnamon. *Finish* – Long and chewy with a dark peaty note & a very complex tail. *Notes* – D.o.b.

1946, 46.6% abv

Sweetness – 4	Peatiness – 5	Availability – 2

Colour – Mid-amber with gold highlights. *Nose* – Big, medium-sweet and nuttily mature with full notes of oaky vanilla and quite a heavy peat note. *Palate* – Medium-dry, with an edge of richness, chewily tannic with a sweet oak character and quite delicately peated. *Finish* – Long and chewy with just a hint of sweetness; quite elegant, if a little austere. *Notes* – D.o.b.

MACALLAN GRAN RESERVA, 18 yrs, 40% abv

Sweetness – 7	Peatiness – 4	Availability – 2

Colour – Deep amber with ruby/bronze highlights. *Nose* – Full-bodied, nutty, a dried raisiny note, a rich, deep, soft peatiness with an Armagnac-like note and a fresh, slightly green citrus edge. *Palate* – Full-bodied, round, medium-sweet, nutty and gently chewy, delicately peated and elegant. *Finish* – Long, fresh, gently, nuttily chewy and quite ethereal. *Notes* – D.o.b., bottled in 1999.

MACALLAN MILLENNIUM DECANTER, 1949, 50 yrs, 43% abv

Sweetness – 7	Peatiness – 5	Availability – 1

Colour – Deep, dark amber with ruby-tinted old gold highlights. *Nose* – Full-bodied, rich, sweet, slightly honeyed and almost syrupy, with notes of demerara sugar, green coffee, toffee and soft vanilla. *Palate* – Full-bodied, medium-sweet, round, smooth, quite ethereal and rich with pleasantly chewy oaky tannins, liquorice and quite soft with a hint of butterscotch and toffee. *Finish* – Long, very elegant & well-balanced, almost vinuous with a spicy note, peat at the back and very complex. *Notes* – D.o.b.

PROVENANCE MACALLAN, 11 yrs, 43% abv

Sweetness – 8	Peatiness – 3	Availability – 2

Colour – Straw with pale lemon highlights. *Nose* – Fresh, slightly mashy & young with a green vegetal aroma, full-bodied, rich, sweet, almost sugar-encrusted, fruit notes of citrus/honey & ripe dessert pears and a little floral touch. *Flavour* – Quite full, but soft, round, fruity, sweet & very clean with lemon & tangerine notes & delicately peated. *Finish* – Long, quite ethereal, fruity and clean. *Notes* – Douglas Laing & Co bottling.

Macduff

Built 1962–3 by a consortium which included George Crawford, Morty Dykes and Brodie Hepburn. Acquired by William Lawson in 1972, which in turn became part of the General Beverage Corporation, the Luxembourg company which controls Martini & Rossi's world interests. Extended from two to three stills in 1966 and to four in 1968. Now a subsidiary of Bacardi Ltd, Hamilton, Bermuda.

Location – Situated to the east of Banff on the east bank of the River Deveron, about half a mile from the Moray Firth.

Notes – William Lawson bottlings take the name *Glen Deveron* from the River Deveron valley rather than that of the distillery itself, which is known as Macduff. A five-year-old version is sold in Italy. It can be obtained bottled by independents as *Macduff*.

Water – The Gelly Burn

GLEN DEVERON, 10 *yrs*, 1988, 40% *abv*

Sweetness – 6	Peatiness – 4	Availability – 6

Colour – Amber with light gold highlights. **Nose** – Fresh, malty, quite full-bodied and medium-dry with delicate, but solid peat with a slight fresh, green edge, a touch of liquorice & a hint of nuttiness. **Palate** – Medium-sweet, quite full-bodied, very clean and creamily smooth with a nice dark peaty character. **Finish** – Long, soft, very fresh & clean with a touch of spice. **Notes** – D.o.b.

20 *yrs*, 1976, 43% *abv*

Sweetness – 6	Peatiness – 4	Availability – 2

Colour – Very pale, watery straw with pale lemon highlights. **Nose** – Quite light and peppery with a spicy, delicate, herby oakiness, medium-dry with a round fruitiness. **Flavour** – Medium-dry with smooth and gently chewy oaky tannins. **Finish** – Quite delicately peated and medium-dry. **Notes** – Blackadder International bottling as *Macduff* from cask no. 1683.

Mannochmore

Established by SMD in 1971 and licensed to John Haig & Co, Mannochmore was built on the same 25 acre (10 hectare) site as the older Glenlossie (1876). Mannochmore does not utilise a purifier between the lyne arm and condenser as does Glenlossie. Part of Diageo plc. Mothballed in 1985, but reopened in 1989.

Location – Sited next to Glenlossie at Thomshill on an unclassified road to the west of the A941, two miles south of Elgin.

Notes – Previously not often available as a single, *Mannochmore* is important to a number of blends, including *Haig*. Owners UDV are now finishing certain whiskies in very heavily charred casks, which helps give a very dark style of whisky. See below.

Water – The Bardon Burn.

LOCH DHU, THE BLACK WHISKY, 10 yrs, 40% abv

Sweetness – 4	Peatiness – 6	Availability – 5

Colour – A very deep black heart with an amber/garnet edge and a ruby hue. *Nose* – Full, rich, dark & nutty with a slight winey sweetness. *Flavour* – Quite full-bodied, medium-dry and smooth with slightly chewy tannins. *Finish* – Long and gently chewy. *Notes* – D.o.b., it has been finished in a heavily charred oak cask.

12 yrs, 43% abv

Sweetness – 5	Peatiness – 3	Availability – 6

Colour – Very pale, almost watery with lemon highlights. *Nose* – Quite full, cerealy and yeasty with green fruit, medium-dry and quite lightly peated. *Flavour* – Medium-dry, mashy, quite fresh, clean and aromatic. *Finish* – Light and clean with a hint of coffee, lasts well. *Notes* – D.o.b.

Millburn

MILLBURN ROAD, INVERNESS [H] EST. 1807

S aid to have been founded by a Mr Welsh. The earliest recorded reference dates from 1825, when James Rose and Alexander Macdonald were named as the licence holders. Used as a flour mill in 1853, it was rebuilt and reopened on 28 September 1876. It was then remodelled internally in late 1898. Owned from 1921 to 1937 by gin distillers, Booth's, who were themselves taken over by DCL in that year. Management was transferred to SMD in 1943. There were two stills.

Location – Millburn was located about one mile east of the centre of Inverness, on the banks of the Mill Burn from which the distillery and the district take their name.

Notes – Fire broke out on 26 April 1922, but the local fire brigade, "greatly assisted" by the Cameron Highlanders, saved the still house and storage warehouses. The commander of the 3rd Battalion, Lt-Col David Price Haig, had owned the distillery until 1921. The site was sold for property development in 1988 and the buildings remain as the Beefeater Distillery Restaurant.

Water – Loch Duntelchaig.

18 *yrs*, 58.9% *abv*

Sweetness – 5	Peatiness – 7	Availability – 1

Colour – Very pale amber with pale lemon highlights. *Nose* – Medium to full-bodied with a dark, deep smoky character, quite pungent and medium-dry. *Flavour* – Quite round with good peaty smokiness and a touch of bitter chocolate. *Finish* – Long and clean with an edge of richness, quite smoky with quite gentle oaky tannins. *Notes* – D.o.b.

11 *yrs*, 1983, 59.7% *abv*

Sweetness – 7	Peatiness – 4	Availability – 3

Colour – Mid-amber with yellow/gold highlights. *Nose* – Medium-bodied with a slight richness, medium-sweet with a green smokiness. *Flavour* – Medium-sweet, rich and round with gentle peatiness and a slight nuttiness. *Finish* – Sweet and rich, quite full and smooth. *Notes* – Wm Cadenhead bottling.

1971, 40% *abv*

Sweetness – 6	Peatiness – 5	Availability – 3

Colour – Mid-amber/straw with gold/yellow highlights. *Nose* – Rich, medium-sweet, delicately peated with touches of oily nuttiness. *Flavour* – Medium-dry, gently smoky, medium to full-bodied, smooth and round. *Finish* – Soft with a touch of spiciness, quite long and gently smoky. *Notes* – Gordon & MacPhail bottling.

1966, 40% *abv*

Sweetness – 6	Peatiness – 6	Availability – 1

Colour – Deep, syrupy golden. *Nose* – Woody, spirity and dryish. *Flavour* – Round and medium-sweet, slightly woody with a touch of fruit. *Finish* – A little flat spot, then finishes well and dry. *Notes* – Gordon & MacPhail bottling.

Miltonduff

Said to have been founded by Pearey & Bain, Miltonduff came into the ownership of Hiram Walker in 1936 and is now a part of the Allied Domecq group. The distillery was extended in the mid-1890s and was largely rebuilt 1974–5. Licensed to George Ballantine & Son Ltd and operated by Allied Distillers Ltd. Six Miltonduff stills and two Lomond stills, which were installed in 1964 and dismantled in 1981. The Lomond stills produced a different style of malt known as *Mosstowie.*

Location – West of the B9010 to the south of Elgin. A short distance away across the River Lossie are the ruins of Pluscarden Priory.

Notes – In the 18th and 19th centuries, the waters of the Black Burn supplied scores of illicit stills in the Glen of Pluscarden, the fertile barley-rich plain being ideal for their situation. *Miltonduff* is the principal malt associated with Ballantine's Scotch whisky.

Water – Reputedly the Black Burn.

12 yrs, 40% abv

Sweetness – 9	Peatiness – 3	Availability – 5

Colour – Straw/golden with greenish edges. *Nose* – Medium to full-bodied, fragrant, slightly floral and sweet. *Flavour* – Sweet, fruity, full and round. *Finish* – Almost delicate, refined and long. *Notes* – D.o.b.

MOSSTOWIE, 1975, 40% abv

Sweetness – 6	Peatiness – 4	Availability – 3

Colour – Amber with old gold highlights. *Nose* – Medium-bodied and medium-sweet with a touch of toffee and quite delicately peated. *Flavour* – Round, smooth and medium-sweet with a slight fruitiness, a touch of spice, good weight and softly smoky. *Finish* – Long, clean and delicately smoky. *Notes* – Gordon & MacPhail bottling.

Mortlach

DUFFTOWN, BANFFSHIRE [S] EST. 1823

The first of Dufftown's "seven stills". Founded by James Findlater. For a time it was owned by J & J Grant of Glen Grant who removed the distilling utensils. It lay unoccupied for some years, the barley granary serving as a Free Church during the Disruption until a Free Church building could be erected. Extended from three to six stills in 1897. Acquired by John Walker & Son in 1923, by which time it was the largest distillery in the area. Walker's joined DCL in 1925 and management of Mortlach passed to SMD in 1936. The old Mortlach was demolished and rebuilt in the early 1960s, re-opening in 1964. Now part of Diageo plc.

Location – Sited at the junction of the A941 and B9014 on the eastern outskirts of Dufftown.

Notes – In the hollow in which the distillery lies ("Mortlach" means bowl-shaped valley) was fought the battle, in 1010, at which the Scots King Malcolm II defeated the Danes. Tradition has it that the distillery is on the site of an illicit still which drew its water from a spring called Highland John's Well. Except in 1944, Mortlach had permission to stay open during the Second World War.

Water – Springs in the Conval Hills.

16 yrs, 43% abv

Sweetness – 7	Peatiness – 5	Availability – 6

Colour – Deep amber with old gold highlights. *Nose* – Full-bodied, deep, dark and nutty, gently peated. *Flavour* – Full, rich, dark and nutty, big-bodied, smooth and round with soft oaky vanilla notes. *Finish* – Long, full-flavoured, smooth and darkly sherry cask-nutty. *Notes* – D.o.b.

COOPER'S CHOICE, 1990, 43% *abv*

Sweetness – 7	*Peatiness* – 7	*Availability* – 2

Colour – Quite full amber with old gold highlights. *Nose* – Rich, quite nutty & full-bodied, warm with a soft, sweet vanilla character – almost hazelnut ice-cream with hints of honey, apple & chocolate. *Palate* – Quite big-bodied, medium-sweet, rich, round and nutty with a good, dark peat note and a soft chewiness. *Finish* – Long, dark, rich, quite walnutty & complex, the finish explodes & expands. *Notes* – The Vintage Malt Whisky Co Ltd bottling.

1984, 40% *abv*

Sweetness – 6	*Peatiness* – 6	*Availability* – 3

Colour – Straw with yellow/pale lemon highlights. *Nose* – Medium-bodied and medium-sweet with a good dollop of dark peatiness and a slight green apple character. *Flavour* – Quite big-bodied and medium-sweet with a dark peatiness and gentle tannins. *Finish* – Long and elegant with a touch of spice and a good balance between sweetness and peatiness. *Notes* – 1995 Gordon & MacPhail *Centenary Reserve* bottling.

12 *yrs*, 1984, 43% *abv*

Sweetness – 6	*Peatiness* – 6	*Availability* – 2

Colour – Straw with yellow highlights. *Nose* – Quite big-bodied, rich and medium-sweet with unctuous vanilla and a slight floral note, medium peat. *Flavour* – Medium-sweet with a fresh, firm and fragrant peatiness and of good body. *Finish* – Long and clean with a floral note to the sweetness. *Notes* – Signatory bottling from cask no. 2941 distilled 11 October 1984.

19 *yrs*, 1980, 59.3% *abv*

Sweetness – 7	*Peatiness* – 6	*Availability* – 2

Colour – Deep amber with old gold highlights. *Nose* – Quite big-bodied with a solid, dark, charred oak peat character, medium-dry with a touch of caramel. *Palate* – Medium-sweet, quite a big peaty character, slightly medicinal and gently chewy. *Finish* – Long, quite powerful & pungent, with chewy caramel/toffee. *Notes* – Adelphi bottling from cask no. 2166.

50 *yrs*, 1942, 40% *abv*

Sweetness – 5	*Peatiness* – 5	*Availability* – 1

Colour – Full amber with old gold highlights. *Nose* – Full, rich and dark, medium-sweet, oaky vanilla with a lightly charred smoky character. *Flavour* – Full-bodied, round and rich with an edge of dryness, medium-dry with oaky tannins. *Finish* – Long, spicy and delicately smoky with firm tannins. *Notes* – Gordon & MacPhail bottling.

North Port

Founded by David Guthrie, a local farmer, Alfred Barnard referred to it as Brechin distillery. It originally traded as Townhead Distillery Co, the company name changing to Brechin Distillery Co in 1823. Barnard wrote "The district around Brechin being highly cultivated, barley of the highest quality is grown and carted" to the distillery, "where nothing but the best barley is malted." Run by SMD since 1922 and licensed to John Hopkins & Co Ltd, the distillery had two stills. It was closed in 1983 and has since been demolished.

Location – Sited north west of the town centre of Brechin.

Notes – North Port took its name from the north gate in the ancient city walls, now long since vanished. It was very much a "family" employer, with sons following fathers into the business.

Water – Loch Lee, which is also the town's supply.

CONNOISSEURS CHOICE

Connoisseurs Choice, a range of single malts from various districts of Scotland.

In the Highlands are situated the greatest number of malt whisky distilleries.

SINGLE HIGHLAND MALT SCOTCH WHISKY
DISTILLED AT
NORTH PORT-BRECHIN
DISTILLERY
Proprietors: Mitchell Bros. Ltd.
DISTILLED 1974 DISTILLED
SPECIALLY SELECTED, PREPARED AND BOTTLED BY
70cl GORDON & MACPHAIL 40%vol
ELGIN SCOTLAND
PRODUCT OF SCOTLAND

1970, 40% *abv*

Sweetness – 7	Peatiness – 6	Availability – 1

Colour – Gold with yellow highlights. *Nose* – Sweet with heather honey aromas and rich. *Flavour* – Medium-sweet, full and round. *Finish* – Strangely slightly astringent, but lasts well. *Notes* – Gordon & MacPhail bottling.

17 yrs, 1976, 64.1% *abv*

Sweetness – 4	Peatiness – 6	Availability – 3

Colour – Pale amber with yellow highlights. *Nose* – Quite light with a burnt oak tang and a touch of perfume, a slight earthy peatiness and medium-dry. *Flavour* – Quite big and medium-dry with slightly bitter oaky tannins. *Finish* – Long with a tail of richness and toffee. *Notes* – Wm Cadenhead bottling.

Oban

STAFFORD STREET, OBAN, ARGYLL   [H] [V]   EST. 1794

Oban distillery was built, fortress-like, jammed between the cliff, on which sits McCaig's Folly, and the main street, by the Stevenson family, founders of the town of Oban. It was rebuilt between 1883 and 1887 by Walter Higgin. It became part of DCL in 1925 and has been operated by SMD since 1930. The still house was rebuilt 1969–72 and has two stills. Now part of Diageo plc.

Location – In the centre of Oban overlooking the harbour.

Notes – During enlargement in August 1890, a cave was discovered which contained bones from the Mesolithic era (4500–3000 BC). These remains are now to be found at the National Museum of Antiquities in Edinburgh. *Oban*'s nose and flavour are reminiscent of *Bowmore*. One of United Distillers' *Classic Malts* portfolio.

Water – Two lochs in Ardconnel, one mile inland from the town.

14 yrs, 43% abv

Sweetness – 5	Peatiness – 7	Availability – 7

Colour – Very pale straw with gold highlights. *Nose* – Medium-sweet and lightly peated, quite rich with a slight burnt heather character. *Flavour* – Smooth, lightly sweet and creamy with a very delicate peatiness. *Finish* – Smoky, dry and delicate. *Notes* – D.o.b.

OBAN DISTILLER'S EDITION, 1980, 43% abv

Sweetness – 4	Peatiness – 7	Availability – 6

Colour – Quite full amber with old gold highlights. *Nose* – Quite full-bodied & rich, but delicate with an elegant smoked note, a hint of the sea, a touch of sweet vanilla & a slight walnut note. *Palate* – Full-bodied, medium-dry & nutty with an edge of unctuously rich fruitiness & a smoked ham/cheese flavour. *Finish* – Long, elegant & restrained with a good balance between peat & malt. *Notes* – D.o.b. Double-matured, finished in a Montilla Fino cask.

Ord

Ord distillery was founded as the Ord Distillery Company, which was taken over by James Watson & Co of Dundee in 1896. Watson's in turn was acquired by John Dewar & Sons of Perth in 1923. Dewar's joined DCL in 1925, and the management of the distillery was taken over by SMD from 1930. The floor maltings were converted to Saladin maltings in 1961. Extensively rebuilt and extended from two to six stills in 1966. A large drum maltings was built on an adjacent site in 1968 and supplies malted barley to many other distilleries in the north of Scotland. Ord is now a part of Diageo plc.

Location – About 15 miles to the north of Inverness on the western side of the A832, immediately to the west of Muir of Ord.

Notes – *The New Statistical Account of Scotland* recorded in 1840 that "distilling of aquavitae" was the sole manufacture of the district. Ord, which was built on the site of a smugglers' bothy, is the only distillery remaining in the area. There were nine other licensed distilleries operating during the last century. The distillery was lit by paraffin lamps until it gained access to the national electricity grid after the Second World War, but water power was still used for some operations as late as the 1960s. A visitor centre was opened in 1992. In the late 1950s and early 1960s, Ord was used for a programme of experiments which studied the differences between batches of spirit produced respectively by heating with coal, oil and steam. A colourful local smugglers' tale tells of excisemen taking a confiscated cask of whisky upstairs to their room for safe-keeping while staying overnight in a local inn, the Bogroy Hotel, in nearby Beauly. A hole was drilled through the ceiling under the cask from the bar below and the whisky was "liberated" while the excisemen slept.

Water – Loch nan Eun and Loch nam Bonnach.

12 yrs, 40% abv

Sweetness – 6	Peatiness – 5	Availability – 6

Colour – Mid-amber with yellow/green highlights and just a tinge of green. *Nose* – Quite fresh and lightly peated with a green fruitiness, medium-dry with a hint of creamy richness. *Flavour* – Medium-dry, quite rich and fresh, full and round with a touch of pepperiness. *Finish* – Long, fresh and quite rich with a dry tail. *Notes* – D.o.b. as *Glen Ord*.

12 yrs, 40% abv

Sweetness – 7	Peatiness – 5	Availability – 0

Colour – Gold/straw with amber tints. *Nose* – Full-bodied, slightly dry, but with an overlying richness. *Flavour* – Quite full, big-bodied, round and medium-sweet. *Finish* – Very smooth, long and smoky. *Notes* – DCL (pre-Guinness) bottling as *Ord*.

27 yrs, 1962, 55.4% abv

Sweetness – 7	Peatiness – 5	Availability – 1

Colour – Amber with good gold highlights. *Nose* – Full, round, medium-sweet and quite mellow with a touch of oily-nuttiness. *Flavour* – Fresh, clean, soft, a touch oaky, quite round and full. *Finish* – Dry, smooth, slightly austere and nutty. *Notes* – Wm Cadenhead bottling.

Pittyvaich

Built by Arthur Bell & Sons Ltd as a sister to Dufftown and operated in conjunction with it. Four stills. Now part of Diageo plc. Closed in 1993.

Location – Situated in the Dullan Glen on the outskirts of Dufftown near the 6th-century Mortlach Parish Church.

Notes – The make uses the same water source as Dufftown and gives a similar whisky.

Water – The distillery draws its process water from two springs, Convalleys and Balliemore.

12 yrs, 43% abv

Sweetness – 4	Peatiness – 6	Availability – 6

Colour – Amber with old gold highlights. *Nose* – Round, quite full and malty, spicy, peppery and almost meaty with a coffee tang at the back. *Flavour* – Medium-dry, quite full-bodied and dark flavoured with a touch of tannin. *Finish* – Long, chewy and quite big. *Notes* – D.o.b.

12 yrs, 56.6% abv

Sweetness – 4	Peatiness – 7	Availability – 2

Colour – Straw/amber with pale gold highlights. *Nose* – Quite peaty and soft with a damp oak character and a touch of green, unripe coffee. *Flavour* – Medium-dry, a coffee/chocolate character and smoky peatiness with a touch of spice. *Finish* – Long, lingering, spicy, smooth and nutty. *Notes* – Wm Cadenhead bottling.

12 yrs, 54% abv

Sweetness – 5	Peatiness – 7	Availability – 3

Colour – Medium to pale amber with lemon highlights. *Nose* – Medium-bodied, spirity and a hint of toffee/coffee with a greenness at the back, medium peated. *Flavour* – Medium-dry with a coffee flavour, quite full-flavoured, round and smooth. *Finish* – Creamy, quite sweet, tangy and long with a soft touch of smokiness on the tail. *Notes* – James MacArthur bottling from cask no. 15096.

13 yrs, 58% abv

Sweetness – 4	Peatiness – 7	Availability – 4

Colour – Deep, cough linctus-amber with bronze highlights. *Nose* – Big-bodied, dark, rich, malty, cerealy and a touch of rubber with a smoky burnt character. *Flavour* – Big, dark, rich, cerealy and smoky with a little spice. *Finish* – Quite spirity, long and smoky with a rich centre. *Notes* – Wm Cadenhead bottling.

18 yrs, 1976, 53.3% abv

Sweetness – 8	Peatiness – 2	Availability – 2

Colour – Pale straw/amber with pale gold highlights. *Nose* – Fresh and sweet with an almost grapey richness, a slightly unctuous lanolin aroma, a ripe apple character and lightly smoky. *Flavour* – Quite sweet, full and smooth with a green ripeness. *Finish* – Long, sweet and clean with a light smokiness on the tail. *Notes* – Blackadder International bottling.

Port Ellen

PORT ELLEN, ISLAY, ARGYLL   [I]   EST. 1825

Founded by Alexander Ker Mackay, with the support of landowner Walter Campbell, shortly after the Excise Act of 1824. Acquired by John Ramsay and run by him, and his heirs, until 1920, when sold to John Dewar & Sons Ltd and James Buchanan & Co, both of which companies merged with DCL in 1925. Port Ellen's management was transferred to SMD in 1930. Although silent from 1929 to 1966, the maltings continued in use. The distillery was extensively rebuilt in 1967, when it was increased from two to four stills. A large new maltings was erected in 1973. The distiller's licence was held by Low, Robertson & Co Ltd. Although the distillery ceased production permanently in May 1983, the maltings now serves all the Islay distilleries, and also nearby Jura, following an historic concordat between the producing companies in 1987.

Location – Situated about half a mile from the centre of Port Ellen, the maltings building now dominates the shoreline.

Notes – The Excise Act of 1824 enforced the introduction of the spirit safe in distilleries. Tests had to be made to ensure that it had no harmful effects on the make. The official experiments were carried out in Port Ellen. The maltings were visited by Her Majesty Queen Elizabeth on 11 August 1980 and a commemorative bottling was produced.

Water – The Leorin Lochs.

DISTILLED

1978

CASK

63.3% VOL·

NATURAL HIGH STRENGTH

SINGLE MALT
SCOTCH WHISKY
FROM
PORT ELLEN
DISTILLERY

LOW ROBERTSON & CO LIMITED

SPECIALLY SELECTED, PRODUCED AND BOTTLED BY
GORDON & MACPHAIL
ELGIN·SCOTLAND

PRODUCT OF SCOTLAND

NATURAL
CASK
STRENGTH

1978

63.3%
VOL

70cl

CASK No.
2698

DISTILLED
21/4/78

BOTTLED
September 1994

16 yrs, 1980, 59% abv

Sweetness – 2	Peatiness – 9	Availability – 2

Colour – Pale straw with pale yellow/lemon highlights. *Nose* – Big-bodied and sea-influenced (ozone & salt spray) with dry notes of cereal and a dark, smoky peatiness. *Flavour* – Big, powerful and dry, but with a richness, very smoky and with quite chewy tannins. *Finish* – Long and smoky with just a hint of sweetness. *Notes* – Signatory bottling.

14 yrs, 1977, 59.7% abv

Sweetness – 0	Peatiness – 9	Availability – 3

Colour – Mid-amber with old gold highlights. *Nose* – Big, pungently smoky and dry with an earthy burnt peat character. *Flavour* – Big, powerful dark peatiness, a real "peat reek", and dry with a slight richness. *Finish* – Long and very peaty. *Notes* – Gordon & MacPhail bottling; cask no. 2017, distilled 14 April 1977.

1971, 40% abv

Sweetness – 1	Peatiness – 9	Availability – 3

Colour – Bright gold/amber with golden/yellow highlights. *Nose* – Smoky peat, ozone, burnt heather roots with a very slight hint of sweetness. *Flavour* – Quite full, round, smoky, quite smooth and almost medicinal. *Finish* – Dry and smoky with the burnt heather roots lingering. *Notes* – Gordon & MacPhail bottling.

1970, 40% abv

Sweetness – 2	Peatiness – 9	Availability – 2

Colour – Peaty/gold with bright highlights. *Nose* – Big-bodied, pungent and peaty with a slight rubbery character and dry. *Flavour* – Big, powerful, burnt peat with an edge of sweetness, very distinctive. *Finish* – Long, pungent and smoky. *Notes* – Gordon & MacPhail bottling.

Pulteney

WICK, CAITHNESS [H] EST. 1826

Established by James Henderson. Became part of DCL in 1925, having been purchased by John Dewar & Sons a couple of years earlier. Closed between 1930 and 1951, then revived. In 1955 it was bought by Hiram Walker, now part of Allied Domecq, who rebuilt the distillery in 1959. Pulteney distillery was sold to Inver House Distillers in June 1995. It has two stills.

Location – The most northerly distillery on the UK mainland, it is sited on the southern side of Wick, close to the North Sea coast.

Notes – The wash stills give the impression of having been truncated to allow the roof to fit onto the building. The lyne arm comes off below the top of the still, resulting in an elegance in the spirit.

Water – The Loch of Hempriggs.

12 yrs, 40% abv

Sweetness – 6	Peatiness – 5	Availability – 5

Colour – Very pale straw with pale, watery-green highlights. *Nose* – Soft, medium-bodied and medium-dry with a fresh, gentle, east coast touch of the sea and an almost grapey richness. *Flavour* – Medium-dry, fresh, clean and smooth, with good richness and an edge of sweetness. *Finish* – Very clean and fresh; lingering with a slightly salty touch on the lips. *Notes* – D.o.b.

15 yrs, 59.9% abv

Sweetness – 7	Peatiness – 5	Availability – 6

Colour – Straw/yellow with yellow highlights. *Nose* – Dry, quite full-bodied, malty & quite rich with a fresh hedgerow greenness, a herbal note and a distinct character of seaweed-covered rocks. *Palate* – Rich, medium-sweet, smooth and full-bodied, intense, fruity and gently peated. *Finish* – Long, rich, complex, fruity – apricots – tangy & salty. *Notes* – D.o.b.

Rosebank

FALKIRK, STIRLINGSHIRE [I] EST. 1840

The distillery, established by James Rankine, was converted from the maltings of the earlier Camelon distillery. It was rebuilt by his son in 1864. It was Rankine's objective to distil a whisky which would stand comparison with his competitors' finest makes. By the 1890s, there was an extraordinary demand for *Rosebank* and customers were put on allocation. In 1914 the Rosebank Distillery Ltd, as it was then called, was one of the original founders of Scottish Malt Distillers Ltd. Now part of Diageo plc, Rosebank was closed in May 1993.

Location – Sited on the banks of the Forth and Clyde Canal where the A803 intersects with the canal to the west of Falkirk.

Notes – The make was triple distilled with one wash still and two spirit stills. The licensees were The Distillers Agency Ltd.

Water – Carron Valley Reservoir.

LOWLAND
SINGLE MALT
SCOTCH WHISKY

Established on its present
site at *CAMELON* in 1840

ROSEBANK

distillery stands on the
banks of the *FORTH*
and *CLYDE CANAL*.
This was once
a busy thoroughfare with
boats and steamers
continually passing by;
it is still the source
of water for cooling.
This single *MALT
SCOTCH WHISKY* is
triple distilled which
accounts for its *light
distinctive nose* and *well
balanced* flavour.

A G E D **12** Y E A R S

Distilled & Bottled in SCOTLAND
ROSEBANK DISTILLERY
Falkirk, Stirlingshire, Scotland.

43% vol 70 cl

12 yrs, 43%abv

Sweetness – 2	Peatiness – 4	Availability – 6

Colour – Straw/light amber with gold and lemon highlights. **Nose** – Medium-bodied and spirity with a touch of greenness, lightly oily, medium-dry with a good edge of richness. **Flavour** – Light and smooth, dryish with a mashy character. **Finish** – Smooth, dry and oaky with a pleasant lightness. **Notes** – D.o.b.

Sweetness – 2	Peatiness – 5	Availability – 2

Colour – Very pale straw with very pale lemon highlights. *Nose* – Fresh with a youthful greenness, medium-bodied, almost dry and slightly perfumed. *Palate* – Dry, almost a bubble-gummy fruitiness, fresh, lightly malty and of good body. *Finish* – Long & malty with a hint of richness. *Notes* – The Vintage Malt Whisky Co Ltd bottling.

1990, 46% *abv*

Sweetness – 4	Peatiness – 5	Availability – 2

Colour – Pale, watery straw with pale lemon highlights. *Nose* – Quite full-bodied, a mashy, cereal character, medium-sweet & floral with quite a rich, fresh, slightly green peaty note. *Palate* – Rich, medium-dry, quite delicately peated, round, smooth & fresh. *Finish* – long, fresh & rich with an almost milk chocolate note. *Notes* – Murray McDavid bottling.

1989, 58.9% *abv*

Sweetness – 2	Peatiness – 5	Availability – 2

Colour – Pale straw with pale lemon highlights. *Nose* – Dry, quite fresh hedgerow character – almost nettley – a touch of menthol, medium-weight peat & quite malty. *Palate* – Dry with a fresh leafy greenness, quite a dark peat character, a clean menthol note & a touch of liquorice. *Finish* – Long, with good, softly smoky peat & very clean. *Notes* – Blackadder bottling from cask no. 842.

1969, 51.7% *abv*

Sweetness – 5	Peatiness – 3	Availability – 2

Colour – Pale straw/amber with pale gold highlights. *Nose* – Malty, cerealy and soft with a slight oily oakiness and quite full with an edge of richness. *Flavour* – Quite full-bodied, sweet and rich, lightly peated with a green, fresh edge. *Finish* – Long, sweet and rich with a touch of chocolate. *Notes* – Signatory bottling.

Royal Brackla

CAWDOR, NEAR NAIRN [H] [V] EST. 1812

Founded by Captain William Fraser of Brackla House. A map of the Cawdor Estate dated 1773 shows a "malt brewhouse" on the site. The distillery was sold to John Bisset & Co Ltd, which became part of DCL in 1943, when management was transferred to SMD. It was rebuilt between 1964 and 1965 and the number of stills was increased from two to four in 1970. Closed in 1985, Royal Brackla reopened in 1991 and was sold to Barcardi in 1998.

Location – Sited to the north west of the B9090, one mile south of Nairn.

Notes – Despite being regularly fined by HM Customs & Excise for irregularities, Brackla was the first distillery to be granted a Royal Warrant in 1835. It was referred to at that time as *Brackla* or "The King's Own Whisky". Some of the older buildings were converted to a visitor centre in 1982–3, the distillery being three-quarters of a mile from Cawdor Castle. During demolition in November 1994 of no. 4 warehouse, which had not been used for some years, a hive of wild bees was discovered in one of the warehouse walls. The hive was between 10 and 15 feet across and it was estimated that the bees had inhabited this site for approximately 70 years. Demolition of that wall was postponed until the spring of 1995, when the queens were temporarily removed to another site. The bees have been returned to beehives in the shape of pagoda roofs which are sited close to the original site of no. 4 warehouse.

Water – The Cawdor Burn.

HIGHLAND
SINGLE MALT *SCOTCH WHISKY*

ROYAL BRACKLA

distillery, established in 1812, *⅞* lies on the
southern shore of the MORAY FIRTH at *Cawdor* near *Nairn.*
Woods around the *distillery* are home to the *SISKIN;*
although a *shy bird,* it can often be seen *feeding* on *conifer* seeds.

In 1835 a *Royal Warrant* was granted to the *distillery* by King William IV,
who enjoyed the *fresh, grassy, fruity* aroma of this *single malt whisky.*

43% vol   AGED **10** YEARS   70 cl

Distilled & Bottled in *SCOTLAND.* ROYAL BRACKLA DISTILLERY, Cawdor, Nairn, *Scotland.*

No age statement, 40% abv

Sweetness – 6	Peatiness – 7	Availability – 7

Colour – Pale straw with pale yellow highlights. *Nose* – Medium-bodied, quite peaty and round with a slight liquorice character. *Flavour* – Medium-sweet, rich and slightly spicy with a good smoky peatiness and good body. *Finish* – Quite clean and fresh with almost a hint of bitter chocolate on the end. *Notes* – United Distillers bottling.

10 yrs, 43% abv

Sweetness – 7	Peatiness – 5	Availability – 6

Colour – Quite pale straw with yellow highlights. *Nose* – Fresh, clean and medium-sweet with a fruitiness and a floral note, with gentle peat in the background. *Flavour* – Round, medium-sweet and quite full-bodied with a green fruity character. *Finish* – Long, fresh and clean. *Notes* – United Distillers bottling.

18 yrs, 1979, 43% abv

Sweetness – 6	Peatiness – 6	Availability – 2

Colour – Amber with yellow highlights. *Nose* – Full-bodied, rich and dark with a walnutty character, medium-dry with a slightly perfumed note to the peatiness. *Flavour* – Big, round, rich, medium-sweet and full-bodied with a slightly tarry note to the tannins. *Finish* – Long and elegant with a slightly chewy smokiness. *Notes* – Blackadder International bottling from cask no. 5279, distilled 9 January 1979.

1975, 46% abv

Sweetness – 5	Peatiness – 7	Availability – 2

Colour – Amber with pale old gold highlights. *Nose* – Big-bodied, fruity & a touch perfumed, round with a slight Christmas cake richness & quite a dark peat note. *Palate* – Quite big-bodied & darkly peaty, smooth, softly unctuous with vanilla flavours. *Finish* – Very long, quite powerful, a touch perfumed & smoky. *Notes* – Murray McDavid bottling.

1970, 40% abv

Sweetness – 6	Peatiness – 6	Availability – 3

Colour – Pale mid-amber with yellow gold highlights. *Nose* – Good body with oak, cold apples and a peaty smokiness. *Flavour* – Medium-dry, oaky, quite mellow and smooth with a slight oiliness and a medium peatiness. *Finish* – Reasonable oaky finish with a touch of richness. *Notes* – Gordon & MacPhail bottling.

Royal Lochnagar

Originally known as New Lochnagar, as another Lochnagar distillery had been built nearby in 1826. This had closed by 1860. Lochnagar obtained the Royal Warrant after its owner, John Begg, had invited Queen Victoria and Prince Albert to view the distillery in 1848. The distillery was rebuilt in 1906 and acquired by John Dewar & Sons Ltd in 1916, passing to the DCL in 1925 and operated by SMD, now UMGD, from 1930. Part of Diageo plc.

Location – On Royal Deeside overlooking Balmoral Castle and about one mile from the Queen's bedroom, from which the young Queen Victoria is said to have looked out at the distillery.

Notes – The story the locals tell is of John Begg looking out of the window one evening and seeing a few figures making their way towards the distillery through the gathering dusk. The figures turned out to be Queen Victoria, her husband, children and lady-in-waiting. The Royal party had just arrived for their first stay at Balmoral, and Begg had delivered the Queen a note inviting her on a not-to-be-missed tour round his new distillery. Prince Albert was particularly interested, being enthusiastic about all new technology. Royal Lochnagar is now the only remaining distillery of the several that used to operate on Deeside. There is a very popular visitor centre, converted from the old distillery farm steading. Scottish children try to trick one another by asking how deep Lochnagar is. The catch is that Lochnagar is not a loch, but a mountain. At 3,789 ft (1,155m) its bulk dominates the countryside around Balmoral.

Water – Springs in the foothills of Lochnagar.

12 yrs, 40% abv

Sweetness – 7	Peatiness – 4	Availability – 5

Colour – Mid-amber with old gold highlights. *Nose* – Medium-bodied, soft and round with creamy sweet vanilla oak notes. *Flavour* – Soft, gently peated and round with creamy sweet vanilla oak notes. *Finish* – Fresh, lingering and medium-sweet with a slightly smoky tang. *Notes* – D.o.b.

12 yrs, 40% abv

Sweetness – 8	Peatiness – 4	Availability – 0

Colour – Pale straw with bright gold highlights. *Nose* – Pleasantly sweet, slightly peppery and fruity. *Flavour* – Sweet, clean, creamy and slightly peppery. *Finish* – Smooth and with good length. *Notes* – DCL (pre-Guinness) bottling.

ROYAL LOCHNAGAR SELECTED RESERVE,
No age statement, 43% abv

Sweetness – 8	Peatiness 3	Availability – 3

Colour – Deep peaty amber with good gold highlights. *Nose* – Rich, wet oak, vanilla, sweet and lightly sherried. *Flavour* – Full, round and rich, mellow, nutty and creamy. *Finish* – Long, slightly spicy and very smooth. *Notes* – As *Royal Lochnagar Selected Reserve*, it has no age statement because it is produced from selected casks and the age varies from bottling to bottling.

St Magdalene

LINLITHGOW, WEST LOTHIAN [L] EST. PRE-1797

S aid to have been founded in the 18th century on the lands of St Magdalene's Cross, the former site of an annual fair and of St Magdalene's Hospital. The earliest record is of Adam Dawson as distiller in 1797. It was taken over by DCL on 16 November 1912, prior to which the owning company was A & J Dawson Ltd. St Magdalene was one of the five founding distilleries of SMD in July 1914.

Location – Sited at the eastern end of Linlithgow, where the railway line, running alongside the Union Canal, intersects with the A706 to Edinburgh.

Notes – Linlithgow was a centre of milling and malting in the 17th century and brewing and distilling in the 18th century. The distillery closed in 1983 and its buildings have been converted into housing.

Water – The town's domestic supply, which comes from Loch Lomond.

RARE MALTS
SELECTION

Each individual vintage has been specially selected from Scotland's finest single malt stocks of rare or now silent distilleries. The limited bottlings of these scarce and unique whiskies are at natural cask strength for the enjoyment of the true connoisseur.

NATURAL CASK STRENGTH
SINGLE MALT
SCOTCH WHISKY

AGED **23** YEARS

DISTILLED IN 1970 AT THE
ST MAGDALENE
DISTILLERY
ESTABLISHED 1765
LINLITHGOW
58.43%vol 70cle
PRODUCE OF SCOTLAND
LIMITED BOTTLING

23 yrs, 58.1% abv

Sweetness – 2	Peatiness – 3	Availability – 1

Colour – Amber with gold highlights and a tinge of green. *Nose* – Gentle, soft and medium-dry with a bread yeasty aroma and a slightly oaky acetone character. *Flavour* – Big-bodied, quite dry, but with an edge of richness, tannic and yeasty. *Finish* – Long, quite powerful and quite tannic. *Notes* – D.o.b.

10 yrs, 1982, 62.3% abv

Sweetness – 2	Peatiness – 2	Availability – 2

Colour – Pale straw with lemon/yellow highlights. *Nose* – Fresh, clean, fruity and spirity, medium-dry with a slight touch of oak and a light mashy character. *Flavour* – Medium-dry with good richness and round with quite good body. *Finish* – Good length, rich and smooth. *Notes* – Wm Cadenhead bottling.

1980, 40% abv

Sweetness – 3	Peatiness – 3	Availability – 1

Colour – Straw with pale lemon/pale gold highlights. *Nose* – Quite good body with a fresh, almost fruity richness, off-dry, lightly peated and green with a slight edge of sweetness. *Flavour* – Smooth, mashy, malty, clean, medium-dry and quite rich. *Finish* – Quite long and rich with a slightly green freshness. *Notes* – 1995 Gordon & MacPhail *Centenary Reserve* bottling.

1965, 40% abv

Sweetness – 1	Peatiness – 4	Availability – 2

Colour – Light to mid-amber with gold highlights and just a tinge of green. *Nose* – Quite fresh with a light oak character, quite lightweight and dry, a little spirity. *Flavour* – Dry with oaky tannins, of medium weight and lightly smoky. *Finish* – Dry, oaky and chewy with dry tannins. *Notes* – Gordon & MacPhail bottling.

Scapa

Built by Macfarlane & Townsend. Owned by Hiram Walker (now part of Allied Domecq) since 1954. Two stills. The wash still was replaced by a Lomond still in 1959, this producing a heavier spirit than the more traditional long-necked stills. Operated by Allied Distillers Ltd.

Location – Sited on the Lingro Burn two miles south west of Kirkwall on the A964 at the head of Scapa Bay.

Notes – Scapa Flow was where the German fleet was scuttled at the end of the First World War. When whisky chronicler Alfred Barnard visited the distillery in 1886, it had been open for just a year. He wrote about it as being "one of the most complete little Distilleries in the Kingdom". The stills were described as being of "the newest type and heated by steam instead of fire, and are both fitted with 'collapse' valves, which allow air to enter in the event of a vacuum being formed". For a malt with such a pronounced astringent nose in its youth, the palate is, unusually, surprisingly sweet. Scapa is one of the main malts associated with *Ballantine's* blended Scotch whisky.

Water – The Lingro Burn and nearby springs.

12 yrs, 40% abv

Sweetness – 8	Peatiness – 5	Availability – 4

Colour – Amber with old gold highlights. **Nose** – Fresh, medium-dry, quite malty, herby & grassy with quite a dark peat note and grapey/gooseberry fruit notes. **Palate** – Sweet, quite full-bodied, rich, & round with a ripe grapefruit character & a nice caress of peat. **Finish** – Long, very rich & mouth-fillling with butterscotch on the tail. **Notes** – D.o.b.

8 yrs, 57% abv

Sweetness – 8	Peatiness – 7	Availability – 2

Colour – Peaty/amber with good gold highlights and a greenish tinge. *Nose* – Spirity, somewhat astringent, young and peaty. *Flavour* – Sweet, rich, full-bodied, lightly oaky and malty. *Finish* – Good, spicy and long lasting. *Notes* – Gordon & MacPhail bottling.

1983, 40% abv

Sweetness – 2	Peatiness – 4	Availability – 4

Colour – Mid-amber with old gold highlights. *Nose* – Fresh, clean, malty and slightly green with a slight nuttiness and medium-dry. *Flavour* – Almost dry, quite full-bodied, slightly spicy and tangy, gently smoky. *Finish* – Long and clean with a touch of richness. *Notes* – Gordon & MacPhail bottling.

14 yrs, 1979, 43% abv

Sweetness – 6	Peatiness – 5	Availability – 0

Colour – Pale straw with yellow/lemon highlights. *Nose* – Round, smooth and medium-sweet, slightly unctuous with a fresh floral character and rich with a maltiness at the back. *Flavour* – Medium-dry, quite full and round, quite smooth with tannic oak. *Finish* – Long and full, quite rich with a toffee tail. *Notes* – Master of Malt bottling from cask no. 3851/2, distilled 9 May 1979.

1979, 56.3% abv

Sweetness – 8	Peatiness – 6	Availability – 1

Colour – Straw with yellow/lemon highlights. *Nose* – Full-bodied, fruity (strawberries), bubble-gummy, medium-sweet and finely peated. *Flavour* – Sweet, round, quite spicy, smooth, almost grapey. *Finish* – Long, sweet and clean. *Notes* – Scotch Malt Whisky Society bottling, cask no. 17.13, bottled May 1994.

24 yrs, 1965, 50.1% abv

Sweetness – 8	Peatiness – 6	Availability – 1

Colour – Straw with lemony gold highlights. *Nose* – Sweet, quite fresh and rich with a creamy peatiness and an underpinning of oak. *Flavour* – Quite sweet, softly peated, light and quite delicate. *Finish* – Smooth and smoky with a lanolin character. *Notes* – Wm Cadenhead bottling.

Speyburn

ROTHES, MORAY [S] EST. 1897

Built by John Hopkins & Co for the Speyburn-Glenlivet Distillery Company Ltd. Local tradition has it that the walls were built of stones "extracted by man and beast" from the bed of the River Spey. DCL bought John Hopkins & Co in 1916, but the Speyburn-Glenlivet Distillery Co Ltd was not wound up until 1962, when Speyburn's management was transferred to SMD. It was the first distillery to install a drum maltings, this unit being closed in 1968. The distillery has two stills and is now owned by Inver House Distillers, who purchased it in 1991.

Location – Situated a quarter of a mile north west of the B9105 on the northern outskirts of Rothes.

Notes – Speyburn started up in the last week of December 1897. Doors and windows still had not been fitted to the still house and, as a severe snowstorm was sweeping the district, employees had to work in overcoats. Just one butt of spirit was bonded with 1897 on its head.

Water – The Granty (or Birchfield) Burn.

10 yrs, 40% abv

Sweetness – 8	Peatiness – 2	Availability – 7

Colour – Very pale straw with lemon highlights. *Nose* – Fresh, clean and aromatic with a rich lemony fruitiness, medium-bodied and quite lightly peated. *Flavour* – Fresh, clean, rich and medium-sweet; quite full-bodied. *Finish* – Long and sweet with a touch of spice. *Notes* – D.o.b.

21 yrs, 61.9% abv

Sweetness – 7	Peatiness – 6	Availability – 4

Colour – Deep, dark mahogany with ruby/crimson highlights. *Nose* – Full-bodied, round, medium-sweet, sherried & nutty; almost vinuous with a quite solid smoky peat note at the back, a really rich, nutty Oloroso note. *Palate* – Big-bodied, mature, medium-sweet, quite powerful and rich, with chewy tannins and a touch of spice. *Finish* – Long, sherried, smoky, a serious sippin' whisky. *Notes* – D.o.b.

15 yrs, 1975, 60.1% abv

Sweetness – 7	Peatiness – 5	Availability – 4

Colour – Straw with pale gold highlights. *Nose* – Medium-sweet and fresh with a touch of greenness, light, nutty and biscuity. *Flavour* – Medium-sweet with a good dollop of creamy freshness, fresh, clean, smooth and round. *Finish* – Sweet, fresh and creamy with an edge of greenness and good length. *Notes* – Wm Cadenhead bottling.

1971, 40% abv

Sweetness – 8	Peatiness – 5	Availability – 4

Colour – Rich, peaty, amber with good gold highlights. *Nose* – Sweet, fruity and slightly spirity. *Flavour* – Medium-sweet, quite light and smooth. *Finish* – Mellow, of reasonable length with oak on the end. *Notes* – Gordon & MacPhail bottling.

Speyside

The malt from the new Speyside distillery is bottled as *Drumguish* by its owners. Speyside was built in 1956, opposite the former distillery of the same name (1895–1911) on land purchased by the Christie family, together with stretches of the Spey and Tromie rivers. In the previous year they had formed the Speyside Distillery & Bonding Co The driving force behind the company, whisky blender George Christie, gradually built the new distillery, starting in 1962 and finally completing the work in 1987. The first spirit ran from the distillery's two stills on 12 December 1990. In September 2000, Speyside was taken over by a consortium of shareholders.

Location – At the confluence of the Tromie and Spey rivers.

Notes – The distillery is said to have a maximum capacity of 200,000 gallons a year, although it is planned to produce just 50,000–100,000 a year, all of which is intended for the company's own use. The company produces a blended whisky called *Speyside* and a single malt, *Glentromie*. The first of the new single malt takes its name, *Drumguish*, from that of its precise location. George Christie lives in the house previously owned by G. McPherson Grant who, as well as building the original Speyside distillery, also built Tomatin and Newtonmore. Only Tomatin of this original trio today exists.

Water – A spring on the neighbouring Gaick Deer estate.

8 yrs, 40% abv

Sweetness – 7	*Peatiness* – 4	*Availability* – 4

Colour – Rich amber with old gold highlights. *Nose* – Quite full, malty & fresh, medium-sweet & quite youthful with a hint of orange & honey. *Palate* – Medium-dry, good body, malty, quite rich with a sweet edge, soft vanilla & slight creamy toffee/tablet notes. *Finish* – Long, smooth & creamily rich with lingering toffee vanilla notes. *Notes* – D.o.b.

Springbank

CAMPBELTOWN, ARGYLL [C] EST. 1828

Said to have been originally licensed to the Reid family. It was acquired by John and William Mitchell in 1837 and run by various members of the family until 1897 when the present owning company, J & A Mitchell & Co was incorporated. Springbank's stillhouse contains three stills which has created rumours that it is triple distilled. It is, in fact, distilled two and a half times. The whiskies *Hazelburn* and *Longrow* are also produced from the same stills, *Hazelburn* being traditionally triple distilled.

Location – The distillery is in the centre of the town.

Notes – The family owners of Springbank are direct descendants of the illicit distillers who established the once-numerous Campbeltown distilleries, and the present chairman is the great-great-great-grandson of its founder. The Campbeltown area once boasted around 30 legal distilleries, but the years of Depression after the First World War and prohibition in the USA almost brought about the total demise of Campbeltown whisky. Springbank is now one of only two survivors. Fortunately Springbank now continues to go from strength to strength, its reputation and renown being second to none. It is the only distillery where everything from malting through to bottling is carried out on the premises for all of the distillery's own production.

Water – Crosshill Loch.

7 yrs, 59.1% abv

Sweetness – 7	Peatiness – 5	Availability – 1

Colour – Deep, full amber with ruby-tinted bronze highlights. *Nose* – Full-bodied, rich, nutty, sherried and medium-sweet, with quite fresh, green apple, and dried apricot/banana notes, a hint of beeswax and quite delicately peated. *Palate* – Medium-dry, slightly spicy and quite full-bodied with gently chewy tannins and delicately peated. *Finish* – Long, elegant, quite tangily nutty, slightly tarry and finally salty. *Notes* – Bottling by Luvian's Bottle Shop, Cupar.

9 yrs, 61.2% abv

Sweetness – 5	Peatiness – 6	Availability – 4

Colour – Very pale watery straw with pale mint green highlights. *Nose* – Young, spirity, mashy, quite full-bodied with a dark peatiness and almost dry. *Flavour* – Almost dry, but with a developing richness and a dark smokiness, good body, a lanolin smoothness and mashy. *Finish* – Spicy, elegantly smoky with a salty tail and a sweetness to the edge. *Notes* – Wm Cadenhead bottling.

10 yrs, 46% abv

Sweetness – 7	Peatiness – 6	Availability – 6

Colour – Amber with pale gold highlights. *Nose* – Big-bodied, medium-dry & fresh with quite a solid & gently earthy peat note, a slight tarry character & a light melon touch. *Palate* – Big-bodied, medium-sweet & rich with quite a dark peaty touch. *Finish* – Long, fresh, rich & salty. *Notes* – D.o.b.

12 yrs, 57% abv

Sweetness – 5	Peatiness – 6	Availability – 3

Colour – Deep amber with bronze highlights. *Nose* – Quite full-bodied, with a slightly tarry rope character, a note of lightly charred oak and a rich peatiness. *Flavour* – Big-bodied with good richness and quite chewy vanilla tannins, medium-dry with kindly peatiness. *Finish* – Long and gently chewy with a salty tang on the tail. *Notes* – D.o.b. as *Springbank 100° Proof.*

15 yrs, 46% abv

Sweetness – 7	Peatiness – 5	Availability – 6

Colour – Light mid-amber (honey-coloured) with lemony highlights. *Nose* – Medium weight, rich, oily oak with a touch of greenness, quite lightly peated. *Flavour* – Clean, smooth, medium-dry with good creamy oak and a touch of sweetness and greenness. *Finish* – Long and smooth with a touch of tannin and hints of richness and saltiness on the tail. *Notes* – D.o.b.

Sweetness – 8	Peatiness – 5	Availability – 5

Colour – Deep amber. *Nose* – Definite fruity notes, stickily sweet in their richness, also floral notes and a suggestion of coconut and medicinal cloves. *Flavour* – Silkily smooth, full-bodied and creamy with a salty tang. *Finish* – Very fine, long, dark and oaky. *Notes* – D.o.b.

Sweetness – 7	Peatiness – 6	Availability – 2

Colour – Full, peaty amber with bronze highlights. *Nose* – Rich, ripe, sweet and full-bodied, smoky with a touch of ozone and oak. *Flavour* – Full, round, smoky and medium-sweet with oaky tannins and a salty tang. *Finish* – Long, smoky-oak and tangy with a touch of spiciness. *Notes* – D.o.b.

Sweetness – 8	Peatiness – 6	Availability – 2

Colour – Full amber with old gold highlights. *Nose* – Full and rich, almost raisiny with a touch of liquorice, almost tarry and medium-dry. *Flavour* – Sweet, and rich with a good peaty character, flavour of bitter chocolate and a salty tang. *Finish* – Long and tangy with good sweetness. *Notes* – D.o.b.

Sweetness – 5	Peatiness – 7	Availability – 2

Colour – Pale amber with yellow highlights. *Nose* – Medium-bodied, quite a rich vanilla note with fairly dark peat, medium-dry, quite soft & a slightly meaty character. *Palate* – Medium-dry, round, quite soft & smooth, of good body & with a gently tarry peatiness. *Finish* – Long, quite ethereal & smooth. *Notes* – Murray McDavid bottling.

Sweetness – 7	Peatiness – 5	Availability – 2

Colour – Pale straw with watery lemon highlights. *Nose* – Quite full-bodied, medium-sweet with a slight green peaty note. *Palate* – Quite full-bodied, round, clean, smooth & medium-dry with a slightly perfumed note to the peat. *Finish* – Very long, rich, tangy, quite tarry & salty. *Notes* – Blackadder bottling from cask no. 95, distilled March, 1990.

17 yrs, 1975, 55.8% abv

Sweetness – 7	Peatiness – 4	Availability – 1

Colour – Mid-amber with gold highlights. **Nose** – Dry, fresh, smoky and rich, quite full-bodied with a good richness at the back. **Flavour** – Big-bodied, medium-sweet and rich with gentle tannins and delicately peated. **Finish** – Tangy and rich with good length and a touch of spice. **Notes** – Signatory bottling from cask nos. 3592/3, distilled 17 December 1975.

18 yrs, 1975, 43% abv

Sweetness – 7	Peatiness – 4	Availability – 1

Colour – Pale amber with pale yellow highlights. **Nose** – Quite full-bodied, rich and medium-sweet, underpinned by peat and with a hint of green coffee. **Flavour** – Fresh, green, rich, round and medium-sweet, almost grapey with a vanilla note. **Finish** – Long, salty, lingering and gently smoky. **Notes** – *The Ultimate Collection* bottled for Van Wees of Holland from cask no. 3596, distilled 17 December 1975.

1965, 46% abv

Sweetness – 7	Peatiness – 5	Availability – 1

Colour – Quite deep amber with ruby-tinted old gold highlights. **Nose** – Full-bodied, quite intense and medium-sweet with creamy vanillin, quite solid dark, almost tarry, but delicate peat character. **Palate** – Quite full, round, smooth, rich & medium-dry with gently chewy oak tannins & a good peat note. **Finish** – Long, quite fresh, quite ethereal & salty. **Notes** – Murray McDavid bottling.

28 yrs, 1965, 53.2% abv

Sweetness – 7	Peatiness – 5	Availability – 2

Colour – Full amber with old gold highlights. **Nose** – Full, warm, nutty (hazelnuts), medium-sweet with a fruitcake richness and a green peatiness at the back, a lanolin oaky unctuousness and a slight medicinal touch. **Flavour** – Medium-dry, very rich, quite big-bodied with chewy tannins, good body and quite delicately peated. **Finish** – Powerful with good richness – even a sweetness at the end – and a salty tang on the tail. **Notes** – Adelphi Distillery bottling; bottled 1993.

Strathisla

KEITH, BANFFSHIRE [S] [V] EST. 1786

Built in 1786 as Milltown (Keith was the centre of the Scottish linen industry) and later known as Milton, Strathisla was originally the name of the make and subsequently also became that of the distillery. It was converted into a flour mill in 1838. After reconversion to distilling, the distillery was twice badly damaged in the 1870s: first by fire in 1876 and three years later by an explosion. Extensive modernisation took place after these events and again in 1965, when the distillery was enlarged from two to four stills. It is today owned by Chivas Brothers Ltd, which was a subsidiary of The Seagram Company of Canada until sold to Pernod Ricard in 2001.

Location – Half a mile from the centre of Keith.

Notes – On 15 June 1993 Strathisla received an unexpected visitor from Louisville, Kentucky; a young black and white cat fell asleep among some Bourbon barrels in a container awaiting shipment to Scotland. On opening the container some four weeks later, the cat staggered out, weak from hunger and drunk from the Bourbon fumes in the enclosed space. After six months' quarantine, the cat, for obvious reasons called Dizzy, is now employed by Chivas Bros as a "mouser".

Water – The Broomhill Spring. The reservoir which holds the distillery's water supply is said to be visited nightly by the "water kelpies" which could account for its special flavour.

8 yrs, 40% abv

Sweetness – 8	Peatiness – 3	Availability – 2

Colour – Amber with good gold highlights. *Nose* – Fruity, spirity and sweet with a lanolin oiliness. *Flavour* – Spicy, quite smooth and medium-sweet with a touch of oak. *Finish* – Good body, although perhaps a little short because of its youth. *Notes* – Gordon & MacPhail bottling.

12 yrs, 43% abv

Sweetness – 5	Peatiness – 5	Availability – 6

Colour – Mid-amber with yellow/gold highlights. *Nose* – Quite big and round, a dark hazelnut character with good richness at the back, just a hint of sweetness and a delicate burnt peaty character. *Flavour* – Medium-dry with a smoky nuttiness and a touch of dark, oaky tannins with a nice green edge. *Finish* – Quite long, hazelnut and smoky. *Notes* – D.o.b.

21 yrs, 40% abv

Sweetness – 8	Peatiness – 4	Availability – 4

Colour – Amber with bright copper highlights. *Nose* – Medium-sweet and malty, lightly peated and oaky. *Flavour* – Medium-dry, oaky and spicy and creamy. *Finish* – Long and spicy with hints of bitter chocolate. *Notes* – Gordon & MacPhail bottling.

1989, 60% abv

Sweetness – 7	Peatiness – 4	Availability – 2

Colour – Straw with pale gold highlights. *Nose* – Medium-sweet and quite full-bodied with a young spiritiness, quite delicate peatiness and a slight hint of toffee richness. *Flavour* – Medium-sweet and smooth with a gentle peatiness. *Finish* – Long, fresh, clean and quite sweet. *Notes* – Clydesdale Original bottling from cask no. 9408.

18 yrs, 1974, 57.8% abv

Sweetness – 6	Peatiness – 7	Availability – 3

Colour – Amber with old gold highlights. *Nose* – Full-bodied with a dark nuttiness and medium-dry oaky vanilla. *Flavour* – Smoky with a dark nuttiness, medium-sweet with gentle oaky tannins and a slight astringency. *Finish* – Long, creamy & smoky with a background of sweetness. *Notes* – Gordon & MacPhail bottling, distilled 23 March 1974.

Strathmill

KEITH, BANFFSHIRE [S] EST. 1891

Originally a corn and flour mill, it was converted in 1891 as Glenisla-Glenlivet. Acquired by W & A Gilbey in 1895, when it was renamed Strathmill. Became part of IDV in 1962 and now absorbed into Diageo plc. Four stills.

Location – Just off the B9014 from Keith to Dufftown.

Notes – Very rare as a single malt, most of the make goes into the *J&B* blend. The label below has not been used for over 30 years.

Water – A spring at the distillery.

12 yrs, 55.5% abv

Sweetness – 6	Peatiness – 3	Availability – 0

Colour – Very pale watery with watery green highlights. *Nose* – Light and cerealy, lightly smoky with a touch of perfume and a delicate nuttiness. *Flavour* – Medium-sweet, smooth and quite round with good body. *Finish* – Long and spicy with a pleasant leafy greenness. *Notes* – A cask sample kindly supplied by J&B Scotland Ltd, who also supplied the above label from their archives. The whisky is not now available bottled by J&B.

11 yrs, 1980, 60.6% abv

Sweetness – 7	Peatiness – 3	Availability – 4

Colour – Pale straw with lemon highlights. *Nose* – Fresh, young, mashy vegetal greenness with an edge of richness, medium-sweet and lightly peated. *Flavour* – Cerealy, corn flake-like, medium-sweet with soft tannins, smooth and quite round. *Finish* – Good sweetness, quite good length, clean with a mashy vegetal character and a green edge to the tail. *Notes* – Wm Cadenhead bottling.

Talisker

The distillery was originally sited at Snizort, to the north of the island, but was closed and mysteriously moved. The current buildings were founded by Hugh and Kenneth MacAskill in 1830. Rebuilt 1880–7 and further extended in 1900. Merged into Dailuaine-Talisker Distilleries Ltd in 1898, under which name it still trades although absorbed fully into DCL in 1925. Rebuilt again 1960–2 after the still house was destroyed by fire on 22 November 1960. Operated by UMGD. Five stills.

Location – Situated in a gentle bowl which forms a lonely, very sheltered glen on the west coast of Skye.

Notes – The only distillery on the island of Skye, it took its name from a farm about six miles distant. The make was triple distilled until 1928. One of UDV's *Classic Malts* portfolio.

Water – A burn on the slopes of Cnoc nan Speireag (Hawk Hill), cooling water comes from the Carbost Burn.

10 yrs, 45.8% abv

Sweetness – 1	Peatiness – 10	Availability – 8

Colour – Straw with gold highlights. **Nose** – Pungent, peaty with a burnt heather character and hints of ozone. **Flavour** – Peaty, dry, spicy and quite creamy. **Finish** – Smoky, spicy, smooth, almost salty at the end. **Notes** – D.o.b.

14 yrs, 1979, 64.3% abv

Sweetness – 2	Peatiness – 9	Availability – 2

Colour – Straw with gold/yellow highlights and just a tinge of green. *Nose* – Quite big and pungently smoky with a medicinal burnt oak character and a slight touch of richness. *Flavour* – Big, powerful with quite gentle pungency, earthily oaky and quite soft richness. *Finish* – Long, smoky with a touch of fresh greenness and pungent with a salty tang. *Notes* – Wm Cadenhead bottling.

38 yrs, 1955, 53.6% abv

Sweetness – 2	Peatiness – 9	Availability – 1

Colour – Deep amber with bronze highlights. *Nose* – Deep, dark, nutty and woody with a medicinal character and just an edge of richness. *Flavour* – Big, dark and tannic, quite pungent with an almost burnt peaty character and a touch of richness. *Finish* – Long, tannic, chewy and pungent. *Notes* – Gordon & MacPhail bottling, cask nos. 1257, 1310 & 1311, distilled 12 and 28 May 1955.

TALISKER DISTILLER'S EDITION, 1986, 45.8% abv

Sweetness – 3	Peatiness – 10	Availability – 6

Colour – Deep amber with bronze highlights & a hint of ruby. *Nose* – Rich, deep, darkly peated with a sweet edge, big-bodied, soft & mellow with a fruity note. *Palate* – Big-bodied, round & dry, but with good richness & an edge of sweetness & quite big peatiness. *Finish* – Long, very characterful & malty with good smoky pungency & a little hint of honey. *Notes* – D.o.b. Double-matured, finished in an Amoroso cask.

Tamdhu

Built by the Tamdhu Distillery Company Ltd which was owned by a consortium of blenders. Owned by Highland Distilleries Company since 1898. Closed from 1927 to 1947, but extended in 1972 from two to four stills and again to six stills in 1975. A feature is Tamdhu's Saladin maltings which have been largely rebuilt.

Location – Sited on the banks of the River Spey south of the B9102 between Knockando and Archiestown.

Notes – The old railway station at Knockando has been converted into a visitor centre for Tamdhu. Tamdhu does not have the traditional pagoda heads atop its kilns, having instead a short, square concrete chimney. The visitors' centre was closed at the time of writing, and it is not known if it will be reopened.

Water – A spring under the distillery.

No age statement, 40% *abv*

Sweetness – 7	Peatiness – 4	Availability – 8

Colour – Straw/amber with yellow highlights. *Nose* – Medium-bodied, fruity and a touch floral, medium-sweet with a greenness. *Flavour* – Medium-sweet, quite light, mashy, biscuity and quite smooth. *Finish* – Quite short; spirity and sweet. *Notes* – D.o.b.

42 yrs, 1958, 40.8% *abv*

Sweetness – 6	Peatiness – 4	Availability – 2

Colour – Amber with pale old gold highlights. *Nose* – Big-bodied, rich & sweet, with a slightly unctuous oily-oak character, touches of vanilla, toffee/tablet, caramel and hints of banana & melon. *Palate* – Medium-dry, smooth and delicately peated with gently chewy oaky tannins. *Finish* – Long, clean, gently chewy & creamily toffeeyed. *Notes* – Hart Brothers bottling.

Tamnavulin

TOMNAVOULIN, BANFFSHIRE [S] [V] EST. 1966

Built by the Tamnavulin-Glenlivet Distillery Company, a subsidiary of Invergordon Distillers and now owned by JBB (Greater Europe) plc. A very modern distillery, it could be operated by just a handful of technicians. Mothballed early in 1995.

Location – On the B9008 at the village of Tomnavoulin.

Notes – The only distillery actually positioned on the River Livet, from which the cooling waters are drawn. "Tomnavoulin" from the Gaelic means "mill on the hill" and an old carding mill which stands at the riverside just below the distillery has been converted into a very attractive visitor centre, which is still open. The mill machinery has been preserved inside. Equally pleasant are the grassy banks of the river which have been turned into a picnic area.

Water – Subterranean springs at Easterton in the local hills.

12 yrs, 40% abv

Sweetness – 7	Peatiness – 4	Availability – 3

Colour – Mid-straw with pale lemon highlights. *Nose* – A dark nuttiness and a gentle peaty character, medium-sweet with a rich, charred oak note. *Flavour* – Dark and medium-dry with nice weight and a good dollop of peat at the back. *Finish* – Smooth, long and nutty with a rich, oaky tail. *Notes* – D.o.b.

18 yrs, 46% abv

Sweetness – 8	Peatiness – 3	Availability – 1

Colour – Very dark, teak coloured. *Nose* – Nutty, quite spirity, light and medium-sweet. *Flavour* – Smooth, oaky, quite velvety and nutty. *Finish* – Smooth and spirity, quite long with a dry end. *Notes* – Wm Cadenhead bottling.

Teaninich

ALNESS, ROSS-SHIRE [H]   EST. 1817

Founded by Captain Hugh Munro. Sold to SMD in 1933. When SMD took over, there were four stills, two of which were described as being very small. When production restarted after the Second World War, the two smaller stills were removed. Capacity was increased from two to four larger stills in 1962 and to ten when an entirely new distillation unit named "A side" began production in 1970. The milling, mashing and fermentation part of the old distillery, "B side", was rebuilt 1973. Now owned by Diageo plc.

Location – Sited to the south of the A9 on the western outskirts of Alness and on the west bank of the River Alness, three-quarters of a mile from its outflow into the Cromarty Firth.

Notes – Alfred Barnard recorded in 1887 that Teaninich was the only distillery north of Inverness to be "lighted by electricity". In 1925 both malting floors were of solid clay. "A side" is in production, but "B side" was mothballed in the mid-1980s.

Water – The Dairywell Spring.

10 *yrs*, 43% *abv*

Sweetness – 7	Peatiness – 5	Availability – 6

Colour – Pale straw with yellow highlights and a tinge of lemon. *Nose* – Fresh and quite light with a good green peatiness, medium-sweet with an appley character. *Flavour* – Medium-dry, gently smoky, smooth and round. *Finish* – Clean and fresh with a sweet tail. *Notes* – D.o.b.

18 yrs, 1975, 43% abv

Sweetness – 7	Peatiness – 5	Availability – 1

Colour – Straw/pale amber with pale lemon highlights. *Nose* – Fresh, green, quite cerealy and clean, medium-sweet and quite full-bodied. *Flavour* – Fresh and clean with an earthy smokiness, medium to full-bodied and medium-sweet with a touch of richness. *Finish* – Clean, quite long with an almost perfumed smokiness. *Notes* – Master of Malt bottling, cask no. 13988, distilled 12 November 1975.

17 yrs, 1975, 43% abv

Sweetness – 9	Peatiness – 3	Availability – 1

Colour – Quite pale straw with lemon highlights. *Nose* – Quite full-bodied, spirity and fresh, almost salty with fruity and floral notes. *Flavour* – Quite sweet, round, spicy, full-bodied, rich and delicately peated with a nutty character. *Finish* – Long, sweet and slightly smoky. *Notes* – Master of Malt bottling from cask no. 13984.

21 yrs, 57.2% abv

Sweetness – 6	Peatiness – 6	Availability – 1

Colour – Straw with pale yellow highlights. *Nose* – Medium-bodied, medium-sweet with a slight burnt stick peatiness and an edge of richness. *Flavour* – Medium-dry, with good body and weight of peat. *Finish* – Long and quite darkly smoky, albeit gently. *Notes* – James MacArthur bottling.

In Celebration
500 Years *of* Scotch Whisky
1494 - 1994
TEANINICH
HIGHLAND SINGLE MALT
AGED 21 YEARS
70cl   JAMES MACARTHUR & CO. LTD. EDINBURGH   57.2%vol

Tobermory

TOBERMORY, ISLE OF MULL   [H] [V]   EST. 1798

Established by local merchant John Sinclair. Owned from 1890 to 1916 by John Hopkins & Son & Co, when taken over by DCL. Silent from 1930 to 1972 when revived as the Ledaig Distillery (Tobermory) Ltd. This company went into receivership in 1975 and the business was acquired in 1978 by the Kirkleavington Property Co of Cleckheaton. Tobermory was in production between 1979 and 1981, before closing again until 1989. It was purchased in 1993 by Burn Stewart Distillers for £600,000 plus £200,000 for stock. Four stills.

Location – Situated at the head of Tobermory Bay.

Notes – The only distillery on Mull. Because the distillery was closed for several years, very little Tobermory single malt has been produced until recently, all distilled between 1972 and 1975, and 1979 and 1981. *Tobermory* is now becoming more readily available, however. The older bottlings of *Tobermory* that are available have been bottled as *Ledaig*. Owner Burn Stewart has decided to use only unpeated barley in the production of *Tobermory*, although a few mashes will be produced each year using peated barley. These will be reserved for whiskies marketed under the name *Ledaig*. Independent bottlings are also under the distillery name of Ledaig.

Water – A small private loch close by the Mishnish Lochs.

FOUNDED 1798
TOBERMORY DISTILLERS LTD
THE ISLE OF MULL
PRODUCT OF SCOTLAND

10 *yrs*, 40% *abv*

Sweetness – 4	Peatiness – 5	Availability – 4

Colour – Pale amber with pale gold highlights. *Nose* – Quite soft and round with sweet vanilla, sherbet, citrus & toffee characters and a slight hint of a dark peat character. *Palate* – Medium-dry, sherbetty-sweet, medium-bodied, smooth, quite gently peated & citrus flavoured. *Finish* – Smooth, long, & quite round with a limey tang. *Notes* – D.o.b.

LEDAIG

SINGLE MALT
SCOTCH WHISKY

FROM

THE ISLE OF MULL

aged

Aged 15 years

This rare old single malt Scotch whisky
was distilled at the Ledaig Distillery
on the Isle of Mull by
Ledaig Distillers (Tobermory) Ltd.

PRODUCE OF SCOTLAND

70cl   43%Vol

LEDAIG, 15 *yrs*, 43% *abv*

Sweetness – 6	Peatiness – 6	Availability – 2

Colour – Amber with pale yellow highlights. *Nose* – Quite full and fresh with a citrus-lemon juice character and a slight creamy vanilla touch. *Palate* – Quite pungent, with good medium-sweet richness, round and smooth with a slightly earthy smokiness and a hint of milk chocolate. *Finish* – Long and smokily rich with a hint of cocoa & uncomplicated. *Notes* – D.o.b.

LEDAIG, 20 *yrs*, 43% *abv*

Sweetness – 4	Peatiness – 7	Availability – 2

Colour – Quite pale amber with yellow highlights. *Nose* – Sweet, rich toffee, dark chocolate/cocoa with quite a solid dark peat note. *Palate* – Medium-dry, quite rich & quite big-bodied, with a big, earthy peat character. *Finish* – Very long and expansive, carefully peated with a hint of cocoa on the tail. *Notes* – D.o.b.

Sweetness – 7	Peatiness – 7	Availability – 2

Colour – Pale straw with pale yellow highlights. *Nose* – Quite big-bodied with a hint of sweetness, a dark peat note, a sour, almost cork-taint character and youthfully mashy. *Palate* – Big-bodied, smokily and darkly peaty with a cereal character. *Finish* – Long and dark with a cereal/mashy character & quite tangy. *Notes* – Blackadder bottling from cask no. 119, distilled May 1992.

LEDAIG, 18 *yrs*, 1974, 43% *abv*

Sweetness – 2	Peatiness – 8	Availability – 2

Colour – Medium-pale straw with lemony/gold highlights. *Nose* – Medium-bodied, woody with a slight greenness and smokiness at the back and an almost Christmas cake yeasty character. *Flavour* – Medium-bodied, oaky with a slight greenness and good richness at the back. *Finish* – Of good length with a green smoky tail. *Notes* – Ledaig Distillers (Tobermory) bottling.

LEDAIG SHERRY FINISH, No age statement, 42% *abv*

Sweetness – 7	Peatiness – 7	Availability – 1

Colour – Pale straw with pale lemon highlights. *Nose* – Youthful, quite herby with a green vegetal note, a hint of vanilla & a quite smoky peat character. *Palate* – Quite big-bodied, vegetal, medium-dry with a smoky, almost burnt peat note. *Finish* – Sweet, vegetal, quite tangy & gently chewy. *Notes* – D.o.b.

Tomatin

TOMATIN, INVERNESS-SHIRE   [H] [V]   EST. 1897

Founded by the Tomatin Spey District Distillery Co Ltd. Extended from two to four stills in 1956, to six in 1958, to 10 in 1961, to 11 in 1964 and finally to 23 in 1974.

Location – Sited on the west of the A9 at the village of Tomatin, 12 miles south of Inverness. At 1,028 ft above sea level, it is one of Scotland's highest distilleries.

Notes – The first Scottish distillery to be owned by a Japanese company, when purchased by the Takara and Okura Consortium following its then owner's liquidation in 1985. It has the potential for the greatest output (more than 12 million litres of alcohol) of all the malt distilleries. From the Gaelic, "tomatin" means "the hill of the bushes".

Water – Allt-na-Frithe (a local burn).

10 yrs, 43% abv

Sweetness – 6	Peatiness – 5	Availability – 5

Colour – Honey with straw/gold highlights. **Nose** – Light, slightly sweet, a little spirity, malty and leafy. **Flavour** – Light, sweet, malty and peaty with a hint of pepperiness. **Finish** – Smooth, slightly spicy and grapey. **Notes** – D.o.b.

13 yrs, 1976, 60.5% abv

Sweetness – 6	Peatiness – 5	Availability – 1

Colour – Honey with straw/gold highlights. **Nose** – Light, slightly sweet, a little spirity, malty and leafy. **Flavour** – Light, sweet, malty and peaty with a hint of pepperiness. **Finish** – Smooth, slightly spicy and grapey. **Notes** – D.o.b.

Tomintoul

A modern distillery, production began only in 1965 and it was not until 1972 that the make began to appear in bottle. Built by Tomintoul Distillery Ltd and bought by Scottish Universal Investment Trust (part of Lonrho) in 1973. Managed by Whyte & Mackay, which was itself bought from Lonrho by Brent Walker in February 1989 and subsequently sold to American Brands Inc the following year. Doubled from two to four stills in 1974. Sold by JBB (Greater Europe) plc to Angus Dundee plc, August 2000.

Location – Situated in the valley of the River Avon on the B9136 off the A939 Grantown-on-Spey to Tomintoul road.

Notes – Tomintoul is the highest village in the Scottish Highlands, although the distillery itself, being outside the village, is not quite as high above sea level as Dalwhinnie. Tomintoul is regularly cut off by snow in winter.

Water – The Ballantruan Spring.

12 yrs, 43% abv

Sweetness – 7	Peatiness – 3	Availability – 4

Colour – Peaty straw with gold highlights. *Nose* – Medium-sweet, rich and slightly spirity with vanilla and fruity, almost orangey, notes. *Flavour* – Medium-sweet, lightish, slightly peppery and with an oaky touch. *Finish* – A little spirity, although smooth and the oaky vanilla lingers. *Notes* – Whyte & Mackay bottling.

23 yrs, 1976, 54.3% abv

Sweetness – 7	Peatiness – 4	Availability – 1

Colour – Straw/amber with yellow highlights. *Nose* – Medium-bodied, fresh and quite soft with a distinct lemon oil character and touches of beeswax, honey, apple and vanilla. *Palate* – Medium-sweet, of good body and rich with gently chewy oaky tannins and soft, delicate peat. *Finish* – Long and sweet, with soft vanilla and, on the end, a soft smokiness. *Notes* – Adelphi bottling.

Tormore

Built 1958–60 by Long John Distillers Ltd. Now part of Allied Domecq and operated by Allied Distillers Ltd. Doubled from four to eight stills in 1972.

Location – South of the A95 between Grantown-on-Spey and the Bridge of Avon.

Notes – The first new Highland malt distillery buildings to be constructed in the 20th century. The novelist (and former exciseman) Neil M. Gunn was invited by Lord Bracken to search for a suitable site for this new distillery. The expedition is described in "An Affair of Whisky", published in *New Saltire* (Dec. 1962). Glen Keith, established the previous year, used the buildings of a former mill. Tormore distillery and associated buildings are of a most striking design, the work of Professor Sir Albert Richardson, a past President of the Royal Academy.

Water – The Achvochkie Burn.

10 yrs, 40% abv

Sweetness – 8	*Peatiness* – 3	*Availability* – 6

Colour – Pale golden. *Nose* – Light and quite delicate with a strange dryness which is sometimes described as flintiness. *Flavour* – Slightly sweet, of medium weight and slightly spirity. *Finish* – Fine, distinguished and long. *Notes* – D.o.b.

Tullibardine

BLACKFORD, PERTHSHIRE [H] EST. 1949

There was a previous distillery of the same name near Blackford which was established in 1798, although its exact location is not known. The new distillery was the work of Delme Evans, who also designed Jura and Glenallachie. Owned by Invergordon Distillers since 1971, and Whyte & Mackay since 1993. Rebuilt 1973–4 and enlarged from two to four stills. Mothballed January 1995. Now managed by JBB (Greater Europe) plc.

Location – North of the A9 on the south-western outskirts of the village of Blackford, four miles south of Auchterarder.

Notes – On the site of an ancient brewery, the distillery takes its name from the nearby Tullibardine Moor, home of Gleneagles Hotel and golf courses. This area has always been famed for its water: Highland Spring and Gleneagles mineral waters are both from Blackford. Tradition has it that the fair Queen Helen of Scotland was drowned at a ford on the Allan Water (the local river), hence the name Blackford.

Water – The Danny Burn.

10 yrs, 40% abv

Sweetness – 3	Peatiness – 6	Availability – 5

Colour – Straw with golden-green highlights. *Nose* – Quite full, soft, malty and earthy. *Flavour* – Quite dry and spicy with a richness and roundness, quite smooth. *Finish* – Peppery, warm and quite long with a slight bitterness at the end. *Notes* – Invergordon bottling.

Japan

The history of whisky distilling in Japan has very Scottish roots. In 1918, Settsu Shuzou, a spirit producer, made plans to start distilling whisky. Deciding that the best way to learn the art of distilling was to send a representative of the company to Scotland to study Scottish whisky production techniques, he sent Masataka Taketsuru, who also studied Applied Chemistry at Glasgow University. When he returned to Japan in 1921 (with a Scottish wife), he found the country was in the depths of a recession and Settsu could no longer finance the project. Kotobukiya (now Suntory) appointed him to develop a distillery for that company and the Yamazaki distillery in Osaka started production in 1924. Taketsuru managed Yamazaki until he left to establish his own company (Nikka), and distillery, at Hokkaido. Today there are eight major working distilleries in Japan. The success of Scotch whisky in Japan and other world markets has encouraged Japanese drinks companies to produce Japanese whisky with the characteristics of Scotch.

Y A M A Z A K I   Built at the foot of Mt Tennou near Osaka in 1923 by Shinjiro Torii, founder of Suntory. The water supply in this area is famed for its purity. There are 12 stills producing a wide range of styles of whisky; direct-fired gas heating is used, as is steam-heating. Owned by Suntory.

Y O I C H I   Founded in 1934 close to the sea at the neck of the Shakotan peninsula by Masataka Taketsuru with one pot still – he could not afford a second. The second distillation was carried out in the one still which was washed out between distillations. Taketsuru felt that the humidity and water supply here were similar to Scotland and the buildings have a very Scottish appearance. There is a peat moor nearby and four of the six stills are direct-heated by coal.

HANYU Owned by Toa Shuzou, the distillery was founded in April 1946 in a rice field at Saitama with one pot still. There are now two steam heated stills and a continuous still, as well as the bottling plant within the complex. Water is transported by tanker from Kaminoizumi in Chichibu where the company was originally established.

SHIRAKAWA Originally owned by the Mercian Company, it was bought by Takara Shuzou, which owns Tomatin in Scotland, in 1947. The distillery is currently mothballed, although the bottling plant is working.

KARUIZAWA Built in 1955 by winemaker Daikoku Budoushu to the west of Karuizawa, Nagano, at the foot of Mt Asama, an active volcano, in an area popular as a summer resort. The distillery has four stills and the warehouses are ivy-clad, which keeps summer temperatures down. Only sherry casks are used for maturation. Bottles of *Karuizawa* malt contain 90% malt whisky from Karuizawa distillery and 10% malt whisky from another Mercian- owned distillery in Yamanashi. Owned and run by the Mercian Company. Two warehouses have been replaced by an art museum and visitor centre in 1995.

SENDAI In order to produce different styles from those produced at Hokkaido, Nikka built a new distillery at Sendai, Miyagi in 1969. It has eight stills, all of which are steam-heated. The distillery is located in a mountain area, between the Rivers Nikkawa and Hirose.

HAKUSHU Built, in 1973, by Suntory in a beautiful forest at Yamanashi at the southern end of the Japanese Alps, to the west of Mt. Fuji. Hakushu has 24 stills. Suntory has established a bird reserve which is open to the public. There is also a fascinating whisky museum on the site. Hakushu malt is used only for blending.

HAKUSHU HIGASHI This second Hakushu distillery was built in 1981 to supplement the output of the original Hakushu, but with different styles. There are 12 gas-fired stills. Hakushu Higashi produces the bottled 'Hakushu' malt.

F U J I - G O T E M B A   Completed in 1973 in Shizuoka by Kirin-Seagram Ltd, a joint venture established in 1972 by Kirin Brewery Co, Seagram and Chivas Brothers. Its make is used only for blending. Located in an ancient forest at the foot of Mt Fuji, the buildings also house a grain distillery and blending and bottling plant.

M A R S   S H I N S U   A company which originally produced potato spirit in the south of Japan, Mars Shinsu has two steam-heated stills. Its water supply is from two wells on site and peated malt is imported. Whisky is matured mostly in sherry casks, but Bourbon and brandy are also used. Currently mothballed.

CHICHIBU, No age statement, 43% *abv*

Sweetness – 9	Peatiness – 2	Availability – 2

Colour – Mid-amber with yellow-gold highlights. *Nose* – Medium-sweet, rich & very lightly peated with a nutty character. *Palate* – Sweet, of quite good body, rich & nutty with a delicate peatiness and a fruity, almost winey flavour. *Finish* – Sweet & long with a butterscotch note & a slightly green freshness. *Notes* – D.o.b. from Hanyu Distillery.

CHICHIBU, 60% *abv*, 8 *yrs*, sample from Hanyu

Sweetness – 3	Peatiness – 7	Availability – 1

Colour – Mid-amber with old gold highlights. *Nose* – Quite dark & nutty, unctuously smooth, medium-bodied and dry with a hint of toffee & honey. *Palate* – Quite big-bodied, dark & nutty, dry with quite solid tannins and a good, green peat note. *Finish* – Quite long and tangy with a big belt of smokiness on the tail. *Notes* – D.o.b.

CHICHIBU, 10 *yrs*, 59% *abv*, sample from Hanyu

Sweetness – 6	Peatiness – 6	Availability – 1

Colour – Amber with old gold highlights. *Nose* – Dark, quite full-bodied & rich, with a slightly green edge to the peat, round & dry with a slight note of acetone & beeswax & vanilla oak characters. *Palate* – Medium-sweet, sprightly & fresh with a good, dark peat note, cocoa & good body. *Finish* – Long, fresh, clean & gently chewy. *Notes* – D.o.b.

FUJI-GOTEMBA, 12 *yrs*, 40% *abv*

Sweetness – 5	Peatiness – 3	Availability – 1

Colour – Quite full amber with light bronze highlights. *Nose* – Full-bodied, quite intense & rich, an unctuous oily-oak smoothness & medium-sweet with lime and vanilla notes. *Palate* – Medium-dry, quite full-bodied, rich & gently peated with a chocolate flavour. *Finish* – Long and rich with cocoa notes on the tail. *Notes* – D.o.b. as *Single Cask*.

FUJI-GOTEMBA, 15 yrs, 40% abv

Sweetness – 4	Peatiness – 3	Availability – 1

Colour – Amber with gold highlights. *Nose* – Medium-dry, nutty & medium-bodied with notes of citrus, sherbet & beeswax. *Palate* – Medium-dry, quite light, fresh, clean and perfumed with a delicate peatiness. *Finish* – Quite long, very soft & perfumed. *Notes* – D.o.b. as *Single Cask*.

FUJI-GOTEMBA 20TH ANNIVERSARY PURE MALT, 40% abv

Sweetness – 5	Peatiness – 3	Availability – 2

Colour – Amber with pale old gold highlights. *Nose* – Quite big-bodied, rich bananas & pears with a liquorice aroma to the peat character. *Palate* – Medium-sweet, rich, of good body with vinuous flavours of banana & chardonnay. *Finish* – Quite long, rich & clean. *Notes* – D.o.b. vatted malt.

HAKUSHU, 12 yrs, 43% abv

Sweetness – 6	Peatiness – 4	Availability – 4

Colour – Amber with gold highlights. *Nose* – Light–medium-bodied, fresh, slightly fruity – pear & banana & a touch of citrus, almost pine needles. *Palate* – Medium-dry and gently chewy with a dry peat character. *Finish* – Long, softly chewy, quite fresh & softly unctuous. *Notes* – D.o.b. from Hakushu Higashi Distillery.

KARUIZAWA, 13 yrs, 1981, 58% abv

Sweetness – 3	Peatiness – 7	Availability – 2

Colour – Quite a deep amber with bronze highlights. *Nose* – Full-bodied and medium-dry with a darkly peaty charcoal aroma and a hint of rubberised fabric. *Flavour* – Big-bodied and medium-dry with a dark, peaty smokiness, a good broad edge of richness and slightly chewy tannins. *Finish* – Very long, quite smooth and complex with notes of smoky liquorice and quite rich vanilla. *Notes* – D.o.b. A single malt from Karuizawa Distillery.

KARUIZAWA, 15 yrs, 40% abv

Sweetness – 4	Peatiness – 6	Availability – 3

Colour – Amber with old gold highlights. *Nose* – Fresh, clean and dry with a slight green edge to the peat; smooth, nutty & medium-bodied. *Palate* – Medium-dry, round and medium-bodied with a smooth, lightly toasted note to the peat and a hint of bergamot. *Finish* – Quite long & quite delicate with a green edge to the peatiness. *Notes* – D.o.b.

KARUIZAWA, 17 yrs, 40% *abv*

Sweetness – 3	Peatiness – 6	Availability – 3

Colour –Amber with bronze highlights. *Nose* – Fresh, medium-dry & medium-bodied with a fruitcake richness and a slight pear drop character. *Palate* – Medium-dry, smooth, round, rich and of good body with a dark vanilla character, quite gentle tannins and good peat integration. *Finish* – Long, dark, gently chewy and almost chocolatey. *Notes* – D.o.b.

KOMAGATAKE, 10 yrs, 40% *abv*

Sweetness – 7	Peatiness – 3	Availability – 2

Colour – Amber with old gold highlights. *Nose* – Rich, quite sweet, toffee/coffee, lightly peated, but with a hard charred oak core. *Palate* – Smooth, medium-dry & medium-bodied with a nice richness, a smooth note of vanilla & quite softly peated. *Finish* – Long with a slightly dark peatiness & gently chewy. *Notes* – D.o.b. from Mars Shinshu Distillery.

SENDAI, 12 yrs, 45% *abv*

Sweetness – 6	Peatiness – 6	Availability – 4

Colour – Full amber with deep old gold highlights. *Nose* – Big, dark, firm, almost earthy peatiness with a slightly medicinal note, rich, medium-sweet, honeyed, dark, creamy oak and Brazil nuts with a malty cereal note. *Palate* – Quite big-bodied, rich & medium-sweet with a good coffee/toffee note and a gently chewy nuttiness. *Finish* – Long, quite ethereal & dry, tangy & quite elegantly peated. *Notes* – D.o.b.

SHIRAKAWA, 27 yrs, 55% *abv*

Sweetness – 6	Peatiness – 4	Availability – 2

Colour – Amber with gold highlights. *Nose* – Full, quite round and medium-sweet, rich, malty and nutty with a hint of toffee. *Flavour* – Medium-sweet, quite full-bodied, rich with slightly chewy tannins and a good, quite creamy weight of peat at the back of the palate. *Finish* – Long, smooth and pleasantly smoky. *Notes* – Shirakawa distillery is owned by Takara Shuzou.

YAMAZAKI, 8 yrs, 57% *abv*

Sweetness – 6	Peatiness – 3	Availability – 1

Colour – Amber with old gold highlights. *Nose* – Quite a charred oak note, rich, dark, sweet oak with quite a fresh, green character. *Palate* – Medium-dry, gently chewy, smooth & fresh with good richness & a touch of toffee. *Finish* – Long, rich, gently chewy & clean with ripe red apples on the tail. *Notes* – D.o.b. distilled in a straight head pot still & aged in a puncheon.

YAMAZAKI, 10 yrs, 40% abv

Sweetness – 7	Peatiness – 3	Availability – 4

Colour – Pale amber with yellow highlights. *Nose* – Quite light with an appley, sweet vanilla-oaky nuttiness, medium-dry and delicately peated. *Flavour* – Medium-sweet, smooth, soft and delicately peated. *Finish* – Good length, quite delicate and smooth with a sweet oaky character. *Notes* – D.o.b.

YAMAZAKI, 12 yrs, 43% abv

Sweetness – 2	Peatiness – 5	Availability – 4

Colour – Pale amber with gold highlights. *Nose* – Medium-sweet, of medium weight with good richness, a touch of toffee and tablet with a hint of apples and rich liquorice. *Flavour* – Dry, of medium weight, medium peatiness and a tea character. *Finish* – Very dry, with really quite a tannic dryness, quite delicate, but short. *Notes* – D.o.b.

YAMAZAKI, 18 yrs, 43% abv

Sweetness – 4	Peatiness – 6	Availability – 3

Colour – Amber with old gold highlights. *Nose* – Medium-dry and rich with an almost Riesling-like petrol aroma, good body and delicately peated. *Flavour* – Medium-dry and rich with good body and gentle, but firm, peat. *Finish* – Long and quite flavoursome with a touch of chewy tannin. *Notes* – D.o.b.

YAMAZAKI, 25 yrs, 43% abv

Sweetness – 2	Peatiness – 3	Availability – 3

Colour – Deep, dark amber with bronze highlights. *Nose* – Big, rich and medium-sweet with a dry, vanilla oak character, a note of beeswax and a dark, delicate peat character with a medicinal hint. *Flavour* – Dry, chewy and quite big-bodied, but delicately-flavoured with a touch of perfume and quite lightly peated. *Finish* – Chewy, long, perfumed and very dry. *Notes* – D.o.b. from bottle no. 44/1200.

YAMAZAKI SHERRY WOOD, 15 yrs, 1984, 45% abv

Sweetness – 2	Peatiness – 5	Availability – 2

Colour – Deep, dark amber with bronze highlights. *Nose* – Big, dark, quite powerful & nutty with a slightly perfumed & lightly charred oak note, creamy toffee/honey, vanilla. *Palate* – Medium-dry, quite big-bodied & quite smooth with chewy oak tannins. *Finish* – Long, chewy, slightly perfumed & floral and quite dry. *Notes* – D.o.b. Distilled June 1984, bottled September 1999; bottle no. 1107 of 3600.

YOICHI SINGLE CASK, 10 *yrs*, 45% *abv*

Sweetness – 5	Peatiness – 5	Availability – 2

Colour –Amber with old gold highlights. *Nose* – Medium-bodied and quite intense, medium-dry and delicately peated, a rich fruitiness, with notes of marzipan, hazelnut and toffee with a slight green edge. *Palate* – Medium-dry, quite full-bodied with a touch of spice, soft, rich, toffeeyed and delicately peated. *Finish* – Long & quite creamy with an ethereal peaty note. *Notes* – D.o.b

YOICHI, 12 *yrs*, 45% *abv*

Sweetness – 7	Peatiness – 4	Availability – 4

Colour – Amber with old gold highlights. *Nose* – Full-bodied, medium-dry, with a quite rich fruitiness, toffee, creamy vanilla & coffee notes and a nuttiness. *Palate* – Medium-sweet, quite rich & fresh, round, smooth vanilla-oak, of good body & delicately peated. *Finish* – Long, rich and creamily toffeeyed. *Notes* – D.o.b.

YOICHI, 15 *yrs*, 45% *abv*

Sweetness – 3	Peatiness – 7	Availability – 3

Colour – Mid-amber with old gold highlights. *Nose* – A quite delicate soft maltiness with a dark apple character, gently smoky and medium-dry with notes of rich chocolate, coffee and a winey note at the back. *Palate* – Almost dry, quite full, with gently chewy oaky tannins and a smooth, dark, almost medicinal, peat note. *Finish* – Long, quite tangy, with good richness, quite elegant. *Notes* – D.o.b.

ZEN, No age statement, 40% *abv*

Sweetness – 3	Peatiness – 3	Availability – 8

Colour – Pale amber with gold highlights. *Nose* – Light, slightly spirity, a touch perfumed & delicately peated with a lemon/citrus character to the sweetness. *Palate* – Light, dry, smooth, quite creamy & lightly peated. *Finish* – Quite long, fresh, dry & tails off at the end. *Notes* – A vatted malt from Suntory.

New Zealand

The large number of Scots among the early settlers to New Zealand meant that a thriving distilling industry soon developed, only for it to be crushed by punitive duty rates in 1875. In 1968, Wilson's, a subsidiary of Seagram, opened a distillery on the site of the old Willowbank distillery in Dunedin. The distillery has only one pot still which is used for both stages of the distillation. The whisky produced is sold as *Lammerlaw*, taking its name from the hills, the Lammerlaw Ranges, from which the distillery's water supply, Deep Creek, runs through peat and moss.

Location – At Dunedin on New Zealand's South Island.

Notes – New Zealand has a strong historical link with Scotland, many of the original settlers having come from "God's own country". Dunedin (the Gaelic for Edinburgh) was one of the first landing points for these settlers in 1848. Not surprisingly, these early settlers brought their distillation methods with them.

Water – Deep Creek.

10 yrs, 43% abv

Sweetness – 6	Peatiness – 1	Availability – 2

Colour – Pale amber with gold highlights. *Nose* – Fresh, clean, medium-bodied and medium-dry with a hint of rich liquorice, a slightly green touch and a floral note. *Flavour* – Medium-sweet and smooth with good body, a touch of liquorice, very gentle smokiness and quite a lush texture. *Finish* – Long and clean with a note of fennel on the tail. *Notes* – A single malt from Wilson Distillers in New Zealand.

Vatted Malts

BALLANTINE'S PURE MALT, 12 yrs, 40% *abv*

Sweetness – 7	Peatiness – 4	Availability – 3

Colour – Deep amber with old gold highlights. *Nose* – Quite full & nutty with characters of ripe fruitcake – sultanas, lemon peel, sweet vanilla, good maltiness & a touch of liquorice. *Palate* – Full, round, smooth, medium-sweet & quite gently peated with flavours of vanilla & toffee. *Finish* – Long, tangy & complex with lingering oak & dried fruit characters. *Notes* – D.o.b.

THE BENNACHIE, 10 yrs, 43% *abv*

Sweetness – 6	Peatiness – 5	Availability – 2

Colour – Mid-amber with gold highlights. *Nose* – Medium-bodied, quite delicately peated with a green edge and medium-dry with a slight hint of chewy toffee. *Flavour* – Medium-sweet, with good body and flavours of creamy-smooth toffee vanilla, quite gently peated. *Finish* – Long, medium-sweet and smooth with delicate peat on the tail. *Notes* – A vatted malt from Bennachie Scotch Whisky Co Ltd.

BLACK RIBBON, No age statement, 40% *abv*

Sweetness – 7	Peatiness – 7	Availability – 1

Colour – Mid-amber with yellow and gold/green highlights. *Nose* – Medium-bodied, gently smoky with hints of apple and coffee and an edge of sweetness. *Flavour* – Quite full-bodied and round, smoky, oily smooth and medium-sweet, quite rich with hints of coffee and toffee and with a slight greenness at the end. *Finish* – Full with a hint of spice, a gentle greenness and a dark smokiness. *Notes* – A vatted malt, vatted in Scotland and bottled in Sweden by Vin & Sprit. Available only in Sweden.

BLAIRMHOR, 8 yrs, 40% abv

Sweetness – 4	Peatiness – 7	Availability – 3

Colour – Pale amber with pale straw highlights. *Nose* – Clean with a full, dark, almost charred peatiness, full-bodied, almost dry and with a slight dark richness. *Flavour* – Medium-dry, round and smooth with a good firm dollop of smoky peatiness. *Finish* – Long and chewy with notes of smoke and vanilla. *Notes* – A vatted malt from R Carmichael & Sons Ltd.

EILEANDOUR, 10 yrs, 40% abv

Sweetness – 7	Peatiness – 3	Availability – 2

Colour – Amber with gold highlights. *Nose* – Rich and medium-sweet with a honeyed toffee character, delicately peated and of good body. *Flavour* – Fresh, smooth, quite soft and medium-sweet with a delicate peatiness and of good weight. *Finish* – Long, rich, clean and quite elegant. *Notes* – A vatted malt from Isle of Arran Distillers.

MACDONALD'S GLENCOE, 8 yrs, 58% abv

Sweetness – 4	Peatiness – 7	Availability – 2

Colour – Mid-amber with gold highlights. *Nose* – Quite full-bodied & medium-dry with a rich, soft maltiness, quite a solid peat character & a slight medicinal note. *Palate* – Medium-dry, quite big-bodied, very rich & gently chewy with good peat integration. *Finish* – Long, rich, quite powerful & pleasantly chewy with dark peat notes. *Notes* – A vatted malt from Ben Nevis Distillery Ltd.

OLD ELGIN, 8 *yrs*, 40% *abv*

Sweetness – 7	Peatiness – 6	Availability – 4

Colour – Mid-amber with gold highlights. *Nose* – Medium to full-bodied, medium-dry and smoky with a touch of greenness and dark, appley fruit. *Flavour* – Rich, medium-sweet, quite full-bodied and peppery, fresh, round and smooth. *Finish* – Fresh, medium-sweet and clean. *Notes* – Bottled by Gordon & MacPhail.

POIT DHUBH, 12 *yrs*, 40% *abv*

Sweetness – 6	Peatiness – 4	Availability – 4

Colour – Amber with good yellow highlights. *Nose* – Medium-sweet, slightly green and quite rich. *Flavour* – Smooth with a touch of dryness, lightly peated and quite elegant, although light. *Finish* – Long, smoky and slightly perfumed. *Notes* – Bottled by Praban na Linne.

POIT DHUBH GREEN LABEL, 12 *yrs*, 46% *abv*

Sweetness – 7	Peatiness – 7	Availability – 3

Colour – Light amber with gold highlights. *Nose* – Medium-bodied with good body, firm dark smokiness, a touch of liquorice, a slight rich green touch of citrus. *Flavour* – Quite full-bodied, medium-sweet and rich with a good backbone of peatiness. *Finish* – Long, smooth and smoky. *Notes* – Bottled without chill-filtration by Praban na Linne.

POIT DHUBH , 21 *yrs*, 43% *abv*

Sweetness – 5	*Peatiness* – 4	*Availability* – 3

Colour – Mid-amber with old gold highlights. *Nose* – A rich, almost fruity note, medium-sweet, quite restrained and delicate, gently peated with a soft toffee/vanilla note. *Flavour* – Medium-dry and of good body with a nutty peatiness, slightly chewy and smooth with a soft vanilla flavour. *Finish* – Long, tangy and complex with a final elegance. *Notes* – An unchillfiltered vatted malt from Praban-na-Linne.

PRIDE OF ISLAY, 12 *yrs*, 40% *abv*

Sweetness – 1	*Peatiness* – 10	*Availability* – 4

Colour – Mid-amber with yellowy gold highlights. *Nose* – Full-bodied and smoky with a rich, chocolatey nuttiness. *Flavour* – Big and smoky, quite pungent and bone dry with a slight edge of richness. *Finish* – Full, long and smoky with a slight tang of bitter chocolate. *Notes* – Bottled by Gordon & MacPhail.

PRIDE OF THE LOWLANDS, 12 *yrs*, 40% *abv*

Sweetness – 3	*Peatiness* – 2	*Availability* – 4

Colour – Amber with yellowy gold highlights. *Nose* – Medium weight, fresh, oily-rich and medium-dry with a slight unripe grapey character. *Flavour* – Smooth and medium-dry with a touch of coffee and good richness; medium weight. *Finish* – Quite long and fresh with the tang of coffee on the tail. *Notes* – Bottled by Gordon & MacPhail.

PRIDE OF ORKNEY, 12 *yrs*, 40% *abv*

Sweetness – 2	*Peatiness* – 5	*Availability* – 4

Colour – Light to mid-amber with gold highlights. *Nose* – Quite light and rich with dried fruit characters and hints of honey. *Flavour* – Off-dry, smooth, lightly smoky and malty. *Finish* – Clean with a refreshing greenness. *Notes* – Bottled by Gordon & MacPhail.

PRIDE OF STRATHSPEY, 12 *yrs*, 40% *abv*

Sweetness – 8	*Peatiness* – 3	*Availability* – 4

Colour – Amber with gold highlights. *Nose* – Medium-sweet with a touch of creamy oiliness, rich oak and a hint of nuttiness. *Flavour* – Medium-sweet, quite full-bodied, smooth and round with a hazelnut character. *Finish* – Long and nutty with a dry edge and nice oaky tannins. *Notes* – Bottled by Gordon & MacPhail.

SHEEP DIP, 8 *yrs*, 40% *abv*

Sweetness – 3	*Peatiness* – 6	*Availability* – 5

Colour – Pale amber with good yellow highlights. *Nose* – Dry, softly peated and slightly green. *Flavour* – Dry, but with a nice richness, spicy, a good peatiness, round and medium-bodied. *Finish* – Of medium length and with a gentle smokiness. *Notes* – *Sheep Dip* is said to have become popular with farmers because invoices for "Sheep Dip" could easily be lost in their accounts if they kept a few sheep!

In 1885 Tambowie Distillery produced 48,000 gallons of Malt Whisky,
a fact recorded by Alfred Barnard during his pilgrimage round
Scotlands distilleries. Sadly destroyed by fire in 1920, the taste of
Tambowie has been lost to lovers of Malts for over 70 years,
until now! Using the extensive knowledge we have gained
about this old distillery, we have chosen a Malt which
we feel comes closest to its ancient distillate.
Light, yet full of flavour and character,
we think the ghosts of Tambowie
would approve.

DISTILLED AND BOTTLED IN SCOTLAND

750ml   40% Alc.Vol

The Vintage Malt Whisky Co. Ltd   Bearsden, Glasgow G61 3RW   VS958

TAMBOWIE, 8 yrs, 40% abv

Sweetness – 8	Peatiness – 3	Availability – 2

Colour – Mid-amber with gold highlights. *Nose* – Fresh and medium-dry with good body and touches of toffee and oaky vanilla. *Flavour* – Medium-sweet with a touch of richness, of good body and lightly peated with a smooth vanilla flavour. *Finish* – Long, clean and quite sweet. *Notes* – A vatted malt from the Vintage Malt Whisky Co named after a distillery which used to exist in the Glasgow suburb of Bearsden.

Independent Bottlings

BLAIRFINDY, 20 *yrs*, 1976, 51.8% *abv*

Sweetness – 8	Peatiness – 4	Availability – 2

Colour – Amber with bright gold highlights. *Nose* – Full-bodied, medium-sweet and quite intensely hazelnutty with a slight green edge and a touch of coffee/toffee. *Flavour* – Big-bodied, rich, sweet and round with a smooth, unctuous toffee-like character and a gentle, green peatiness. *Finish* – Long, sweet, smooth and elegant. *Notes* – A single malt from Blackadder International.

FINLAGGAN, 12 *yrs*, 43% *abv*

Sweetness – 2	Peatiness – 8	Availability – 2

Colour – Pale amber with yellow/gold highlights. *Nose* – Quite dry, fresh and slightly perfumed with a burnt heather roots peatiness, good body with a little hint of ozone. *Flavour* – Almost dry and smoky with good body. *Finish* – Full, long and smoky with a fine edge of richness. *Notes* – A single Islay malt from the Vintage Malt Whisky Co named after the ancient stronghold of the Lord of the Isles.

GLEN EASON, 10 *yrs*, 40% *abv*

Sweetness – 3	Peatiness – 7	Availability – 2

Colour – Full amber with old gold highlights. *Nose* – Fresh and medium-dry with a slightly green edge to the almost sooty peatiness and with the cerealy aroma of a maltings floor. *Flavour* – Quite full-bodied, medium-dry, smooth and with a good, firm peatiness. *Finish* – Long and gently smoky with just a hint of sweetness on the end. *Notes* – A single malt from Isle of Arran Distillers.

GLENTROMIE, 12 yrs, 40% abv

Sweetness – 6	Peatiness – 3	Availability – 4

Colour – Mid-amber with gold highlights. *Nose* – Quite light, elegant, medium-sweet & peppery, quite rich with a slight tablet note & sweet vanilla oak. *Palate* – Quite sweet, round, smooth, soft & quite delicately peated. *Finish* – Long, clean, quite ethereal & peppery on the tail. *Notes* – Single Highland malt from Speyside.

GLENTROMIE, 17 yrs, 40% abv

Sweetness – 6	Peatiness – 3	Availability – 4

Colour – Mid-amber with old gold highlights. *Nose* – Quite light, elegant, rich & medium-sweet with notes of toffee/vanilla & demerara sugar & slightly peppery. *Palate* – Quite sweet with gently chewy tannins, a touch of a charred oak character & quite lightly peated. *Finish* – Long, soft, quite smooth & peppery on the tail. *Notes* – Single Highland malt from Speyside.

THE ILEACH, No age statement, 43% abv

Sweetness – 2	Peatiness – 9	Availability – 2

Colour – Amber with pale gold highlights. *Nose* – Big and powerful with a quite earthy peatiness, notes of burnt heather roots & a slight edge of sweet citrus. *Palate* – Big-bodied, round, rich, smooth & earthily smoky with a slight perfumed note. *Finish* – Long, very gently chewy and full, but softly, smoky. *Notes* – A single Islay malt from The Vintage Malt Whisky Co Ltd.

LOCKE'S, 40% abv

Sweetness – 7	Peatiness – 0	Availability – 2

Colour – Amber with pale old gold highlights. *Nose* – Fresh, clean and slightly honeyed with a slight grassy/hedgerow character and sherbet/lemon notes. *Palate* – Fresh, medium-sweet & clean, quite creamy and soft. *Finish* – Long, very clean and grassy. *Notes* – An Irish single malt whiskey from Cooley's.

MACPHAIL'S MALT, 10 yrs, 40% *abv*

Sweetness – 6	*Peatiness* – 6	*Availability* – 4

Colour – Mid-amber with old gold highlights. *Nose* – Quite light, fresh, dark and smoky, medium-dry. *Flavour* – Medium-dry with good body, an earthy peatiness and a touch of spiciness. *Finish* – Fresh, quite smoky and long-lasting with a touch of oak. *Notes* – Single malt bottling under Gordon & MacPhail's own label.

MACPHAIL'S 106, No age statement, 60.5% *abv*

Sweetness – 7	*Peatiness* – 6	*Availability* – 4

Colour – Amber with old gold highlights. *Nose* – Quite full-bodied and medium-dry with a slight earthy peatiness, a rich lanolin note and a fresh greenness. *Flavour* – Full-bodied, medium-sweet, rich, round and smooth with a slight green peatiness, good body and gentle, chewy tannins. *Finish* – Long and complex with a nice, slightly green nuttiness and pleasantly chewy. *Notes* – Single malt under Gordon & MacPhail's own label.

OAK BRANDY CASK, 1970, 40% *abv*

Sweetness – 6	*Peatiness* – 3	*Availability* – 1

Colour – Pale amber with yellow/gold highlights. *Nose* – Quite lightweight, medium-dry with a green fruity character, malty and spirity with a hint of acetone. *Flavour* – Medium-sweet with an oaky dryness, smooth and soft. *Finish* – Quite long with a cough linctus character and lightly smoky. *Notes* – A single Speyside malt matured in a brandy cask and bottled by Gordon & MacPhail.

OAK BRANDY CASK, 1963, 40% *abv*

Sweetness – 5	*Peatiness* – 3	*Availability* – 1

Colour – Amber with gold highlights. *Nose* – Medium-sweet and medium-bodied with a hint of smokiness and a rich, honeyed character. *Flavour* – Medium-dry, soft, quite light and fresh with a touch of richness. *Finish* – Quite long with a dry finish and a touch of honey on the tail. *Notes* – A single Speyside malt matured in a brandy cask

OAK PORT CASK, 1970, 40% *abv*

Sweetness – 5	*Peatiness* – 5	*Availability* – 1

Colour – Amber with gold highlights. *Nose* – Medium-sweet, quite rich with a ripe Christmas cake fruitiness and a slight touch of perfume on the tail. *Flavour* – Medium-dry and quite round with a demerara sugar character, lightly smoky, dark and nutty. *Finish* – Long, quite dry and chewy. *Notes* – A single Speyside malt matured in a port cask. Bottled by Gordon & MacPhail in 1993.

THE OLD MAN OF HOY, No age statement, 43% *abv*

Sweetness – 6	*Peatiness* – 4	*Availability* – 3

Colour – Mid-amber with old gold highlights. *Nose* – Medium-bodied, malty and medium-sweet with a slight herbaceous character and a rich, honeyed edge. *Flavour* – Medium-bodied and quite fresh with a slightly rich greenness and a sweet edge. *Finish* – Long, medium-sweet and rich, a touch tangy with a slight nuttiness on the end. *Notes* – A single Orcadian malt.

RAW CASK BLAIRFINDY, 57.6% *abv*

Sweetness – 8	*Peatiness* – 3	*Availability* – 2

Colour – Rich, dark, nutty, full-bodied & fruity with a slightly charred unctuous oak note & warm, raisin/dried fruit aromas. *Nose* – Quite full-bodied, round, rich & intense with notes of dried fruit/orange marmalade/apples/lemon, underpinned by quite soft toffee vanilla oak & delicate peat at the back. *Flavour* – Big-bodied, medium-sweet, smooth, round & rich with a fruitcake flavour and dark nutty vanilla. *Finish* – Long, smooth & quite ethereal. *Notes* – Blackadder International bottling. The bottle retains some of the cask sediment.

THE VINTAGE MALT WHISKY CO. LTD.

ANTALLAN
Highland
Single Malt

YEARS 10 OLD

SCOTCH WHISKY

DISTILLED AND BOTTLED IN SCOTLAND
THE VINTAGE MALT WHISKY CO. LTD. GLASGOW G61 3RW
DISTILLATO DI CEREALI

70cl ℮   40%Vol

TANTALLAN, 10 *yrs*, 40% *abv*

Sweetness – 7	*Peatiness* – 6	*Availability* – 2

Colour – Very pale straw with pale lemon highlights. *Nose* – Fresh, clean and medium-dry with a gentle floral note and a slightly green peaty character. *Flavour* – Medium-sweet, big-bodied and powerful, round, smooth and clean with a slightly chewy peatiness. *Finish* – Long and clean with a green, spicy freshness. *Notes* – A single malt from the Vintage Malt Whisky Co.

VINTAGE SINGLE ISLAY MALT
No age statement, 40% *abv*

Sweetness – 1	*Peatiness* – 9	*Availability* – 1

Colour – Quite deep amber with old gold highlights. *Nose* – Big-bodied, slightly pungent and dry with a charred smoky character and almost a perfumed note. *Flavour* – Dry, full-bodied, smooth and very smoky. *Finish* – Long and dry with a fragrant peatiness. *Notes* – A single Islay malt from the Vintage Malt Whisky Co.

Specialist Whisky Shops

Although some of the major retail chains offer good selections of single malt whiskies at competitive prices, they cannot hope to compete with the whisky specialist for depth of choice and knowledge. If there is a whisky you particularly want, then the specialist will usually try to get it for you, often being prepared to go to considerable trouble for a customer. Many also offer a mail order service. If you know of others that should be included in this list, please write to us. We are also interested in hearing from specialist shops in other countries. Information should be sent to Malt Whisky File, Canongate Books Ltd, 14 High Street, Edinburgh EH1 1TE.

SCOTLAND
The Cadenhead Whisky Shop, 172 Canongate, Edinburgh EH8 8BN
Cairngorm Whisky Centre, Inverdruie, Aviemore, PH22 1QH
Canape Wines, 85 Main Street, Bothwell, Glasgow G71 8RD
The Cheese and Wine Shop, George Street, Oban PA34 5NT
Clifton Coffee Shop, Tyndrum, Crianlarich, Perthshire FK20 8RY
Eaglesome Ltd, Reform Square, Campbeltown, Argyll PA28 6JA
Gordon & MacPhail Ltd, 58 South Street, Elgin, Moray IV30 1JY
Loch Fyne Whiskies, Inverary, Argyll PA32 8UD
Luvian's Bottle Shop, 93 Bonnygate, Cupar, Fife KY15 4LG
Peter Green & Co, 37 Warrender Park Road, Edinburgh EH9 1HJ
Robertsons, 46 Atholl Road, Pitlochry, Perthshire PH16 5BX
Royal Mile Whiskies, 379/381 High Street, Edinburgh EH1 1PW
Strachan of Aboyne, Balmoral Terrace, Aboyne, Aberdeenshire AB34 5HL
T B Watson Ltd, 11–17 English Street, Dumfries DG1 2BU
Villeneuve Wines Ltd, 1 Venlaw Court, Peebles, EH45 8AE
The Whisky Castle, Main Street, Tomintoul AB37 9EX
The Whisky Shop, Waverley Market, Princes Street, Edinburgh EH1 1BQ
The Whisky Shop, Princes Square, Buchanan St, Glasgow G1 3JX
The Whisky Shop of Fort William, 93 High Street, Fort William, PH33 6GH
The Whisky Shop of Inverness, 17 Bridge Street, Inverness IV3 5PR

ENGLAND AND WALES
Bentalls, Dolphin St, Kingston-Upon-Thames KT1 1TX
Bloomsbury Wine & Spirit Co, 3 Bloomsbury St, London WC1B 3QE
The Brighton Malt House, One North Road, Brighton BN1 1YA
Byrne Ltd, 12 King Street, Clitheroe, Lancs BB7 2EP
Constantine Stores Ltd, 30 Fore St, Falmouth, Cornwall TR11 5AB
Cornerwise, 13 Lake Road, Keswick, Cumbria CA12 5BS
The County Stores, 52 North Street, Taunton, Somerset TA1 1ND
The Covent Garden Whisky Shop, 3 Russell St, London, WC2B 5JD
Dartmouth Vintners, The Butterwalk, 6 Duke Street, Dartmouth TQ6 9EB
Donnington Wines, The Hollow, Castle Donnington DE7 42PN
Fortnum & Mason, 181 Piccadilly, London W1A 1ER
Harrod's, 87–135 Brompton Rd, Knightsbridge, London SW1X 7XL
Milroys, 3 Greek St, Soho, London W1A 1ER
Pallant Wines, 17 High Street, Arundel, West Sussex BN18 9AD

ADDITIONAL INDEX

Space prohibits us from including a full index of malt whiskies, but most whiskies should be easy to find by their distillery names, which are alphabetically listed. Listed below are local nicknames, alternative or marketing brand names alongside the distillery from which each originates. Names marked with an asterisk are second malts distilled in a slightly different manner from the named distillery; *G are grain distilleries within which the malt stills are/were situated.

Acknowledgements

Our grateful thanks are due to a great many people for their assistance in completing this book:

Jamie Walker of Adelphi Distillery
Bill Bergius of Allied Domecq
Colin Ross of Ben Nevis
Raymond Armstrong of Bladnoch
James McEwan of Bruichladdich
Robin Dods and Alistair Walker of Burn Stewart
Cliodhna Purcell of Bushmills
Allan Murray and Mairi Sih of Cadenhead
Vanessa Wright of Campbell Distillers
Alan Greig of Chivas Brothers
John Harte of Cooley
John Alden of John Dewar
Fred and Stewart Laing at Douglas Laing & Co
Jim Turle and Elizabeth Rose of Edrington
John Grant and Rebecca Richardson of Glenfarclas
Barbara Anne Nimmo and Sharon McLaughlin of Glenmorangie
Ian Whitecross and Leslie Duroe of Gordon & MacPhail
Tina Brown of William Grant
Alistair and Donald Hart of Hart Brothers
Freda Ross of Highland Distillers
Graham McEllen of Invergordon
Margaret Mary Timpson of Inver House
Gordon Mitchell of Isle of Arran
Richard Paterson of J.B.B.
Gavin Durnin of Loch Lomond
Glen Moore of Morrison Bowmore
Gordon Wright of Murray McDavid
Calum Murray of Praban na Linne
Jane Yelloly of Seagram
Andrew Symington of Signatory
Jim Gordon and Rick Christie of Speyside
Neil Clapperton of Springbank
Brian Crook of Vintage Malt Whisky Co
Naomi Proudlove of Cohn & Wolfe
and
Takeshi Mogi, Tokyo, and the following Japanese distillers:
Suntory Ltd; Mercian Co Ltd; The Nikka Whisky Distilling Co Ltd; Kirin-Seagram Ltd; Toa Shuzo Co Ltd; Hombo Shuzo Co Ltd; Takara Shuzo Co Ltd

Our sincere apologies to anyone who has been omitted from the above list, as space is limited. You know who you are – we thank you.